FROM THE MASTER'S MOUTH TO THE STUDENT'S EAR

EDITING

Ilias Lampros Katsiampas
Sophia Ag. Skoumis - Katsiampas
Lampros Vas. Katsiampas
Vassiliki L. Katsiampas
Spiros G. Polizois
Lamprini Sp. Polizois
Anatoli Fitopoulou

Cover designer: Georgia Matsamaki
Production supervisor: Platon Malliagkas – mediterrabooks.com

ILIAS L. KATSIAMPAS
OMAKOIO OF TRIKALA
METAPHYSICAL STUDIES IN YOGA AND SHIATSU
KEFALLINIAS 21, 42100 TRIKALA, GREECE
TEL.: 0030-24310–75505 or mobile: 6974-580768
Web Site: http://www.omakoio.gr
or https://omakoio.blogspot.com
E-mails: omakoio@omakoio.gr
or omakoeio@gmail.com

© 2015 ILIAS KATSIAMPAS

All Rights Reserved. No part of this publication may be reproduced in any form or by any means, including scanning, photocopying, or otherwise without prior written permission of the copyright holder.

First Greek Edition 1995, Trikala, Greece
First English Edition, 2015
ISBN: 978-960-85735-5-0

ILIAS L. KATSIAMPAS
ESOTERICISM FOR ALL

FROM THE MASTER'S MOUTH TO THE STUDENT'S EAR

Revealing Metaphysical Correspondence -
a Modern Greek Mystic,
Nikolaos Margioris (author of 189 works)
and his student Ilias Katsiampas (14 works)

Significant Esoteric Essays

With a thorough philosophical dictionary
of Sanskrit - 400 words for the students
of Yoga

OMAKOIO OF TRIKALA, GREECE
FIRST ENGLISH EDITION

I dedicate this first work of mine to my Spiritual Father and Master, **Nikolaos A. Margioris (1913-1993)**, with all my sincere love and my eternal gratitude for everything he tirelessly and unfalteringly offered me on my Esoteric journey, and to the Truth that he whole-heartedly represented.

**His student till the End
Ilias L. Katsiampas**

Contents

EDITING	2
DISCLAIMER	11
ACKNOWLEDGEMENTS	13
REQUEST	13
PART ONE - CORRESPONDENCE WITH THE MASTER	19
PREFACE	21
ACQUAINTANCE WITH THE MASTER	21
CORRESPONDENCE WITH THE MASTER	23
1st Letter	25
1st Answer	27
2nd Letter	28
2nd Answer	31
ANSWERS	31
3rd Letter	34
3rd Answer	36
4th Letter	38
4th Answer	42
5th Letter	44
5th Answer	48
6th Letter	49
6th Answer	51
ANSWERS	52
7th Letter	54

7th Answer	55
RECOMMENDATIONS	56
8th Letter	57
8th Answer	58
9th Letter- part a	62
9th Letter-part b	65
Answer 9a and b	69
ANSWERS	69
10th Letter	71
11th Letter	77
11th Answer	80
12th Letter	84
12th Answer	91
13th Letter	95
NOTES	101
PART TWO - ESSAYS	**103**
PREFACE	105
1st Essay	107
2nd Essay	126
3rd Essay	134
4th Essay	146
5th Essay	153
7th Essay	167
PART THREE - GLOSSARY OF SANSKRIT (ANALYTICAL PHILOSOPHICAL DICTIONARY OF 400 WORDS)	**173**

PREFACE	175
GLOSSARY OF SANSKRIT	179
A	181
F	209
G	209
H	210
I	213
J	214
K	216
L	224
M	225
N	232
O	236
P	236
R	242
S	246
T	261
U	264
V	267
Y	273
PART FOUR - DROPS OF WISDOM	281
PREFACE	283
DROPS OF WISDOM	285
PART FIVE - DEDICATION TO MODERN GREEK MASTER NIKOLAOS A. MARGIORIS	317
PREFACE	319

NIKOLAOS MARGIORIS
THE PATRIARCH OF GREEK OCCULTISM 321

THE PATRIARCH OF GREEK OCCULTISM
AND MYSTICISM HAS LEFT 325

A few words about his Multi-dimensional Work 327
ONE YEAR WITHOUT MASTER 330
NIKOLAOS A. MARGIORIS 330

100 Great Greeks
THE GREATEST OF ALL TIME 334

NIKOLAOS A. MARGIORIS (1913-1993) 335
Biographer's Notes 340
A Letter to Master 342
OMAKOIO SCHOOLS IN OPERATION
IN ATHENS, LAMIA AND TRIKALA 346
THE WRITER'S BIBLIOGRAPHY 351
PUBLISHED BOOKS BY NIKOLAOS A. MARGIORIS 351

BOOKS BY ILIAS L. KATSIAMPAS
(N. MARGIORIS' STUDENT) 357

PRESENTATIONS ON YOUTUBE AND IN FACEBOOK
OF 189 WRITINGS OF MODERN GREEK MYSTIC,
NIKOLAOS A. MARGIORIS (1913-1993) 360

CURRICULUM VITAE
OF WRITER ILIAS KATSIAMPAS 363

SUMMARY OF THE WORK 367

DISCLAIMER

Ilias Katsiampas, the author of this book, has attempted to convey some basic and important knowledge from the year-long, personal relationship he had with his spiritual Master Nikolaos Margioris, in order to properly inform anyone interested in the deeper matters of **Esoteric Metaphysics**, derived from the true experiences of a few of his fellow Mystics, and particularly from the important and decisive role of the relationship between **Master** and **Student** throughout the path of improvement and spiritual evolution.

It is the author's firm belief that this book, along with any specialized information and analysis it offers, assists people in realizing and seeing the great value that the esoteric cultivation of one's self holds for themselves, and for society, as well; it also guides them to commune with and reflect on the ethical and societal values and heritage of **Humanity's Greatest Minds**, so that every person may take individual responsibility as a social and spiritual being towards themselves and the Living and Inanimate Creation- in other words, God.

Any type of instruction, especially in Metaphysics, requires the close and structured relationship between Teacher and Student in the daily practice (The title of this book is inspired by the second principle of **Niyama** in **Raja Yoga**, which in the modern age is construed-presented as *The*

Study of Books that deal with human spirituality and salvation. In the past, with no such books at hand, the perpetual, intimate tutelage *From the Mouth of the Master (Guru) to the Ear of the Student (cela)* existed, instead.) so that the initiation may be reliable, constantly evolving, of high quality, substantial, vibrating and more effective. Any other relationship, like the one described in this book, has a purely informative character for the potential growth and moral-spiritual evolution-completion of every person, for the ones who will actually want it and willingly follow it not only in the context of a special education and disciplined application, but also in their daily life.

The author has made every effort to make his subject matter easily understood by the reader, and bears no responsibility for any errors, inaccuracies, omissions, or inconsistences that might be found in this book, due to its being freely translated from Greek into English.

He also assumes no responsibility for any misunderstanding, misinterpretation and side effect, because this book is not a personal life counselor, but a descriptive - informative medium of information and the conveyance of the author's knowledge, on which everyone is free to meditate - reflect upon, to judge, accept or reject.

It is everyone's wholehearted wish that the readers find an interesting, enjoyable, and useful study-course in the **Esoteric Empirical Knowledge of the Mystics** contained in this book.

Greece, Trikala, 1-12-2014
Ilias L. Katsiampas

ACKNOWLEDGEMENTS

I would like to thank all those who have contributed in any way to the publication of this book; the students of the Athens, Lamia and Trikala Omakoio who have pre-bought it, and those who have helped with the editing. My special thanks are extended to my sister Vassiliki L. Katsiampa for her cooperation in and her contribution to the presentation and the performance of the Kriya Yoga exercises contained in the Sanskrit glossary of this book; Lamprini Sp. Polizoi who, from the first day of my apprenticeship by the side of Nikolaos A. Margioris, undertook to supply me with the recordings of Master Nikolaos A. Margiori's speeches and lectures that contributed to my global and holistic esoteric education. I would also like to thank my wife Sophia Skoumi who undertook the typesetting, the layout and the editing of this book.

REQUEST

Those who wish to use parts of this book are kindly requested to acknowledge the source of the quoted material and its author.

First Greek Edition 1995

*Photos from the dinner organized by **the author** for **his Master Nikolaos A. Margioris** and for the students of **the Omakoios of Athens, Lamia** and **Trikala**, after the **inauguration** of the **Omakoio** of Trikala on the 18th of January, 1992. The first photo shows author **Ilias Katsiampas with his Master**. The second photo shows a general view of those who were present at the dinner.*

A photo from an excursion with **Master Nikolaos A. Margioris** *to* **Nafpaktos**, *in June 1991. From left to right are shown:* **Spiros Polizois, Aspassia Polizoi, Lamprini Polizoi, Nikolas Blanas, Dimitris Tsaparas, Ilias Katsiampas, Master Nikolaos Margioris, Smaro Kosmaoglou, Giannis Tsaparas, Georgia Christodoulou** *and below,* **Anthi Purnara.**

Master **Nikolaos Margioris**, *while writing Volume II of his three-volume work* **Mystical Teachings.** *It is noted that during the writing of his works –except for two or three necessary exemptions– he didn't use a bibliography because he used to write directly from within him, in an "automatic" way, with* **the power**, **the knowledge** *and* **the light** *of* **his soul** *for every matter that he analyzed. A photo of Master Nikolaos Margioris during holidays with his students in Githio (Greece), in August 1992.*

PART ONE

CORRESPONDENCE WITH THE MASTER

PREFACE

ACQUAINTANCE WITH THE MASTER

In 1983, after a five-year-period of intense esoteric exploration, various studies and experimentation with different Schools, I became acquainted with Master **Nikolaos A. Margioris'** personal work when I read his book *Eastern and Western White and Black Magic* which I had come across in a bookshop in Athens.

From that moment on- along with my other studies- and in less than four years, I acquired and studied all his works, about **189** in total, extensively. In these works, I discovered an inexhaustible well of Esoteric Knowledge which greatly impressed me as, on the one hand, they were something unprecedented especially in the tradition of Greek writing, and, on the other hand, because in spite of the numerous books of similar content which I had read at times, this was the first time that I encountered such concentrated Knowledge expressed so analytically in layman's terms by a real Mystic who was, in fact, Greek!

I immediately contacted him by phone and we began to have frequent telephone conversations, a custom that went on for the many years I spent in Yugoslavia for my studies, but which continued when I returned to Trikala. In 1985, we met face to face for the first time in Lamia and fell into the habit of seeing each other whenever I went to Athens. Of course, the purpose of all our discussions was to sate my unquenchable thirst for the subjects of Esotericism.

In 1987, while still a student abroad, I recognized my need for a more substantial esoteric education at the «feet of the Master», so I enrolled in the school which the Master kept in Athens and attended the Raja Yoga and other lessons diligently. In 1989, I became a member of the Master's narrow circle of students and was given the opportunity to have regular and direct personal contact with the Master during our frequent all-day gatherings. This also gave me the chance, until his passing (6/5/1993), to ask more and more burning questions about the inexhaustible panorama of Esotericism (Occultism and Mysticism) and resulted in invaluable answers on subjects which had not been deeply analyzed until then and on some that had not even been touched upon.

Through his teachings, I saw the path which leads to Truth, that road which suited - if you wish - my idiosyncrasy. I followed it and continue to do so without feelings of disappointment. On the contrary, it gives me the answers I ask for, it fulfills me and it never ceases to open vast spiritual horizons for me. And I am continuing my journey on the ascending path...

Through his teaching and for the first time in my life, I achieved something rare and significant. I recognized, I realized, I became conscious of and I felt the Christic element that exists within me and within all of us. I gained profound insight into our Religion. To put it more simply, I became a conscientious Christian, a truly faithful and sensible follower of our beloved Jesus Christ, of whom my Master was a humble soldier all his life.

In December 1991, after numerous discussions with the Master and with his encouragement, consent and moral assistance, I proceeded with the establishment of a spiritual school, the OMAKOIO of Trikala, which Master N. Margioris inaugurated himself in the presence of many of his students on January 18th, 1992.

CORRESPONDENCE WITH THE MASTER

At that time, the physical distance that separated me from the Master was a torturous obstacle which blocked my path towards the source of Truth. I found it soothing to express the burning questions I had in long letters addressed to the Master, hoping that he would read and answer them. I knew that he had a heavy schedule (lectures, speeches, treatments, writings etc.), so I was overjoyed and experienced a great sense of relief when he responded immediately. Thus began the very special correspondence we had which lasted the whole time I was a student abroad.

I decided to bring this personal correspondence, which constitutes a rare sample of true and sincere communication between a Master and a student, to light because it does not concern only me, since any other human soul could have been in my shoes at that time. The content of the correspondence which is purely instructive and of an initiatory nature will be of interest to any human being who is searching for the esoteric path of his life, to any man who has probably chosen and is already following his own internal course, to any seeker who is looking for some radical answers mainly concerning Esoteric matters.

As you will see, my letters to the Master include the burning questions that had inevitably arisen in the course of my internal pursuits. I set forth the queries which tortured me, which proved a restraining factor in my evolution and needed an immediate answer or some clarification in order for me to attain a certain level of stability and equilibrium and which in turn enabled me to go on with my personal struggle.

The elucidations and the clear details that were given me, along with additional clarifications over numerous phone conversations and face-to-face meetings played a catalytic role in helping me conceive and integrate the offered Knowledge in such a way as to allow me to steadily, surely and safely ascend the steps of my personal upward course.

I present the Correspondence in its original form so as to bring the particular internal pulse of my Master's vibration to light and sincerely hope and wish that it may constitute an invaluable tool for any soul travelling on its spiritual course, just as it was my main support-basis at that period of my life when I began the significant journey of my esoteric ascension.

1st Letter

Yugoslavia, March 17, 1986

Dear Mr. Margioris,

I am Ilias Katsiampas from Trikala, Greece, who has placed some orders for your books.

I am writing you from Yugoslavia, after having studied enough of your work to confirm that it agrees with all the knowledge I have acquired after 5 years of theoretical studies in Metaphysics and Occult Sciences.

As you may understand, I have some 'reservations' concerning the 'initiation' or 'action'. And as I have some queries, I would be grateful if you could enlighten me about them.

First of all, is it possible for an individual to succeed in one's correct and healthy spiritual development through a correspondence course in Meditation, for instance? Would such an approach, again in reference to Meditation, work without distorting the meaning of the text and without causing the student to make serious mistakes or suffer any harm?

Does Astral travelling or the out-of-body experience, as it has been characterized, belong to any of the branches you supervise?

Can anybody with Astral travelling ability alone be set free from the circle of reincarnation?

Do you have any apprentices in Trikala or in Thessalia that I may contact?

Hoping that I am not taking up too much of your precious time, I would greatly appreciate it if you would give me a brief and clear overview of the success and the results of the following branches: 1) Scientific Spiritualism, 2) Esoteric Initiation, 3) Esoteric Philosophy and 4) Meditation.

Also, apart from your answers, please send me if possible in the same or in another envelope, the application forms for the annual subscription to the OMAKOIO journal and for the subscription to the Esoteric Keys. Also, please inform me of the cost of each subscription.

Besides you or after you, is there a potential successor?

Please send all correspondence to the following address:

Please copy it exactly as it is written.

**Awaiting your letter
with many thanks,
Yours faithfully,
Ilias Katsiampas**

1st Answer

March 3, 1986
to Mr. Katsiampas,
Yugoslavia

Dear Mr. Katsiampas,

I just received your letter of March 17th, 1986 to which I am replying. You may apply the Esoteric Keys of Meditation and at the same time read my two books: *The Secret of Hatha Yoga* and *Raja Yoga*. You will not be at all harmed. You need only not drink nor smoke and you must also follow a frugal diet.

'EVERYTHING IN MODERATION'. Try it and don't be afraid; as long as you desire it. As long as you think morally and honestly. There is no such thing as astral travelling, it is just a myth. There is only the elevation of the Mind to hyperconsciousness. If your Karma allows it, then dare to move forward. At worst, it may take a few years, but you will not suffer any harm.

A pure and honest life is the only thing you need.

1) Meditation will prepare you for the high ascension to the transcendental or to hyperconsciousness.

2) Esoteric Philosophy will prepare you.

3) Esoteric Initiation will teach you.

4) Scientific Spiritualism will bring forth other issues that are different from Meditation.

The publication of the OMAKOIO journal has been interrupted. But you may buy it year by year. Every 6 issues per year cost one thousand two hundred drachmas. Please see the prospectuses.

For the Esoteric Key. Enrolment 1.000 GRD.

The three lessons cost 1.500 GRD. The thirty lessons cost 15.000 GRD.

You may attend one triad at a time at a cost of 1.500 GRD. Three lessons, in other words. As you wish. However, enrolment will cost 1.000 GRD. I have many students all over Greece. Lamia is nearer to you. If you wish, write me so that I may send you their addresses in the event you wish to come into contact with them.

Enclosing herewith a prospectus for you with many wishes and love.

N. A. Margioris

2nd Letter

Yugoslavia, May 20, 1986

Dear Mr. Margioris,

I received your parcel and I have sent you a check of 2.000 GRD to cover the cost of the books.

I am writing you from Yugoslavia to ask you some burning questions that have preoccupied me during my studies in Esotericism and in Metaphysics.

I believe that your replies will reflect reality, as I see the invaluable support and love emanating through your books, and your desire to spread as much knowledge and as many stimuli as possible to all those who respond to them.

Here are some of my questions:

1) Why does the evil spirit try to take the legitimate man soul with it during catalepsy when it is being chased away

or exorcised? What does it gain by doing so? Through what procedures or factors can catalepsy attack a man? I mean the evil and not the good catalepsies.

2) You have said that there are sub-etheric and sub-astral worlds with their respective sub-levels. Are there also sub-intellectual, sub-buddhic worlds etc.? Where and what is the end of these worlds? Do any - and what kind of – beings live there? What is the purpose of all the sub-etheric or existing worlds?

3) Does Satan or the Devil or Beelzebub or Lucifer with his following of demons or of negative powers exist? More specifically, the Key of Solomon and the Kabbalah refer to all this as being the ancient secret tradition of Jews. What are all these entities the black magician calls on to assist him in his evil work? The black magician, with his thoughts and his actions serves evil, the negative, involution. What happens in the end? Does he lose his soul? Does he finally become a pawn, a demon himself, since he has removed the good from within himself and descends to involution?

4) Can you free yourself from the Law of Karma by proceeding to spiritual completion through your evolution (reincarnations) on Earth, by simply following a moral and honest life, without having to be initiated? In fact, I think this is the message given to us by Jesus Christ.

5) What can you tell me about the Antichrist or the Beast of Revelation (666), to which the New Testament makes reference in the Apocalypse of John, saying that he will come to you in sheep's clothing, but inwardly he will be a ravenous wolf and also about the return of Christ or of some Avatars?

Is Christ a man who attained union or is he the Word of God that became flesh to guide us? God expresses himself through the Divine Triad; therefore He could not be a man, since the Triad existed before Creation.

6) Two of my books mysteriously disappeared, the first one at the beginning of January 1986 and the other one about 2 years earlier. The first one was a document-type book that analyzed the Rosicrucians and the second one was the Key of Solomon of which I was always particularly afraid. And though it was one of the first books that fell into my hands, I avoided it (I had also heard that one must not burn it or throw it away etc., which further added to my fear). I shall not describe the event in detail, suffice it to say that when I looked for them, I did not find them at the specific place where I keep most of my books of this kind. It was as if they had vanished. This is the explanation I received by a female acquaintance of mine who had been an apprentice to a master for 5 years. She said that they had probably dematerialized or that somebody else had made them dematerialize. In any case, I mention it as an event that puzzled me and about which I await your answer.

7) What is the stellar world of animals? Where can we place it? Can there be spiritual attacks by animals on man, as there are by man on man, voluntary or not?

I must confess that your answers to the above questions will be of great help to me. I intend to send you another letter in continuation to this one. Also, if you have not sent issue number 6 of the first year of the *OMAKOIO Journal* to Trikala, please send it here (Yugoslavia) along with your response. I thank you sincerely for taking the trouble to answer my queries. I am looking forward to receiving your response.

**Yours truly
Ilias Katsiampas**

2nd Answer

Athens, May 27, 1986

Dear Ilias,

Today I received both your letters. Despite my heavy workload, I decided to reply. I am sending you the books you have asked for by post. You will receive the 6th issue in the autumn, unless I find it and I mail it to you.

ANSWERS

1) The expelled spirit cannot take the soul with it, as the spirit-soul is based upon some higher laws that are not disturbed by evil spirits. Besides, the evil spirits are just some souls that have strayed either from our Dimension (the 13th) or by deceived, old angelic beings (the Black Prince accomplished his work), see my book *The Birth and Death of the Worlds*. Catalepsy takes place in the appropriate vessel. When man leans towards evil, he attracts the so-called evil beings near him, through the respectively appropriate vibrations. Like attracts like.

2) In my books you will find many of these. More specifically, every Dimension has 7 sub-dimensions. Our dimension has 4 Etheric and 3 Physical ones. For this reason it is called the Etheric-physical or 13th Dimension. Immediately within is the Thymoastric with 7 sub-dimensions. Deeper inside we find the Intellectual with 7 more Dimensions. See my books *The Birth and Death of the Worlds* and *Posthumous Life*.

3) Satan or the Black Prince or Beelzebub or Helot or Antichrist or Devil or or or..., is the antithesis to the Thesis,

it is the opposite of Perfection and Goodness. Man fights against the evil existing within and without him, day and night, in order to elevate his Pure, his Perfect and his Divine Element. Every wicked man or every unevolved soul continually seeks to pulsate, to be fed or to attract vibrations of a lower type that satisfy him, since he himself is, lives, feels and exists within it.

4) Karma is itself the story of your lives. You will get what you have given and you will build what you have demolished. Your every action brings either a good or a bad result. You must return both to their original position. You will succeed in this when you are enlightened and elevated. When you have managed to restore everything you have disturbed to harmony, then you will have managed to free yourself. To leave rebirths behind.

5) The Antichrist is the antithesis, he is the other side of the Divine and of Beauty. The spirit is Perfection but matter, all matter is imperfection. The more we approach the Divine, Perfection, Justice, Love, and our spiritualization, the farther away we get from imperfection, from evil, from the antichrist, from the antithesis, from chronicity. Everything uniting us with Eternity unchains us from vanity, from matter, from evil.

6) Though materializations and dematerializations take place from time to time, in the case of your books a hand took them away. But I think it did very well. Because books which upset the soul and prepare it for something evil should be kept at a distance until man has acquired sufficient KNOWLEDGE on LIFE. When you too arrive at the place you seek, then no book will alter your views about the Truth surrounding us. You must learn that 'it takes time for fruit to ripen' and that 'little by little does the farmer plant a vineyard.'

7) The Stellar world of animals is the astral dimension, the 12th one where the Stellar world of man is found as well. There we can also find the Stellar regions of the human souls. Everything that leaves our 13th Etheric-physical Dimension, as soon as it sheds the representation of its form, enters the Stellar world, clad in the stellar clothes one wears beneath the rejected physical clothing.

My dear friend Ilias, you must read the books which you have bought from me continuously. In them, you will find the answers to your just and remarkable questions. What I write you is less than the least I should write you.

I do so because of a lack of time on my part. In my encyclopedia, in my 49 journals, in my essays, in my Esoteric Keys, you will find in-depth answers to your burning questions. In essence, our world is composed of new and old souls. The primitive ones have not yet recovered from the drunkenness of Matter and occupy themselves with bad thoughts, words and actions.

While the old souls have learned of the superfluous, the evil, the harmful, the vain, the futile, the useless and the unworthy. They have turned to the Beyond. They seek the Divine, Goodness, Perfection, Beauty, Truth and Eternity.

Our Greek Mythology teaches us this in its own way, in the myth of HERCULES where Virtue and Vice tried to entice him. When the man-mind, this material construction becomes perfect, it turns to Intelligence and the soul, seeking to enter perfection. Turn your eyes within yourself and allow your introspection to discover the old soul that awaits you.

Wishing you spiritual elevation,
Margioris

3rd Letter

Yugoslavia, May 29, 1986

Dear Mr. Margioris,

I shall take up some of your time once more to ask some questions, concerning the basics in the branch of Meditation.

1) In your book *RAJA YOGA*, p.177, you write that in order for the elevating completion of Meditation to be achieved, the three last steps are sufficient:

a) DHARANA (Concentration), b) DHYANA (Meditation) and c) SAMADHI (Theosis).

Does this mean that the following five preparations you refer to are not needed?

a) YAMA (restraints) **b)** NIYAMA (discipline) **c)** ASANA (poses - positions), **d)** PRANAYAMA (control of Prana – energy through rhythmic breathing) and **e)** PRATYAHARA (withdrawal of the senses from the Mind):

However, on pages 175-176, where you refer to DHARANA, analyzing its technical side, you also talk about the use of PRANAYAMA and PRATYAHARA.

Finally, are the first five steps needed or not? If not, are some of them needed and which of them do you analyze in the *ESOTERIC KEY*?

2) Applying the *Esoteric Key* (Meditation Branch), how should I deal with the matter of love? Should I see it only as a way of bearing children or should I apply the saying you wrote me in your previous letter? 'EVERYTHING IN MODERATION'. And what is MODERATION, especially in Meditation?

3) Is the Kundalini for elevation applied in the Esoteric Key (Meditation Branch)?

4) What is the difference between the expansion of con-

sciousness and the withdrawal of consciousness? Where do you go or where are you with the one and where with the other?

5) With the successful elevation to hyperconsciousness do we get in touch with reincarnated and more evolved human-entities, Guides or Masters? What can you tell me about the reincarnated Master who is supposed to guide a group of students?

6) When I called you from Trikala, you told me that you knew where I was; what did you mean? And if you really knew it, what is your opinion-advice, regarding the branch of meditation or other meditations?

Mr. Margioris, by asking these and the previous questions, I don't wish to appear clever or naive. I am an individual who is generally searching for some Truth and I believe I will receive responsible answers from you on matters that have been occupying my mind from a very young age.

I believe that before making decisions about the matters that interest me directly, I ought to clarify certain aspects, not only to make sure that the path I will follow is the right one, but also that I will be able to follow it correctly.

If you are too busy, do not answer me immediately.

With much love and appreciation,
Ilias Katsiampas

3rd Answer

June 6, 1986
to Mr. Katsiampas

Dear Mr. Katsiampas,
I have received your letter of May 29th, 1986 and I am replying to you although I am terribly busy. I am doing so because I noticed a particular leaning towards Metaphysics and an effort to speed things up on your part, which I do not particularly agree with. Therefore, I am answering you so that I can have a clear conscience.

1) The three last steps always presuppose the existence of the previous five ones. But nobody can ascend Dharana unless he becomes good and unless he ceases being attached to the worldly and futile. This is common knowledge, since real concentration - Dharana - cannot be achieved if the Mind is preoccupied with material interests. Why do we say that? In order to push the student to search deeply within himself, to forget the external material things and to concentrate. I think you understand what I mean. Only without any attachment can he attain true concentration. In order not to be attached one must learn, become prepared. One must shed the interests of the temporary in order to discover those of Eternity.

2) The Esoteric Key is a strong stimulus. Initiation teaches but does not change man. If you are prepared, you will be assisted in the attainment of elevation. Love (coitus) inhibits de-spiritualization. During the interval of exercises-experimentations, coitus must be abstained from. Afterwards it may return in moderation to love (sex). One must abstain from sex for at least 48 hours before the attempt to Concentrate. But is it only the sex? Feelings of irritation, evil and cunning thoughts, egoisms, desires for glory and dominion,

drinks, food, backbiting and accusations, unwillingness to forgive your enemies, etc.

3) In order for Kundalini to awaken, a certain technique is needed, which means the body needs training. At the same time you need to train the Mind. Meditation with the Esoteric Key stimulates man. The awakening of Kundalini depends on one's inclination, preparation, will, knowledge and education.

4) The expansion of consciousness means that it can follow the subconscious states in some way or that it can be aware of the hyperconscious states.

5) The elevation of Kundalini is one thing. The elevation to hyperconsciousness is another thing. And contact with fleshless beings is yet another. Each has its own purpose which may sometimes apply to another as well. It depends on the quality of the evolution of the potential seeker.

6) Dear Mr. Ilias, if I felt that you were simply toying with the idea or just killing time, I surely wouldn't write to you. Every day, I leave thousands of letters unanswered. I give cliché advice. You must study first. It is still too early for you. You should read the PROPER Metaphysical works to form your axis. Then, you will gradually find out what suits you. Now you can take up Meditation. Certainly not to elevate yourself. It is still too early for you. But you should become informed about what you need for YOGA. Seek higher understanding. Seek MYSTICISM. Of course, you should learn about everything but your Mind must always be in union with YOUR HYPERCONSCIOUSNESS. To attain this, you need to work at it for many years. Become moral. Practise introspection and... act accordingly.

Athens, June 6, 1986
Margioris

4th Letter

Yugoslavia
September 28, 1986

To start with, I consider it necessary to inform you about my personal practical trials and experimentations before I met you, about 3-5 years earlier, when I was at an age that everything impressed me and aroused my curiosity, causing me to do insufficient and perhaps also irresponsible experimentations in relaxation, concentration, hypnotism etc. First of all, I tried Mind control by following a method in a book. In a nutshell, it started with thought control, relaxation and the creation of a mental screen, where you could project whatever you wanted. The degree of my success was mediocre, and after three months of continual efforts, I stopped before I could accomplish the 'mental screen'. Later, I tried Hatha Yoga, centripetal relaxation as you call it, aiming for the splitting of the personality and thus I began suggesting to myself that my fingers are foreign to me and that I do not feel them, and to proceed gradually onwards. When I reached the chest and while my eyes were closed, I felt them closing even more tightly and I could not open them as I had fallen into a deep lethargy. My reaction was immediate and after an effort that seemed to last a century (5-6 seconds), I managed to open my eyes and to escape from the fall into lethargy that made me believe that 'I was lost' (there were two more people in the room).

After a few months, I tried the 'imagination technique'. That is, while I was lying down, I tried to imagine or rather to see myself (division) suspended 2-3 meters over my body. Finally, I felt a strange feeling as if I were sinking into a kind of torpor like before. At the same moment, a little above my chest, I felt an abrupt and continual flight like a fluttering going to and fro and automatically, as in the first trial, I made an effort to return to the world of sensations, before I fell into the bonds of torpor. Both times, I returned terrified, afraid of something worse.

I do not know how successful my attempts at splitting for relaxation purposes could be considered. Anyway, these events kept me at a distance from any practical techniques to this day. I also used hetero-hypnotism with moderate success.

What is your point of view on the consequences of the completion of the afore-mentioned experimentations and what is your advice concerning their correct application?

Furthermore, I would like to mention the case of a friend of mine, a housewife with three children who lives in Trikala. She is also a student of Occultism and trained with a teacher in Thessaloniki for about four years. Her master can't have been very positive for, as she told me, he tried to have an influence over her and she was obliged to leave him, because she did not find that her conscience was in agreement with everything he taught her. After she left, she was obliged to come into "conflict" with him (in order to defend herself).

After successfully liberating herself, she continued on her own for five years and up till today, according to the Christian standards and to the ascending course through the realization of 'personality splitting' (out-of-body state). She has a very good writing and poetic style, especially when it concerns metaphysical issues and problems. She writes weekly articles, mainly on metaphysical matters, for my father's newspaper. Our first meeting was a little strange but since then we have kept in touch and have frequently worked together. What I notice about her is that, in spite of being advanced in practical matters, she sometimes presents one-sided views in our conversations; that is, she is a bit absolute about feelings and authenticity. So, I still have the impression that in the transcendental (etheric, stellar lower intellectual), there has been some kind of deception and that she may have been involved in the Thymic-astral world (clearly personal conclusion). I understand anyway that she needs an expert master for the correct guidance to ascension. I have spoken to her repeatedly about you and I think that I have nearly convinced her. I hope she contacts you soon.

Concerning my own progress, it is as follows: I have made efforts to improve joint flexibility with the application of immobile poses (asanas) that serve meditation. For seven months, I have not smoked nor drank (after five years of use) and for one month I haven't consumed decoctions.

I have no evil thoughts nor a desire for precedence, but I do have issues with my ego which I am trying to fight. Generally, I still need a lot of training before the obstacles are overcome sooner or later. I have not yet started any practical application of Meditation. The reason for this is that I am a little demanding and I want to have a full and detailed picture about every ascension step.

'The unknown attracts me but at the same time it frightens me.' I realize that 'the Mind is the devil' but I do not feel strong enough to make the leap of my salvation-conversion in a moment. First of all, I want to confirm and to listen attentively to the Omnipresence. I wish to have my mind focused on the Divine and Mystic Union of Perfection, of Bliss and of Eternity, without excluding the Omni-Totality of which I will, sooner or later, be a participant. I understand the maya (matter), the vain and harmful things, as I understand the superior, the higher, and the more spiritual things. I am aware of my weakness, as well as of my Will for ascension that lies in the gradual awakening to and the correct and elevating orientation of my inclination. Faith is my guide and my leader who will transfer me 'transformed' to KNOWLEDGE-WISDOM-TRUTH-SPIRITUAL ELEVATION-UNION, through the sentiment of eternal LOVE.

The last 20-22 lines came from deep within me. In this burst of sincere feelings that define the low evolution of my soul but also the sight of Perfection that pushes me to higher paths of perception and achievements for my own Salvation and, in extension, for the salvation of the Whole, which I hope will eventually come.

Below are some questions which I kindly request you answer if you have time:

1) How are somnambulism and demonic possession explained metaphysically?

2) This question concerns 'Donors' who offer their vital organs for transplantation after death to people who need them. Does this cause any difficulties since the vital organs of the deceased continue to operate?

3) If science can construct a computer that can think and feel, does this mean that a computer has an individual soul?

4) At which point in time does the soul enter a new-born or an embryo and in which month?

5) Must Meditation take place every day? Is there a problem when it takes place in different, non- magnetized spots?

Thank you very much for your attention. Awaiting your reply to my letter.

**Yours very truly,
Ilias Katsiampas**

P.S.: Please, inform me if the books *Patapios the Humble, Light in the Dark, Pythagorean Arithmosophy* or others have been republished and also, if *KRIYA YOGA* has been edited.

4th Answer

March 3rd, 1986
to Mr. Katsiampas

Dear Ilias,
I have received your two letters dated September 28th, 1986. First of all, I will deal with the one containing your personal experiences and your questions.

1) It is a phenomenon belonging to the domain of Spiritualism - Hypnotism and... Parapsychology. It is a hypnotic phenomenon in essence and belongs to the sub-conscious state of the sleep-walker. It takes place after natural sleep but also after induced sleep. It can occur automatically and naturally or after hypnotism and the command of the hypnotist to the hypnotee. During somnambulism, the sleep-walker goes about with the eyes of the soul and does not run any danger of walking off the edges of terraces or of steep cliffs in the deep darkness. If the somnambulist is suddenly awakened, he will surely lose the guidance from his subconscious and the conscious that will succeed it will not continue guiding man safely. See Esoteric Key and my other books (Hypnotism - Orthopsychism).

Demonic catalepsy is something different. It concerns a temporary or a permanent possession of the physical bearer-body by an unevolved and primitive spirit-soul existing in man's natural body. This takes place either with the consent of the spirit-soul residing in the physical body or this same spirit-soul is violently driven out by another unevolved one.

2) The donor of a certain vital organ does a good deed.
But the vibration of the organ or skin or bone, is different from the diseased body accepting the corporal piece of the donor. The body of the ailing person always rejects the

attachment of a new part from another physical body, since its own vibration is different. The soul vibrates the body in accordance with its evolution. If the organism accepts the attached foreign piece, this means that its vibrations are similar to those of the body of the donor. It means that they identify with each other and that they are on the same vibratory scale.

3) The Computer symbolizes the Mind. Just like the human mind receives the power of the Intellect and the stimuli from the sensations, so does the computer do what the Mind sets it to through the keys that the computer operator uses to compel the machine to operate. The Soul has no relation to the computer.

The soul is uncomposed because it is an essence. The Computer is a material machine, constructed from matter and by human-intellect. The Computer is made of matter. The Soul is immortal, eternal, since it is uncomposed, made of spirit.

4) The Soul enters the infant as soon as its little head exits the womb. The Spirit-soul, which is the sacred of the sacred, the immortal and the blessed part of God, can never enter the embryo.

5) There is no need for meditation to take place every day. It must happen only when there is disposition and prosperity, when the soul is prepared and moved. The Space is created first with a mental and devout prayer at the venue where meditation will take place. The Space must be purified. It must be considered a holy pedestal where no bad thoughts must reside. All these instructions can be found in my books. I am too busy and I cannot answer the questions that the readers of metaphysical books ask.

I answer your questions only, from time to time and as an exception. I read your letters and understood that you have greatly confused Spiritual-Hypnosis with Holy Meditation. Spiritual-Hypnotism is part of the subconscious. Meditation belongs to the hyperconscious. Their difference is immense. Death - Immortality, Life - Death, corruption- purity, Vanity - Eternity, Deceit - Truth. Please, read my books thoroughly. Beware of misconceptions. Occultism is different from Mysticism, as the vain world is different from the eternal world, as vanity is different from.... eternity.

The greatest error for anyone is to be taught by a semi-literate. Pay attention. Read my books as well as the journal and specially the Esoteric Key.

Your answers to the Esoteric Key are good.

**With warm wishes,
Margioris**

5th Letter

Yugoslavia
October 1, 1986

Dear Mr. Margioris,

I am sending you the following study which is my first attempt at developing certain metaphysical matters, mainly for two reasons:

1) That you may appreciate my position on the subject of Truth and

2) That you advise me on whether I must develop such essays, analyzing terms, such as: morality, faith, love ..., that have a metaphysical dimension.

I believe that all of us (some to a greater and some to a lesser extent) are searching for some form of Truth. There are many means available for its quest, and they range in formation and structure. Some of them are called Dogma, others are called Religion, Metaphysics, Magic, Spiritualism, Occultism, Mysticism, etc.

Some of them are for the large masses, for the coherence of the people, since everything is based on and dealt with through faith, some are for more conscious persons-groups and others are for those who experience Truth or for whom Truth is an experience.

Faith or inclination is the perception, conscious or not, of the internal processes, instincts, tendencies (pre-experiences), impressions, feelings and the will. It is also the most powerful path to Truth.

Consciousness or the Mind or the self or the ego, is finite since it communes with the five insufficient senses, that do not offer us reality (truth) but just a part of it, a reflection that exists for educational, perfectionist, evolutionary, discriminatory (bad-good) purposes only, since our thoughts contain inclinations of a positive and negative nature.

It is recognized by science that there are 76 octaves (608:8 = 76), that is 608 different radiations or pulse-vibrations, of which our senses are able to conceive only the 8, which means only one of the 76 octaves.

Consequently, since Truth is part of our broadest perception, the one beyond our senses, and is diffused through these numerous radiations, if we wish to approach it (since this is our purpose), we must first and foremost have faith and inclination, which means moral wholeness, perfection, ascension, a certain degree of evolution, and the correct cultivation of pre-experiences. Immediately afterwards, there follow any methods or techniques that help broaden consciousness and raise its vibrations in order to gain a greater understanding of the spectrum of Truth, with a focus on the broader Cosmic positioning.

For all those who are not in a position to perceive and to understand, mainly due to the youth of their souls or their intoxication from matter, or because they have been deceived by negative powers or by negative thoughts (thinking figures) – it would be better to say their 'crystallization'. It is for all these people that dogmas, world theories, spiritualism, and at a higher level religions and so on, were created.

These are only, more or less, distorted versions of Truth that favor biases, material interests, pseudo freedoms, lower inclinations for education-knowledge, and that will bring about profits, egoism, hate, abuse, exhibitionism, false prototypes of moral values etc.

All the above represent the individual's satisfaction with or inclination towards slightly or completely distorted parts of Truth, that may reach the point of becoming lies, hypocrisy, crime etc., since they all represent the imperfect that leads to perfection, eternity, de-spiritualization.

Truth cannot be limited within matter; it exists in forms of great or smaller perception.

TRUTH: The right, the perfect, the real, the infinite, that which truly IS, it is beyond the relativity of man, since it cannot be conceived and understood by our finite senses. It is spiritualism, liberation, joy, beauty, happiness, eternity, revelation, transcendence, the perfect and true Knowledge - Wisdom.

Everything in the World (the earthly - unearthly) are parts-pieces that compose the Truth and that can only be approached through Knowledge, which can be attained using different techniques of varying degrees of suitability at different time periods. What's more, the correct Knowledge brings immense changes to the BEING of man.

Every human and imperfect Mind can interpret the doctrines, the world theories, the religions as they serve him or as he narrowly perceives Truth.

For this reason, in every religion there are numerous heresies, together with world views and dogmas, because the finite perceives Truth according to its degree of evolution. Only by attaining Knowledge (broadening) and certainly the acquired aptitude through one's continual educational experiences, can one escape the illusions of matter, of vanity, of the unreal, of the senses, of imperfection and find his true Esoteric Self, by realizing one's potential for introspection and the attainment of Truth.

For this reason, true Sages have been characterized as prophets, initiates, saints, etc. They have actualized the 'Know Thyself' Truth itself.

These conclusions are my personal appreciations, written in an effort to interpret the meaning of the word 'Truth' metaphysically, as I perceive it and as comprehensively as possible. They were written on June 11th, 1986.

Thanking you for your hospitality,
With love,
Ilias Katsiampas

5th Answer

Athens, October 7, 1986
to Mr. Katsiampas

Dear Mr. Katsiampas,

I have received your two letters of October 10th, 1986. One refers to the answers of the first triad of Scientific Spiritualism and the other to your study of a metaphysical matter, where you develop the meaning of Truth. You request my opinion and, in a way, correction. At first sight, you appear a novice. However, this shouldn't be disappointing to you. Your readers or your listeners do not have sufficient knowledge to judge you. So, you may express your Metaphysical knowledge freely...

The Truth is as follows:

The world we exist and live in is the other end of Truth. It is the Lie. Everything is a lie. We live in an illusion that does not represent any Truth, since the place-time and the causality constitute and form the whole area, whose foundation is deception. Then, where is Truth? Exactly at the other end of this Omniuniverse, where place-time is absent and causality does not exist. Only here, in the limited place-time, where causality acts, only here in Maya (matter) is the untruth born and does it exist, since everything is an unsuccessful, crude, blotted copy that distorts Truth and represents one thing instead of something else.

Consequently, it is a fact that there is no Truth in the world of form we exist in. To find or to see Truth, we must communicate with the True field of the Omnipresence. That's where, according to Plato, the ideas, the Perfection of everything lie. But Perfection does not apply here, in the area of the representation of form, in the imperfection of our world.

No one has found Truth or Perfection here. Everything is an unsuccessful copy. It is part of the imperfection, of the deceit and of the untruth. Can anyone find Truth in the world of illusions and untruths? Certainly not. Here, everything is a lie and the Truth has never arrived here in this world of forms, in this place-time, in this causality.

Man strives to attain the inexistent Truth. In this way, great men such as Buddha, Plato, Socrates, Ammonius Saccas, Plotinus, Porfirius, Iamblichus and other more recent ones have perceived it, when they managed to set their hyper-senses into motion, a function of the mind that helps in the conception of higher vibrations. These vibrations belong to the world beyond ours, where Truth resides, as True metaphysics describes it.

Athens, October 7, 1986
With love,
Margioris

6th Letter

Yugoslavia, June 11, 1986

Dear Mr. Margioris,

I send you my best regards.

I was particularly glad about the establishment of the Jnana Yoga school. I would very much like to assist in the practical lessons of Raja Yoga and I may be able to visit you in the middle of December, in order that I come into my first basic contact with the practical procedure of Meditation, which is so necessary. For it is different for someone to have the Master who will teach him the procedure and how to overcome obstacles by his side than to try to copy and apply what one reads in a book. Of course, a strong theoretical background is necessary, but once one wishes to apply the theory, one faces unforeseen impasses and obstacles. I think that at least at the beginning, one must be instructed by a Master.

If I come to Athens in the middle of December for a few or even more days, will you be able to give some practical advice; that is, will you have free time for a few basic lessons?

Below follow some metaphysical questions:

1) How does science perceive the existence of Ether and how does metaphysics perceive it?

2) In the ascending process of Meditation, are lower soul powers such as telepathy, telemotion, far-hearing, far-sight, elevation and so on developed?

3) Many people in Metaphysics say that they do not believe if they do not see something with their own eyes and say: 'All this is fine but can you prove it?' One can try to convince them with different facts and after realizing the impossibility of making them understand (believe), finally one ends up talking about Meditation. However, from my observations till now, I realize that Meditation does not appeal to them very much either because of how difficult it is to grasp its theoretical and technical foundation, or due to the necessary time period required for its implementation. As a rule, they ask for immediate results, through a mediating factor such as: hypnotism, parapsychological phenomena, spiritual meetings; phenomena that only a true Expert can prove and not an inexperienced and incomplete student who controls himself with difficulty. I would like to ask you

if it is necessary to provide the whole spectrum of proof or just a part of it such as relaxation or hypnotism, in order to impress people.

4) Is Meditation a partial or a total out-of-body state? What is it until the stage of Identification?

5) During the practice of Meditation is there any danger of catalepsy by black entities, by souls bound to Earth, by black magicians and so on? What are the precautions or countermeasures that should be taken?

6) Besides the Esoteric White Hierarchy, is there also a Black Hierarchy in the Esoteric universes, or at least in the external 6-7 Dimensions - worlds of the 7th founding Ray of the 7th Dimension to our own external 13th Physical etheric world?

Thanking you very much,
With love,
Ilias Katsiampas

6th Answer

Yugoslavia, November 13, 1986
to Mr. Katsiampas

Dear Ilias,

I am replying to your letter, despite my heavy workload of writing and teaching.

This year, the school of Raja Yoga is not open. It operated for about 4 years and in the last year it collaborated with the Karma Yoga school. That is, there were three years of pure

Raja Yoga and one year of a mixed type with Karma Yoga. Then, one year of pure Karma and this year, Jnana Yoga. So, there is no Raja Yoga school. Private lessons are offered at a high cost.

Unfortunately, life and action do not allow us any luxuries. This year it is Jnana's turn. Some other year, God willing, the Raja Yoga school may re-open.

ANSWERS

1) Up until the time of the unforgettable William Crookes, the discoverer of Thallium, everybody accepted the existence of ether, particularly this great English scientist, chemist, philosopher, and researcher in Metaphysical problems and especially Spiritualism. But gradually, as scientists left the nineteenth century behind them, they abandoned ether for a new theory, QUANTUM. In order to prevail, Quantumism suffered many trials. However, more pro-quantum theories appeared, thus distancing external science from Ether. Concerning Metaphysics, it accepts ONLY ETHER, because it knows that everything derives from it.

2) During the ascending process of the meditating person, only the superior-soul powers, such as far-hearing and far-sight develop. This takes place because the Mind tries to open the hyperconscious. Concerning telepathy, telemotion and elevation, they are actualized by the SUBCONSCIOUS and not by the path (MEDITATION) which goes to the hyperconscious. As I have already told you in the past, you confuse the conscious, the subconscious and the hyperconscious.

3) Those who deny the Metaphysical Truth have not yet developed and are still in a state of evolution. The true path is the path of Meditation, because it starts from Socrates' concentration or thought. Here is the truth. Beyond concen-

tration-thought, Meditation awaits us and then Theosis or Participation or Union of the lower self of the apparent man, with the infinite and substantial self existing within him.

Hypnotism, Spiritualism, the parapsychological phenomena are the products of the subconscious. They are half-truths; the light of the moon. Hyperconsciousness is the light of the sun.

Do not accept the half-darkness. Choose, as difficult as it may be, the luminous Helysia, where Socrates went after his Death.

4) Meditation has nothing to do with the out-of-body state. This belongs to the subconscious achievements. Meditation unites man and God directly. Stop making this mistake. You implicate the subconscious (material worlds) with the hyperconscious (spiritual worlds). You have not yet clarified in your mind the material worlds that the subconscious in its own right possesses and understands. Through Meditation, the Hyperconscious meets only the Spirit.

5) As you can see, you once again confuse the subconscious with the hyperconscious, Occultism (subconscious) with Mysticism (hyperconscious). One has no relation to the other. Only during the use of the subconscious (hypnotism, spiritualism) do the dangers you refer to appear. Not through the hyperconscious course of MEDITATION.

6) Only in our own world do good and evil exist. Here in this place-time and in our little world, in the lower and the most exoteric Dimension of Omnicreation does Karma or the Law of Retributive Justice exist or act. Higher above, neither good nor evil exists, only Truth exists; Truth that is foreign to good and evil, to happiness and unhappiness, to life and death, etc.

Wishing you the enlightenment of God,
Your Master
Margioris

7th Letter

Yugoslavia, November 10, 1986

Dear Mr. Margioris,

I felt the necessity to write you in relation to something that has often happened to me and that I have realized in the last two years. This 'something' always appears to me during sleep and especially when I sleep on my back, and either some clear dream unfolds or I do not remember any dream.

So, while I am sleeping and dreaming, I feel a shake and something like a weight or a pressure, paralyzing and benumbing my whole body, and creating a state of full undesirable immobility (though I am aware of the whole situation that prevents me from escaping from this suffocating pressure and the paralysis). From the first moment that this phenomenon appears, I react with will power, knowing that if I succeed in moving one centimeter, I will escape from the suffocating bonds of the weight and the paralysis that suddenly overwhelmed me. Now, the last time this happened to me, I thought that I had begun to see, before managing to open my eyes, the wall beside me, definitely a little changed and dim, very briefly while at the same time, I was struggling to wake up.

Every time this happens to me, perhaps from the shock I suffer, I somehow awaken, but I can neither open my eyes, nor move, feeling the pressure of a power that is nailing me down and immobilizing me or of a more powerful weight with the same results. So, reacting by instinct, I try to wake up by provoking a movement in my body, in order to escape from the suffocating pressure and the tingling in my limbs.

I truly experienced all that I have narrated to you in the

specific moment that they appeared. It is difficult to describe the whole experience but I hope that I have managed to convey to you this strange phenomenon that can be expressed in words only with difficulty.

Please, inform as best you can and enlighten me on this phenomenon or advise me on measures that must be taken.

Thanking you very much,
With love,
Ilias Katsiampas

7th Answer

Athens, November 14, 1986
to Mr. Katsiampas

Dear Ilias,

I received your letter of October 10th, 1986 and I am replying to you. Many other people feel what you feel in your sleep. They call it MORA or pressure or spiritual pressure and so on. It is the common phenomenon of the absence of the soul from the body. When the soul leaves the body, the body remains with its etheric body, which continuously supplies our physical body with life. When the etheric body leaves, when the connecting umbilical cord between the etheric and the physical body is cut, then man dies, since he does not revive the physical body with ever-living fire. But when the soul is absent, the etheric physical body is subject to different states. The 'mourmoulikia', (mourmoulikia: Inferior creatures that live in the etheric world and enjoy deceiving, annoying and laughing at people during their sleep), which live on etheric food, find the etheric body of man ready in front of them and start picking at it as they themselves are also composed of etheric matter. But every removal of a molecule from the etheric body of man creates the sensation of pain-pressure-strangulation.

When we sleep, the conscious is replaced by the subconscious and the former falls into lethargy until the sleeping person awakens and becomes vigilant once more. The 'mourmoulikia' or the beings of etheric nature, try to keep man in a state of subconsciousness, so that the sleeping person does not wake up. But as soon as the soul descends with incredible speed, then the 'mourmoulikia' disappear. This happens because the brightness of the soul burns these beings, which disappear from fear.

RECOMMENDATIONS

Man must sleep on his right side. He must be trained so that during hypnotism, the subconscious may move only one muscle of the body, any muscle, so as to alert the soul, which is connected to the etheric body (etheric - physical), to immediately descend in a flash to its place, in the physical body (etheric physical body of the sleeping person).

I have also received answers of different Keys.

I remain with love,
Your Master
N. Margioris

8th Letter

Yugoslavia, November 17, 1986

Dear Mr. Margioris, my best regards.

As I am in a particularly esoteric state, where I feel the need for practical confirmation and elevation and since I am in no position to actualize the achievement of the long-term aim of Meditation, I considered it a good idea to enroll in a school of the Western 'Esoteric Tradition (Kabbalah)' which may express me more. I believe it contains a true initiating system which derives from ancient years and achieves the Unity with the Superior Self or Hyperconsciousness. In this way, I believe that my time will not be wasted and that I may realize that this system does not suit me.

I thought it best to inform you about my decision as well as to express my desire not to discontinue the work we do together, since I still have many things to learn or I may even have made a wrong choice.

You may think that I am in a great hurry or that I am a thick-headed person. I recognize this to some extent, but deep down I am a very restless soul-searching spirit who is not satisfied with theory alone, as in actual fact, all theory ends in dogma and offers man a one-sided view. I do not refute anything by these words of mine, but I just wish to point out man's natural desire to become attached to something, so that he may feel safe and have the impression that he has attained his actualization as an individual, judging and condemning everything he may find in front of him with 'Divine' certainty.

I agree that practice is difficult and requires a particular sensitivity, but with methodical training and a true will, it can become a reality. So, since I cannot receive training in your school and I am unable to apply your Meditation key, which is not accompanied by a sufficiently-guiding analysis, I decided to try a completed system of 'Western Occultism' that 'sounds' closer to my idiosyncrasy and to my knowledge of its stages in general.

Though I think that, after mature consideration and appreciation, I have made up my mind, I would still like to hear your opinion. Please send me your answer to Yugoslavia.

Thanking you very much
With love and appreciation
Ilias Katsiampas

8th Answer

Athens, November 20, 1986
to Mr. Katsiampas

Dear Ilias,

I have received your letter of November 17th, 1986 and I felt your disquiet.

You ask my opinion about... new horizons... of practical applications etc.

Since you have already chosen and made up your mind, why do you ask me? I believe that you must go to the school you mention and acquire this experience as well. Nobody represents Truth exclusively. Truth exists within us. When the time is ripe, it will emerge from within you.

Meanwhile, you need the knowledge that is given by a responsible person and not by a SYSTEM.

But you must taste every fruit of the Earth. Sweet or bitter. This is what you need at this moment. Afterwards, you will see the vanity of your decision. From a distance, I gave you or rather I sent you the motives. You see, I never had you near me... to teach you practically and to pull your ear when necessary...

Now, you feel obliged to follow, as you write to me, the system of WESTERN OCCULTISM...

OMAKOIO will forget you and will delete you as its student until Easter 1987, so that you may find complete serenity in your new orientation. I hope you find what you desire. But I am 75 years old and you are still... a child.

May you not realize the vanity of your fraudulent pursuits and... despair.

Truth (God) needs work and faith, perseverance and sacrifice. Otherwise everything is a mistake...

I beg you not to contact OMAKOIO before Easter 1987. When you find what you are seeking, do not contact us anymore, even after Easter...

Wishing you full success,
I bless you, invoking Jesus Christ
With my wishes for rapid progress,
N. Margioris

NOTE: On the following two pages there are photographs of Master Nikolaos A. Margiori's manuscripts, so that the reader may get a clear sample of his hand-writing.

ΟΜΑΚΟΕΙΟ ΑΘΗΝΩΝ
ΝΙΚΟΛΑΣ ΜΑΡΓΙΩΡΗΣ
ΜΕΤΑΦΥΣΙΚΕΣ ΕΡΕΥΝΕΣ ΚΑΙ
ΓΙΟΓΚΑ - ΕΚΔΟΣΕΙΣ ΒΙΒΛΙΩΝ
ΚΑΙ ΠΕΡΙΟΔΙΚΟΥ
ΧΟΥΡ. ΤΡΙΚΟΥΠΗ 17 - ΕΞΑΡΧΕΙΑ
ΤΗΛΕΦ. 3608365
ΤΚ 10683

Αθήνα 20/11/86
Κύριον
Ηλίαν Καζιόφκα
Γιουκοσλαβία

Αγαπητέ Ηλία.

Έλαβα το γράμμα σου της 17/11/86 και είδα την ανησυχία σου. Μου ζητάς τη γνώμη μου για .... νέους δείχνοντες ... πρακτικώς εφαρμογήν. Αφού ήδη έχης ωρομείνει και διαβεβαιώσει τι θέλω τους; Η γνώμη μου είναι να πας και να δώσεις καυτή συνέχεια. Κανένας δεν αλησμοσώκεν ει δεσμεύθεις με την αλήθεια. Η αλήθεια πρόκειται μέσα μας. Από μέσα σου, σαν ερωδιός και αλλά ζώγζα, θα τη βγάζεις. Εν τω μεταξύ χρειάζεται γνώση σου δίνεται από έναν υπεύθυνο άνθρωπο και όχι ΑΠΟ ΣΥΣΤΗΜΑ. Αλλά πρέπει να γνωθείς και σε καιρό και σε γης. Γυσώ τι θέμα. Είναι κυβέρνη αυτή η ανάγκη σου. Ύστερα θα δώσεις το μαθαίνω της πράξης σου. Από ... παρουσά σου έδωσα ή μάλλον σου έπεμψα το έσωθιθ μαθα. Από και δεν θα είχα ωδεξωγιά ... να σε διδάζω πρακτικά και να σου σφυρίζω δίκαια και σε κει σου. ......
Τώρα εν των πραγμάτων υποχρεωνίθαι να παρασμοιωθίκες καθώς μου γράφεις το σύστημα ΑΥΤΙΚΟΝ ΑΠΟΚΡΥΦΙΣΜΟΥ. ...

Τό ὁμακοεῖο θά σέ ξεχάσει καί θά σέ
ξεχρεώσει ἀπό ὅλα ἐκτός ἕως τή Λαμ-
πρή τοῦ 1987, ὥστε νά βρεῖς ἀπό ὅλην
ἡσυχία σέ ὥρα ὁμακοεῖο... ἀροβαναλογιά τό
εὔχομαι νά βρεῖς τό ποδαρικό ν σ.
Ὅπως εἶναι 75 χρόνων καί εἶναι
ἀσέλα..... παιδί...
Εἶδε νά τή ἀντιμετωπίσεις τό
θάρρος τῶν ὅσο μικρῶν ἐστ......
δικηγόρου καί... ἀποφάσισές ....
Ἡ ἀγνθεια (Θεόι) χρειάζεται δου-
λειά καί ὅτι: ξεκαθαρίζριου
καί πασία. Ἀλλιώς, ὅτι εἶναι
γάδι......
Παρακαλῶ θερμά πρό τοῦ Πάσχα 1987
μήν ἀπασχολεῖς τό ΟΜΑΚΟΕΙΟ.
Ὅταν βρεῖς τό μ-πούλινο, μήν ἀπασχολήσεις
ἀπό δελῆς, ἐσύ κι ἐμᾶς γιά τό Πάσχα....
Εὔχομαι ἀπό ὅλη ψυχή ἡσυχία
σέ ἐλογω, ἐδῶ ὅπου εἶναι ἀπό
καί ἄν ὄσο χρειάσω.
Καλή πρόοδο

9th Letter- part a

Yugoslavia, November 28, 1986

Dear Mr. Margioris,

I have received your letters.

I realize that you are fulfilling a divine if not unique calling and this is exactly the reason why you are actually compelled to rely perhaps solely on your work, living your life in order to spread, as widely as possible, the Unique Esoteric Truth and the real purpose of man.

This means that your life is a continuous struggle for the improvement and for the development-actualization of the human race.

This is my belief about your person through the direct contact I've had with you, through your written work (books-correspondence) and the one face-to-face contact that has taken place. I also see you as a person who attained self-actualization-Union and is now striving for the good of all, for the elevation of man. This is my opinion of you so far, regardless of whether I am wrong.

I would like to ask you some questions:

1) In which ray dimension can we place the Superior Self-Hyperconsciousness?

2) Is Hyperconsciousness the Spirit-God in Metaphysics - Esotericism? That is, is it the Superior Self-Ego-Mind? However, is the Superior self or the True Self-Spirit really the Global Consciousness or the Universal Ego or the Universal Mind?

3) During our earthly life, the only self-actualization-union that can be obtained is the one of our lower self (consciousness) with hyperconsciousness or the superior self. Is there perhaps another superior union and if so, which one?

Where does it reside? What is the difference between this one and the previous one?

4) In your letter, you inform me that a correspondence course in Raja Yoga is possible but it will involve a high cost. Please give me more details about how long it will last and how much money will be needed? What are the lesson topics that will be dealt with?

5) Please, provide me with a theoretical and practical comparative analysis of the following systems: Raja Yoga and Kabbalah. In general, I know the following: First of all, Raja Yoga follows the path of the negative and of the repulsion of matter, which it considers an error, a lie, not real, realizing, of course, that this leads to the union with the Superior Self.

Its practical technique involves a life of 'abstinence' and morality that, with the practice of Meditation (Samadhi) and through Karma Yoga, actualizes the union with the Superior Self in the right way. I am not aware of what visions or breathing exercises it uses.

As for Kabbalah, it recognizes all the schools that lead to spiritual elevation as equal in value, accepting that every seeker has his own idiosyncrasy and his own level of esoteric cultivation, which means that in accordance with his qualitative evolution, he is attracted by one or the other of the most important systems offered.

It also accepts matter in its system as the 'bright clothing of the eternal' and not as something dirty, but as something important for the correct and controlled elevation. As it says, we must step firmly on matter, for the obvious reasons that such careful and controlled contact is for beneficial purposes towards our fellow-humans. Thus, the so-called expression of the Superior Self is attained in the initiated individual of Kabbalah.

Also, its teachings are based on the so-called symbolic 'Tree of Life', through which the trainee harmonizes and ennobles its vessels (sentiments etc.). Thus, it attains the control- taming of the Mind, so that the expression of the Superior Self (Enlightenment) may be undertaken harmlessly.

Would you please give me a more objective and substantial analysis.

6) According to Western Occultism, what is the meaning of the names that characterize the initiated who follow the unbalanced development without taking into consideration the tides (stellar influences) and so on? And who follows the destiny of all those who are called the Sons of Loss, roaming stars etc.?

I await your analytical answers. As I recognize that you are busy, please answer when you find the time, as I am interested in the details and my questions are substantial.

Please send your letter to Trikala in December.

Thank you very much,
Yours very truly,
Ilias Katsiampas

P.S.: After I wrote you the two letters, I received your reply for my possible choice of Western Occultism.

Once again, I have confirmed my initial opinion of you, that you respect the Freedom of Will and the different ways to access Truth. As I acknowledge that you are one of the few ascended Masters, I am still considering my choice of Kabbalah.

That is the reason why I asked you all those questions: because I am seeking and want to clear up the details and the main approaches that define a trainee's main idiosyncrasies.

I know that my attempts at ascension will be realized, which means that I shall start changing myself fundamentally and substantially, internally as well as externally.

I am also asking for guidance with specific instructions as to the practical application, for that is what holds appeal to me and my attempts at ascension; I do not wish to be repulsed or made passive. This is the major incentive I need, at least as I see it, and provided that the other obstacles such as memories of fear, of superstitions, of prejudices and so on, are overcome. Only with a specific, daily and consistent method may I be able to ascend the necessary steps of elevation.

I, the above-signed

9th Letter-part b

Yugoslavia, November 28, 1986

Dear Mr. Margioris,

In a letter dated November 7th, 1986 that I sent to my female friend seeker, whom I mentioned in one of my previous letters, I informed her about as many Metaphysical matters as possible to which I believe I have discovered a solution that defines esoteric Truth.

I felt encouraged to spread the Truth to an individual who has all the necessary prerequisites to conceive of Metaphysical matters and who can perceive the Truth, though she has formulated some errors in thinking (for example, dogmatic ones); I analyze to her the most important elements that define the correct way of seeking and understanding Truth.

So, with my relatively poor writing, I will make an effort to briefly summarize certain matters.

At its depth, our world is composed of all kinds of souls that, as a rule, are either involved or sunk in matter or crystallized or recently arrived. The mature souls that are not satisfied with their fellow-man's way of life and are roaming and continually seeking the answers to philosophical or ontological questions or are vibrated by an unselfish love for their fellow-man, society and for HIM, the Divine Substance itself that only Love, especially Universal Love can approach since he is the seed of every individualized Ego, of every man (personality-Ego).

All of us are ONE and from ONE we all derive. Nearly all religious teachings talk about the impending return of every spark-atom-Ego to the Singularity itself from which it has come.

This is the UNION (Yoga) that the most mature souls sought and seek, where partiality will be united-deified with ENTIRETY, the temporary with the Eternal element. We had similar mystical souls in the Greek Orthodox Church, such as Gregory the Sinaite, Gregory Palamas, Nikodemus of the Holy Mountain and so on.

To every apprentice two paths are open. The first one is for those who encounter the Esoteric Truth for the first time along with the transcendent world of the Esoteric Pulse Depth, who seek and remain in the endless search for the knowledge of the Esoteric Universes since they are new souls that are trying for the first time to connect with the visible and the invisible, and with the Worlds and the Beings that hide within them.

They seek to flock together until the necessary experience has been gained, through the continual understanding of vanity.

The second path is the direct contact image-union of the prepared Mystic with the Divine and Supreme Substance that cannot be described since it is the full actualization of man's purpose. It is the return itself of the Prodigal Son to his home and to his Father.

The mystics are distinguished by their particular sensitivity and religiosity that emanates from them at all times. It is they who constitute the Father's real children or his Words.

Matter is a maya (error), a crude copy, an illusion, an untruth, it is the temporary and the past element.

Man always tries to 'appear' good, superior, rich, clever etc. and not 'BE' as he ought to.

Personality is not our true self; but the lower, the external self, lost in its passions, weaknesses, stresses, fears, inhibitions, desires to dominate or receive support from his fellow-men. Man tries to move within the limits of the moral values of his people (traditions, customs), overcome by superstitions and prejudices that constitute his temporary and erratic personality, in a kingdom where his passions reign and rule. He moves forward, unrestrained, in the same deep waters, thinking that he will remain afloat forever, until he sinks and... one day he will be reborn, to do what? To be dogmatized, to support, to judge and to condemn and certainly, to depend on the status quo and on authority.

The true or Superior Self or Hyperconsciousness or Esoteric Self is the Spirit, the spark, our true Self. The eternal sensation of the Ego, of Existence, of Being, but without the feeling of 'who am I?' It is beyond morals, customs, dogmatisms, judgments, accusations, prejudices, knowledge, etc.

It is about our esoteric voice, our feelings that are stirred up when we face a bad or a tragic event. It is the superior controller and guide of our inferior and mortal self. All the real seekers must have this union of the exoteric with the esoteric self as their principal aim, so that man may become the sovereign of his personality, and not its blind slave, his assistant in his self-actualization. It is the fulfillment of 'KNOW THYSELF.'

That was the principal part of the letter which I submit to you for correction and so that you can have a more complete idea about what I write in my other letter. I think I was able to clearly express my own beliefs about the above-mentioned matters.

In any case, I want to assure you that my main interest is the Metaphysical quest and understanding. And more precisely, during the last 5 years, in order to fulfill this purpose, I have collected numerous books on topics ranging from parapsychology to Science to Occultism and Metaphysics. I wish to have a spherical and well-founded view and not only a theoretical or abstract one.

I want to grasp as many matters as possible so as to attain a complete understanding. So, I am studying psychology, philosophy, parapsychology, history, archaeology, medicine, physiology, nuclear physics etc. to fill the terrible gaps I feel I have. This means that most of my money goes to the purchase of relevant books that open new horizons of thought and comprehension to me. I may send you some books or articles written by my friend, so that you may see her truly advanced evolution. Please send me your reply along with the other letter to Trikala, where I shall be during all of December.

Thanking you for paying attention to my letter,
Sincerely yours
Ilias Katsiampas

Answer 9a and b

Athens, December 5, 1986
to Mr. Katsiampas
Trikala

Dear Mr. Ilias,

In spite of the punishment that I have imposed on you in my previous letter, I am replying to your two letters dated November 28th, 1986, which I just received. I will answer both your letters together because I do not have enough time available to answer them individually.

ANSWERS

1) Hyperconsciousness is a means that conceives vibrations superior to our diffused Universe. It is not our superior or our esoteric self. It is not found in any RAY or in any Dimension. According to man's evolution, it receives vibrations: a) from our Etheric world, b) from the Thymo-astral Dimension and c) difficult and rare vibrations of the 11th Intellectual Dimension...

2) Nothing is true of all these. It is the highest organ of the Mind that manages to conceive, IF IT IS USED in the proper way, the spiritual vibrations, which are foreign and unknown to our world. Everything else you write is irrelevant to this.

3) There are TWO unions. The union of the inferior self or consciousness with the superior self or the Mind with the soul, through the Intellect. The second union is the one of the soul-spirit and God. The difference between the two is immense...

4) I reply only to you. I never said that Raja Yoga taught

as a correspondence course could lead to actualization. It would only supply encyclopedic knowledge. Now you are completing your studies. You have no time for actualizations in Raja Yoga. Actualization can only be taught at the feet of a Master. The succession of steps in Raja Yoga are:

YAMA, NIYAMA, ASANA, PRANAYAMA, PRATYA-HARA, DHARANA, DHYANA, SAMADHI, KAIBALAYA.

What do you understand of all that you ask about? Someday, when you learn about it, you will laugh at yourself.

Now, no school for Raja yoga is in operation. One will operate in two years again. You may study on your own in a private tutorial course. However, this is difficult and expensive. You have to wait for your time to come and for your Karma's permission. You're running ahead of your Karma. Everything will come in due time. You are trying hard and suffering hardship in vain. There are unbreakable laws of the soul.

5) Your fifth question is immense and extends to judgments about Raja and... Kabbalah... What is the relationship between two unlike things? This is where you go astray and err. You're comparing potatoes and carrots. You do not yet understand that Metaphysics is an immense field in which both wild and gentle grasses grow.

The human soul is **FREE** to learn everything that is presented to it. But I am surprised by the haste with which you make decisions about matters you do not YET grasp.

Now, listen to my advice for the last time. Where are you going, without having trained your body and your Mind? Matter gave us the body. The body gave us the soul through its Intellect. The soul will allow us to grasp the SUPERIOR SOUL or our Eternal Father and God. Pay attention not to encounter the disappointments that many other people encountered during their passage on Earth.

First of all, you must learn:
KARMA YOGA
BHAKTI YOGA
JNANA and then **RAJA YOGA**.

You will learn how to use your Hyperconscious to accomplish what you want. It should bring you to vibrations or to esoteric dimensions/worlds where **LIGHT EXISTS**.

6) Since you know that YOUR ELEVATION will be attained only by you, QUO VADIS? WHERE ARE YOU GOING?

I shall give you ONLY advice:
AWAITING
PATIENCE
KNOWLEDGE
JUDGMENT
DECISION
ACTUALIZATION

Afterwards, you will be free to do whatever your soul wishes. This means two things:

a) The needed experience for your soul

b) Your Karma. Your past and current obligations.

To conclude, follow the dictates of the proverb: 'A rolling stone gathers no moss.' Did you find the source? Stay near it. Otherwise you will enter the Labyrinth of many different views. This is a serious reason that will help you make up your mind...

Wishing you Enlightenment,
Happy Holidays,
N. Margioris

10th Letter

Yugoslavia, January 5, 1987

Dear Mr. Margioris,

Though belatedly, I send you my wishes for a Prosperous New Year, for happiness and health.

To start with, I must inform you that I have enrolled in the school of Kabbalah and that I am taking my first steps in the training that it offers for the apprentice's elevation.

I feel the obligation to assure you that my motives are pure, and that my only aim-purpose-ideal is the knowledge-approach-union with my superior self or my esoteric self or soul, in order to be able to know (live) and to be able to offer my services to my fellow-men. I realize that this is a long and fundamental journey and that after persistent efforts, I will arrive there... one day. Of course, this is not my final target-ideal, though it will one day become a reality and perhaps only then will I be able to say with certainty that I know and... will act accordingly.

I also recognize and am trying to live a virtuous, moderate life, with a successive-gradual purging of wishes-habits, with a clear understanding of why, and not just because a certain system or religion etc. imposes it on me as an ideal; fully understanding the value and the necessity for this experience. I believe you understand me. I will inform you below about the reasons for my 'going astray.'

In recent years, my quests led me to change many opinions and to adopt many philosophies-theories and especially Yoga that is represented by you and that is one of the most important systems of esoteric development, a completed path leading to the self-discovery of Truth. So, by studying Yoga-Metaphysics, I have comprehended as much as possible, who I am, the reason for existence and my purpose - to return to the Source. It is not easy for me to state to you what speculations and thoughts I have made and I am still making. Anyway, though I realized the necessity for elevation and completion, I thought hard during this past semester. This summer, especially, I suffered a state of great frustration and inactivity toward my environment, the people and especially toward the wide range of discussions that focused mainly on material subjects. I was asking myself, 'what's the matter?' And I was allowing myself to sink into passivity and inactivity.

Almost nothing was important to me, everything was empty talk, full of void, unsatisfied passions, illusions, hypocrisy and egoism (even mine). I made many efforts to reinstate some form of communication, but continued to shut myself in. So, I started avoiding many of my 'friends' because I clearly saw that we did not suit each other and that there was nothing in common in our pursuits and in our interests.

Although I suffered a serious sense of futility, I did not judge it right to 'escape' from life but to obtain a balance and to act in a positive way.

This is when I began wondering as to how much the philosophy of Yoga is helping me and I thought to turn my quests in other directions, such as that of Kabbalah, which I had known about and had looked into even before I came into contact with you.

But even if Kabbalah represents Occultism - vanity, its purpose is clear: it is the actualization of the superior or esoteric self which will be attained after many years of preparation and hard work taming and controlling the Mind, so that the ascension may be realized, correctly, actively and effectively, for the initiated person himself, but also for his fellow-men and the prevailing unhappiness.

Besides this, Alice Bailey in her book *Letters on Occult*

Meditation mentions the differences between the Mystic and the Occultist and points out that when the two types (souls) pass by the four rays (initiations) and end in the fifth one, their development will be completed respectively for both of them.

Also, after having studied Krishnamurti, I was literally overwhelmed, seeing everything from an unprecedented perspective but also noticing the 'sluggish application' of its cultivation that he so comprehensively advocates, but is so unattainable, even for seekers, as men are not prepared for the full freedom of their thought that they always limit and bind. So, even in this school of thought, they are compelled to ask for assistance from a Guru, who can help teach them ways of thinking or how to block thoughts, keeping only one to successfully achieve concentration-samadhi. Essentially, this defines the lower nature of man, as man prefers dependence to free and active thought. And I believe that this happens because we learn what to think and not how to think. I made up my mind about Kabbalah after considerable thought and because I discerned no ulterior motives on the part of the school. I should inform you that it is a non-profit organization that requires no payment and does not bind me to other Metaphysical studies or books but advises against adulterating the practical technical exercises that are taught with the techniques of other systems.

I suspect that somewhere along the evolutionary process some 'enticement' will be applied, perhaps to develop powers in relation to the unharmonized purification process, but I believe that I shall attain my aim with as little deviation as possible.

Anyway, I have discovered a more 'rational-scientific' approach that rather suits me and that is offered to a great extent in Kabbalah. If you happen to have reservations or concerns about the school, the system, me or something else, please let me know. Below, I present you with some important questions and ask you to address them when you have free time.

1) Is God (Universal consciousness) the Ego? Is the Ego the primary unit from which the individualized Egos are created? Is the Ego defined as an eternal sense of existence (I am-I exist), that penetrates everything and is everywhere and nowhere? Is it accompanied by a state of whole love and happiness or is there something else? In fact, is there ever an end? Is this, however, the element that is everywhere and ever-present and that blows life into all the formed lengths and widths of all the Universes and Galaxies?

2) Is everything states of consciousness? Can you give me more information about this?

3) We have 13 Founding Rays/Groves that derive from the Creator, each of which is composed of 13 Dimensions. More specifically, our 7th Founding Ray ends in our formed 13th external Dimension. When somebody manages to return to the unchanged Source, then does he remain there until he is... detached again for a new individualized existence in some future Founding Ray/grove, in order to become a Deacon - Devas - Archangel or to sow new fields of Chaos? Or what else?

4) Does the Unknown Death exist? What happens with the existence (individual - ego) that did not manage to bring order to the chaos within itself, that which we call the second death? Does it concern the death of the etheric body or the End of Time (Pralaya) that finds man's vessel – body unprepared, without the necessary purification – harmonization, destroyed - dispersed of the elements that compose it, leaving the spark – ego unprotected, and dispersed? Isn't Man immortal? That is to say, doesn't he struggle for his immortality through evolution and purification for as long

as he is on Earth? Aren't all the partial elements of the incarnated individual (spirit, soul, body), and especially the qualities constituting the human spirit (thought, will, imagination), immortal? Doesn't individuality as a whole and as consciousness of the Ego ensure immortality, until at least some connection and ordering of the elements of the reincarnated individual is achieved?

I hope that I am not tiring you very much. Please, send me your answers along with the following books: *9th and 10th Meditation lessons* and your book *Patapios the Humble, the Philosopher and Saint from Egypt*, to Yugoslavia.

**With great love and appreciation,
Ilias Katsiampas**

NOTE: There was no reply to this letter (10th).

In October 1987, the writer realizing the mistake of his 'choice', acknowledged his error and returned to his Master, enrolling in the Omakoio of Athens and in the Raja Yoga school which he faithfully attended henceforth, fully resolved and committed. In the beginning, he would come and attend classes from Yugoslavia where he was a student. He continued when he was fulfilling his military service and then, as a civilian.

In the recent period, along with his close apprenticeship with his Master, he became an active instructor in the Omakoio of Trikala that he established on December 1st, 1991. Throughout this period, he concentrated on the extensive study of and training in Esotericism under the direct guidance of Master Nikolaos A. Margioris until the latter's departure on May 6th, 1993. Since then and to this day he has continued His spiritual legacy, responsibly and methodically.

11th Letter

Yugoslavia, April 23, 1988

Dear Master,

With some delay, I send you my wishes for a Happy Easter. The problem with my military service deferment has been resolved, so, I will be near you once again to attend the Raja Yoga course.

I am writing you now from Yugoslavia to ask you some questions on Metaphysical reality, which are preoccupying me.

1) Since November, but more rarely now, I have been seeing something like an eye which might, however, be a cross and the pupil of an eye, sometimes in the center and sometimes the whole shape. When I asked Mrs. Smaro about it, she said that this eye or this cross means the introversion of the Mind, that is that the Mind is starting to become introverted. This happens at intervals, and most often when I am on the verge of falling asleep. What is your opinion?

2) I would like you to inform me about the states that are called: a) 'Guardian of the threshold' and b) 'Dark night of the soul.' Which of these is Raja Yoga influenced by and to which of the 8 steps of Patanjali do the above states correspond?

3) From what I heard, at least by some former female students, every student has some protective covering from the Master. Please, give me more information about the type of protective influence (thought-form or other) and how it helps or offers protection.

4) According to Alice Bailey's books *The Rays and the Initiations* but also to yours, which is the ray you yourself serve, as a Master?

5) Regarding Pranayama: To attain the 320 times that the daily program requires, how do we measure the breathing (the times)? Is a completed time considered according to the inhalation, the holding in, the exhalation or the holding out?

6) Raja Yoga Meditation is the continual focusing of a thought on a certain internal or external point-target-object, without the target being an object of any thought. In other words, is this focusing of the Mind on only one point-topic a thought or not? That is, does the Mind remain motionless-passive and does it accept some internal thought of a similar, but unknown until recently, nature which constitutes the personal or, to the more developed, the racial unconscious? Is Raja Yoga meditation receptive and not active? That is, does it draw on the esoteric knowledge connected with the object-target until it identifies or unites with it? Please, give me more and clearer explanations.

7) When somebody starts realizing, even through reason, that Truth (God) does not exist in the world of relativity, duality and maya, he develops a sense of futility for the world of forms, resulting in a gradual descent into passivity and inactivity. This has a serious social effect, since this person becomes antisocial and without knowing how to swim, he ends up floating on deep waters, with a half-inflated life jacket, being in constant danger.

That is, he loses the low, but nonetheless indispensable, communication with other people, for the very correct but perhaps not very comprehensible reasons of introversion, which may lead some young people who are at a transitional age to extreme acts or even to suicide.

As I wrote to you a year and half ago, I had suffered a serious crisis of purposelessness - certainly not leading to suicide – that lead me to a passivity that has not yet disappeared completely, and as I am also seeking Moderation, I ask you:

Is the confrontation of this event achieved with the non-identification with or with the detachment from the phenomenon-events etc.?

And if so, how do we develop this detachment that calms and helps the Mind to concentrate? Based on these data, what is your opinion and your advice on this subject?

8) I bought and studied the Bhagavad Gita that you recommended to me.

The reason was my question about the war between two countries and about every man's position (whether initiated or uninitiated) towards the destructive war machine. You told me that we had to fight and that it concerned a karmic counter-balance and you had referred me to the Bhagavad Gita which helped me realize what I already knew, but in connection with this specific matter. So, I understood and distinguished between the perishable and the eternal.

But I would like to ask if every effort to abide by AHIMSA (no violence) is lost or is it not important to someone who is initiated? Also, is an aggressive but not defensive war, also considered a karmic counter-balance? On an interpersonal level (disputes, quarrels, oppositions), is the real winner he who applies Ahimsa? But must Ahimsa be practiced in all cases, that is, is it the rule or must we judge for ourselves in which case it applies?

9) In which cases is man charged with Karma and in which cases is he depleted of it? Does Meditation help in the case of Karmic depletion?

All these and many more questions often occupy my mind, so I thought it best to set them before you in order to receive responsible and true answers from you, for you are the Truth on Earth.

Thanking you very much and awaiting your answers in Yugoslavia,

>Yours very truly,
>Ilias Katsiampas

11th Answer

>to Mr. Ilias Katsiampas
>Yugoslavia

Dear Ilias, good day,

I just received your letter of April 23rd, 1988 to which I reply because you are far away, you are thirsty, you want to learn everything and you are in such a hurry that I should scold you. You will find everything in my books and in all my other works. But, as I said, in spite of my immense workload, I will take the time to answer your questions quickly, briefly and a little angrily.

1) This eye or cross you see is proof that you are well-focused on the external target or on the supposed esoteric one. With this steady contact of yours with the object of the target or of the subject of your target, it is the pupil of your own eye that you see reflected with eyes shut or open.

In short, it is as a result of your concentration. Later, with intense concentration, you will see a diamond cross with 5 bright gems. That is the introversion of the Mind. This is where the wavering state of consciousness appears: although it is attracted by the subconscious, the conscious reacts, but the hyperconscious does not slip in, which is fortunate for the inexperienced seeker. The fruit is still unripe and much pain and time is needed to permanently attract the hyperconscious...

2) The dark nights of the soul are, when the tug of war of the conscious-subconscious is underway, and they do not offer the Mind the peace and freedom to elevate to the hyperconscious path, to receive higher matter vibrations. Here the guardian at the threshold appears (Ring-pass-not). The Mind is not let free to use its hyperconscious. Consciousness (vigilance) and subconsciousness (permanent sleep...) keep it imprisoned. The ternary, the trinity of the three hypostases, height, width, length, prevails. Time is absent. There, at its union, the elevation of the Mind becomes four-dimensional.

3) Do not listen to Lambrini or Smaro or anybody else. What I write you is enough.

4) Bailey's words are comprehensible, after an esoteric elevation of 'LOVE'.

5) Pranayama, depending on the case, serves and helps the trainee. In many cases its numerical limits move upwards and downwards.

Notice that Pranayama begins where the naturalness of man's everyday occupation ends. For example, in Raja Yoga one counts seconds.

a) Inhale 18' seconds
b) Hold in 54' seconds
c) Exhale 27' seconds
d) Hold out 18' seconds

Total 117' seconds starting with the left nostril. The same goes for the right nostril. Then we have 117 + 117 = 234 seconds. This will happen only THREE TIMES. Three times 234 X 3 = 702 seconds, before we reach Pratyahara. See my book *Raja Yoga*, page 139 etc.

There is a difference between using Pranayama in preparation for Raja ascension, whereby we use these time durations GRADUALLY; and using Pranayama to help the organism, to strengthen muscles and nerves, muscles etc.

We reduce these time intervals, 18', 54', 27', 18' = 117', as much as we wish according to our level and our endurance. 'Less is more.'

6) This focusing of the Mind on the target of concentration (Dharana) aims to keep the Mind FAR FROM THOUGHTS. Thoughts during concentration is the victory of the conscious, so you can forget about ascension to the hyperconscious (Dharana, Dhyana, Samadhi). No thoughts. We ask for twelve seconds (12').concentration without any thoughts. 12 X 12 = 144'. In the 144th second we enter Meditation or Dhyana. Now 144' X 12 times = 1728' will bring us to the union with the Father, to the elevated four-dimensional coherence of everything, to the much awaited Samadhi.

Here 12' + 144' + 1728' = 1884' and sometimes only with 1728', we enter the four-dimensional space. Place-time, width, length, height, time, cause, effect, a unified system of the roots and basis of our world.

7) Your mistake. No inactivity and no passivity. On the contrary. The seeker develops such activity that he serves as an example. Take me, for example; I am 75 years old and I work hard, not even caring about health problems. The seeker of the four-dimensional state is not at all anti-social. He knows what he wants and what he is asking for. His Mind is healed and functions better than before, ascending the steps of ASHTANGA YOGA and arriving at Dharana to enter Dhyana and Samadhi.

Those who say so, have not been trained in RAJA, in psychological Yoga or mental yoga or the so-called spiritual Yoga.

Man's Mind is cured, quite effectively, in fact. It gives fertility and activity to a great extent. Notice that everything only needs rhythm and order. You must keep a rhythm in Pranayama, a correct line in Pratyahara 73' and 12' + 144' + 1728' at the balcony of the palace you are building. There must be no sometimes high and sometimes low, sometimes quick and sometimes slow, sometimes continuously and sometimes intermittently. You must always follow a program that you will execute with prudence, respect and attention.

8) You must continuously and always read the Bhagavad Gita. Do the same with the New Testament too. You must frequently be on a spiritual course inwards or upwards. Ahimsa is the only path that helps man on the road to the sought after luminous kingdom. Never resort to violence. Always no violence. Then your soul will become serene and will... fly.

This graceful and serene 'PEACE TO YOU' is the great means. That is what every man's non-violent behaviour offers.

You may not yet understand me, perhaps it is still too early. But the path to peace, that is, the non-selfish path leads to OMNIPOTENCE where everything yields to the decisive course of the non-violent initiate. Ahimsa, no attachment to matter.

9) Karma exists as long as it is found in the THREE-DIMENSIONAL world. As soon as one enters the FOUR-DIMENSIONAL world, Karma is diffused and withdraws, because one is so saintly that one is not touched by the fumes of matter. Therefore, when one enters meditation and reaches the end, that is Samadhi; one has burnt one's sins or the so-called KARMA in a cold fire.

10) I am not the Truth on Earth. This is wrong. I am just a philosopher seeking Truth, night and day. I draw the bow

of Love and arm myself with the arrows of Hope, aiming for the heart I love so much, the Beloved Heart of Sweet Jesus Christ, who was so ignored by the people.

I write all this only for you. I consider you a fertile field and I am sowing the good seeds of my Meditation...

Stop asking me, the time will come when you will know the answers. I see that you are already answering your own questions. Read my books and forget about everything else.

With true love,
Your Master
N. Margioris

12th Letter

Yugoslavia September 12, 1988

Dear Master,

I hope my letter finds you in excellent health and full of strength for your activities of the new year.

I am writing to you from Yugoslavia to ask you some questions that are common but important for me. They are the following:

1) Besides the etheric chakras (energy centers), there are the respective stellar, intellectual ones etc. What is their difference and their role in reference to the etheric ones?

2) Three years ago, I spent the summer in Zakynthos. One afternoon, my parents and I visited Saint Dionysius and witnessed a case of demonic possession (catalepsy) that I am in no position to know how authentic it was. It was a

woman who was about 35 years old, with a big bump on her head, dressed in black and looking very sick. She was accompanied by two other women and by one gentleman. When she approached the glass where the corpse of the saint was, I was beside her and heard her saying in a whisper, "Hold me, it is seizing me." Afterwards, she sat on a chair with her hands crossed behind her. She began having seizures, foaming at the mouth and, in general, she was in a state of great tension. Her voice had somehow changed, and had become harder and she began saying different things, insulting the people who were there, with curses, references to the antichrist, 666, threats etc. Finally, at a certain moment, she appeared to relax, as if a burden had been lifted from within her, and with a sigh, she got up completely calm and quiet, and kept saying, "Pray for my soul."

As I was informed afterwards, she had been as strong as an ox in the past.

This situation, as her relatives told us, began at a very young age, when her father had insulted her very harshly with regard to the Divine.

I narrate this case to you as a personal experience that made me think hard. Are catalepsies from 'demonic possessions' that occur to different people and in more severe forms than the one I described to you - as I have been informed by my acquaintances who have witnessed such events - real? Or are they related to disturbances of the Mind?

What are the indicative factors by which we can understand the difference? And what can we do to help people in these cases?

3) Illness, every illness (as you write in your books) from an esoteric point of view, is the disproportionate intake of Life Force (Prana) that disturbs the balance of the positive and negative power forces within us, creating illnesses. Can

an experienced Esoteric Healer, a Meditator, a White Magician and so on, cure any illness? Physical (body illnesses) and psychical (mental illnesses)?

Can he cure even the most cursed diseases (cancers, AIDS) or resist them effectively? What are the limitations of the Esoteric Healer and the possible reasons for his failure and what is the interrelation with the karma of the person receiving therapy? Also, does the interpretation of the new disease AIDS, explain it as the excessive intake of prana or some other external element that has this quantity of prana within it and thus creates the phenomenon of AIDS?

4) At what point can a beginner meditator - esoteric healer start successfully applying self-therapy and eterotherapy for some perhaps simple diseases of the Body and Mind and for 'demonic possessions'? That is, can he start applying therapies from the moment he is successful with his meditation – peeling back the layers and identifying with his target or his purpose or with his subsequent degrees of ecstasy?

5) To what extent does what we call 'exact predetermination' (destiny, fate), or rather predisposition or inclination towards the manifestation of certain events, exist? To what extent is a simple man, with his Free Will, able to control his destiny (karma) or the probable evolutions or how much he is the prey of karma, since he is supposed to have the freedom of choice? What is the difference between him and the initiated one in theory (in Esotericism) and what is the difference on a practical level (completion)?

6) What is the interpretation of the great WHY of Creation? What explanations can be given in approximation with words (symbols) for the reason behind the presence of the Absolute, the Perfect, the Unmanifest, of God, apart from the explanation of the experience, since the perfect would not need it?

7) Matter, all matter, is the phenomenon, the antithesis to the thesis. It is the error, vanity, perishability, imperfection, the past, the unreal. So, talking about the fourth Dimension, about the etheric world (thinner matter), about the world of causes, the invisible, the esoteric levels, the esoteric dimensions and so on, we are talking about the subtler states of matter (maybe more refined), that are perhaps, sometimes and somewhere de-spiritualized. But we are still talking about phenomena and about perishable states.

However, why does Raja Yoga say that in the Etheric world – the fourth Dimension – in Samadhi, we shall find God, that we shall reach Theosis? By developing our hyper-senses and by putting Hyperconsciousness into operation, are we really in a position to conceive finer matter vibrations of the diffused Universe / Etheric world?

Perhaps, in this way we better conceive and realize Its nature. You may tell me that the Etheric world is homogeneous, while the present world is inhomogeneous.

Then, why are the etheric beings living there not actualized, and are, in fact, at a lower evolutionary level than man? Could it be that, through self-concentration and isolation to one and only thought, we leave even if for a moment, the dialectical (intellectual) part of our personality and touch and communicate with the Divine Substance within us which is the spark or the soul and contains the Divine qualities, Eternal Existence - Knowledge - Bliss? And could it be that with the effective exclusion of every thought (every egocentric and personality trait) we achieve the liberation from the bonds of karma with Asamprajnata Samadhi? Under what conditions does the perpetual union, SAHAJA SAMADHI, take place on Earth? I await your explanations through your own experience.

I am expressing below my wish concerning your School.

Dear Master, I wish to become more active in your School, through every possible activity on my part. Of course, as concerns the spread of Esotericism and more specialized probing in some cases, I am doing it with all my heart and with all my knowledge.

But I would like to do the same in more practical matters too. Such as editing texts, books, essays that are to be published and/or any other activity.

I look forward to your response concerning possible activities I could actively participate in.

Hoping that we shall talk personally when the Raja Yoga courses of the 2nd year start.

Awaiting your letter with your answers in Yugoslavia.

**With great love,
Ilias Katsiampas**

P.S.: Dear Master, I set below, as briefly as possible, a most important question that has been occupying and torturing me for over a year.

Can Raja Yoga's Samadhi be achieved in two main ways-methods (perhaps three)?

a) With the elevation of the Mind from Consciousness to Hyperconsciousness that is achieved through Meditation, b) With Special techniques that awaken Kundalini and elevate it to the chakra Sahasrara and perhaps c) With the merging of the two brains, the physical and the etheric. However, in the first case, the Yogi enters the etheric world – the fourth Dimension and can, on an evolutionary level, surpass the astral world and reach the fourth step of the Intellectual world. In order to enter the fifth Intellectual step, the umbilical cords of attachment with the etheric-physical body (death) must be severed, and this presupposes the severing of every karmic bond (it is not subject to reincarnation). So, the Yogi continues his evolution, liberated.

Now, in the second case, the awakening of Kundalini as well as the chakras are mentioned, where the awakened Kundalini rises and 'bites' and awakens these etheric centers of power (or hyperconscious centers), aiming (according to the qualitative evolution of each of us) to reach and to be united with the Sahasrara chakra (Shiva and Shakti or Kundalini).

But, according to your books, *Posthumous Life, Hatha Yoga, Raja Yoga, Kriya Yoga, The Two-Volume Metaphysical Encyclopaedia* and especially in the *Esoteric Key* and your completed works *Meditation and Esoteric Therapeutics* and others, you give every etheric chakra some particular qualities, abilities and so on, that respond, are proportionate and correspond not only to the physical glands of the body but also to other esoteric worlds - esoteric dimensions. And I quote some extracts from your books as examples:

a) The Svadisthana chakra corresponds on a microcosmic scale to the seminal vesicles, but on a macrocosmic scale it corresponds to the etheric world, to the 3rd ray of the outer 13th dimension.

b) The Anahata chakra corresponds, on the one hand to the thymus gland (heart) and on the other hand to the Buddhist world - dimension that is superior to the Intellectual one and certainly has, its 7 sublevels, with its proportion to the 2nd ray of the 10th external dimension.

c) Concerning the Sahasrara chakra which corresponds to the pineal gland on the part of the physical function, it corresponds at the same time to the UNIQUE, to the 1st ray and to the 8th external Dimension. Samadhi is supposed to come about only with the union of Shiva and Shakti, in the Sahasrara chakra. But this probably applies to the highest Samadhi, since the correspondence of the Sahasrara chakra is with the Unique or with the 8th external Dimension, which is the almost pure spirit.

Do all the above mean that, from the moment we awaken any chakra: a) we are able to visually conceive (through visions) the different states of the most perfect Dimensions? b) we become conscious in the world - Dimension the chakra corresponds to? c) we develop and create our action body in that world?

What happens exactly?

Also, how is it possible for the etheric umbilical cords connecting the etheric-physical body with the other worlds, in the 5th Intellectual Step not to be severed? In other words, can the living Initiate (Mystic) continue further on his evolution if he has the time?

Therefore, every chakra awakening is a 'little samadhi' or more than one, since every chakra contains and corresponds to 7 sub-dimensions - sub-levels of every Dimensional plane.

I have also noticed in many Yoga books that there is one more (perhaps even more) chakra, the so-called Bindu, between Ajna and Sahasrara that means sperm of the first vibration, the control center of Nadi and so on, which, however, you do not mention in your books.

What are its parts and what is its microcosmic and macrocosmic correspondence?

And finally, when Kundalini ascends and is to be united with the Sahasrara chakra, does - as you write in your books - a new vessel that collects the Substance of Life, called Antaskarana open up? Then, what does the Mystic catch with this new vessel in the Esoteric worlds (besides colors)? Could he possibly catch or realize the Worlds-

Dimensions, from the 8th outer to the 1st, the seat of the Father? If not, then what else?

Dear Master, I am sure that I have troubled and tired you to the point that you may be 'cursing' me now. But I felt obliged to set these questions which are both just and necessary before you.

The reason is that these questions have been my nightmare and that all these verifications (questions-suppositions-appreciations) that I make are not clearly presented in your books and so on. Perhaps indirect reference was made or there is another reason for them not to appear to the student (metaphysicist). So, now that I have the opportunity, I felt obliged to point them out and to ask for the required explanations. Awaiting your reply in Yugoslavia.

Thank you very much, Please, excuse me for tiring you.

With love,
Your student,
Ilias Katsiampas

12th Answer

Athens,
November 15, 1988

Dear Ilias,

I am replying to your registered letter of November 2nd, 1988.

I am ANSWERING the questions you set forth in your letter. I am doing this only for you because I have no time available as I am writing the necessary books for all the people.

1) There are no Chakras in the stellar or the Intellectual man. These exist only in the etheric one.

2) These are Mind disturbances that Science calls epilepsy, Metaphysics calls them Karmic executions and, Metapsychics (Spiritualism) characterizes them as demonic possessions (catalepsy). All of them are saying the same thing using their own terminology. Put simply, they are Karmic issues that are not cured in a lifetime. Only the great Initiates can undertake this type of therapy, because they take on the responsibility of the Karma, acting upon the patient so that he may be changed, repenting automatically, instantaneously or with the responsibility that the Initiate undertakes.

Paul, Apostle of the Nations, this great superhuman genius, suffered all his life from the slavery of this cursed disease. He did not wish to be cured, because he had to be fully purified of his karmic obligations.

First, become perfect and then become interested in others' imperfections. Then you may offer help with your Divine presence alone. These cases are difficult for the common immortal man. Insight is a rare fruit which sprouts where perfection sprouts.

3) Illness comes from the differentiated and disproportionate quantity of the elements, apart from what mother nature bestows. An Esotherapist and others can cure whatever they are faced with, if they are really accomplished (perfect) and if the case does not contain any Karmic responsibility attribution. As a rule he may, if he is... and if he wants to undertake the... responsibility of his actions.

4) That which signals a beginner to start applying self-therapy and eterotherapy is that he himself must have been purified, he must be able to command his pain to leave him,

to mentally heal the people around him without them understanding it and to cure them correctly and permanently. The following are the points indicating that he knows how to CONCENTRATE and how to transmit the higher vibrational power, which with his thought, will, imagination, he has created as a purified being.

5) Karma is controlled when man escapes from his worldly illusions. He who strengthens the Freedom of his Will, overcomes his destiny. What makes all the difference is your managing to turn your back on conscious reality.

6) The Divine-Unmanifest-Perfect and so on, has the tendency of Its expression in Its very nature and essence.

The human mind conceives only the manifest states and not the unmanifest ones. It is not about necessity but about work. It is at the same time manifest and unmanifest, the existing and the non-existing, the temporary and the eternal. The human mind conceives its external manifest side. The Divine contains the human, which means that the content cannot perceive the whole that contains everything. Only when...well, when through the eyes of the Father he overlooks all Omnicreation. But that's for later...

7) Nobody said that we would find God in the Etheric world. We shall just find fine matter. The Raja Yogi has 13 X 13 Dimensions and sub-dimensions before him in order to approach the spiritual limits. Read *Birth and Death of the Worlds* again. You are wrong. He will just find the four-dimensional world, the Etheric one, the beginnings of a faint and limited truth. The etheric beings which reside there are more evolved than us, since they have no physical body and as incorporeal, as unnatural beings, they have a better Mind, made of a finer matter that operates on and catches finer vibrations; therefore it learns and KNOWS.

Concentration has nothing to do with the area of the

Etheric world. Other vibrations exist there. There, the Etheric Mind operates differently from our physical Mind. There, the Mind is not everything. Only half a step separates us. The earthly (natural) beings may be infinitely more evolved than the etheric beings. Just like we have worms and chrysalises, masters and students, evolved and unevolved people here, in the etheric world there are different steps and the lower steps are infinitely more than the higher steps.

Here, some of our fellow-men may be de-spiritualized. Over there, this is rare. It is a transitional location, higher in vibration than our physical one. But it's not something admirable, exceptional or the all. ON THE CONTRARY, all the 'mourmoulikia', all the diseases and so on, come from the etheric world that, although it pulses a little more than ours, although it has no place-time and causality, it does not cease being possessed by beings of which the greatest percentage is of a low level and is not elevated easily, as is the lowliest of man.

Your time has not yet come. It will come sooner or later, and then you will undertake your responsibilities. You will establish a school of Metaphysics, at the location that the Master will indicate...

SAMADHI: Samadhi is done in many ways. PROVIDED you learn how to concentrate. Concentration is Everything.

Concentration means that you must be in the conscious world and at the same time in the hyperconscious and in the subconscious one. He who learns how to concentrate, will enter samadhi, whether he wants to or not. The other systems are standardized so that the elevated being may know where it is going.

Chakras have no exceptional quality or effectiveness, apart from the solution (therapy) of our natural mummy, of our natural body.

They help the Mind to slip into heightened concentration at some point, if its concentration is functioning SIMULTANEOUSLY. Do not pay further attention to chakras but know their mission as I described it to you.

Antaskarana, in contrast to Sutratma, operates ONLY for the MYSTICS.

Through this, the human soul of the spiritually possessed man comes into contact with the 13 dimensions of the founding Ray, surpassing the whole Universe and arriving at the Superuniverse, where the Seat of the Father resides, the Root, the Throne of the Immovable.

Antaskarana is the product of long struggles, victories, successes of true PERFECTION. Only with SUTRATMA do we struggle to overcome the obstacles with KNOWLEDGE, will, faith and thought, which are the shooting Powers of our Dimension. These however will be given you when your Mind starts operating to a superior spiritual hyperconscious rhythm. I am waiting for this SOON.

Athens, November 15, 1988
N. Margioris

13th Letter

Yugoslavia, March 11, 1989

Dear Master,

I am writing to you from Sarajevo, Yugoslavia to ask you my usual questions and to exchange a few words with you.

You have repeatedly urged us to speak out in order to convey our knowledge to other people.

You must know that my Mind is almost completely orientated towards the Esoteric Truth, towards Esotericism, and to its dissemination to every being willing to listen. And the most important is that every moment, wherever I may be, whatever I may be doing, my priority is to spread, to explain, to dissolve foolish prejudices, superstitions, misconceptions and to offer a spark of Truth and Hope. This fixation of my Mind is so great that every conversation with other people (known or unknown), turns to Metaphysics, most times. Perhaps I'm overdoing it, but on this matter, I have no limits.

I may be reading all day, from morning to night, taking only a few breaks, or studying or trying for hours to transmit whatever I can to anyone. Besides, that's the reason why I record your lectures and so on and I make a list of them or I study your books and I ask you some burning oral or written questions. I am well aware of the fact that there are innumerable idiosyncrasy types in people.

Due to my continual contact with people, I believe that if everyone were offered the Truth with the symbols that suited his own way of thinking and conceiving, many more people would enter the Esoteric Reality. These would help him, initially with the least resistance of his Mind to train and to conceive, first with his intelligence, his capabilities as well as the image of the manifestation of creation and its laws. And then, after he becomes familiar with all this, he will understand and become ready to experience them. I am sure that there are many people who would willingly follow the explanations that agree with and help their thoughts and their beliefs, whether they are religious or social, moral or even scientific and so on, provided they are communicated in the right way and made accessible, so that the opportunity may be given them; otherwise there is rejection on their part. Of course, this may 'smell' of Karma, but the acquaintance with and the appropriate comprehensive education concerning Yoga and its philosophy will sooner or later bear the expected fruit. I say this because I see that what must first be put in order, is man's mind. That is, people's reasoning must first be cultivated in order for them to be able to conceive it and then, perhaps they will become open to it. On the other hand, also from my experience, the 'obvious guide' that brought me here was my reasoning.

Over the last 8 years, I have read hundreds of Metaphysical books. Too many times and especially at the beginning, although I always felt within me that all this was true, I faced and overcame awful disturbances, bonds, superstitions and all types of established rules I had been surrounded by since I was very young. I experienced many weaknesses, sufferings and doubts and it is true that I still experience them, only that now I know, more or less, the external texture of the world, its deepest meaning and I keep hoping to 'see' its internal one that will allow me to talk to other people more openly. If somebody asked me now if I have had a deep Experience, I would not be able to say 'yes, I have,' for it would be a lie. But I can give him a lot of evidence that all this is true. I am working with my intellect at this moment, because I cannot do otherwise. Certainly, I am fighting my internal battle at the same time.

For this reason, every word, every letter, every speech of yours that expresses the unmanifest states are a source of joy, knowledge and hope for me and through me for the few other people who are seeking to quench their thirst as well... So, every phrase and analysis on your part is engraved on my Mind so deeply that I consider it impossible to forget.

This happens because I know that it is the closest replica of Truth.

Also, an idea that I would like to mention to you is about a new book that will outline the Master's personality. That is the writing of a book or a study that will analyze the Master's presence on Earth. That will describe what a true Master is in reality. How a seeker-student can recognize him. If he should test him in some way before he can trust him and distinguish him from the false masters.

What is the potential of a Master, in what way can he help the people around him, visibly but invisibly too. How much he can and how much he cannot help the other people without their consent. How he evolves internally at the same time. How he conceives and transmits his words, the symbols, and the Truth through the intellect to other people. His esoteric experiences. Why he is not able to convey the Truth in words and he asks for the participation and personal actualization of others. What is the difference between a Master who attains samadhi for the first time or even more times and one liberated from Karma who has returned to teach the human race.

What is the potential in each of us to approach the same ideals? What is the aim and the substance of life? I think that such a book would be in great demand and it would have a very wide circulation.

I am stating below the classical questions:

1) During this year's training in integral Pranayama, you instructed us to work on the numbers from four to ten, with 3 as a basis. In the next Pratyahara lesson, you repeat the teaching of Pranayama and you add that after ten, the basis changes and becomes the four, while in Pranayama the limit you gave us was 18 - 54 -27 - 18 with three as the basis. Finally, what is the basis after ten?

2) Does he who operates the Hyperconscious and enters the etheric world see everything as UNIQUE? Does he see the past, the present and the future as a unity-totality? Does this mean that what he sees will definitely happen or will most probably happen, despite man's 'Free Will'? That is, does he know the future? If yes, what are the possibilities he can change it?

3) Matter emits rays, every material object. However, it receives them at the same time by other Planets-Universes and so on. However, it receives radiation by non-material sources as well. Do these 608 radiations you mention in your books come from other material sources? If so, what are they? Scientifically and not, what are these invisible sources that produce radiation of another kind?

4) I notice that Saint Patapios is something like a symbol for you and a basis for your work. After having edited and republished many books in his name, you established the Saint Patapios Association many years ago. Its name is 'The Pious Pilgrims of the Unbuilt Light, Saint Patapios' and afterwards you built a church in his name. Is there any internal reason for your using his name in particular, for your activities, and what is it?

5) You have explained to me that every illness is the result of Karma. But in *Esoteric Therapeutics* you write about and develop quite differently how every kind of disease appears. Is it possible that what you describe so thoroughly in *Esoteric Therapeutics* is just the way in which Karma is expressed and presented to the people? Who, however, handles these Karmic payments and how? Perhaps the Lipika? Do diseases, obstacles, etheric irregularities, storms and so on never appear by chance? Are they perhaps just figures of speech that are simply needed because they help the therapist in therapy?

6) Concerning, once again, therapeutics and the therapies you apply: When I asked you about it, you answered me that there is no miracle in your therapies and that you had told me this because you wanted to be clear with my soul. Afterwards, you mentioned that the therapies you apply are very hopeful and have great success rates, 70%-80%, despite the failures. And you led me to understand that these failures may occur because of the Karmic debts of these specific souls. However, what do you mean when you say that there is no miracle? What does miracle mean to you? When is it possible and what is the difference between miracles and Esoteric Therapeutics? The last time I came to Athens, I asked you how you conceive of a miracle, and you answered that almost every therapy you apply through subconscious or hyperconscious functions, is a miracle. Yet you state that in the therapies you do no miracle exists. Why? Finally, is there a distinction between the two and what is it?

7) In Raja Yoga, in the meditation chapter, you write that he who practices Dharana on a book and attains Meditation, automatically knows the full content of the book but also the causes that produced the inception of this book. Vivekananda mentions that meditation is unbroken Knowledge flowing within the object. Could you please explain this to me more thoroughly?

8) You had asked me to write you in order that you may send me the exact description of the experiment where 14 individuals are needed for aura to appear.

Must the subjects of the experiment be seated or standing? Where should they be facing? North or East? What should they be wearing? Must everybody's Mind be focused and on what exactly? Do they have to sing hymns that prepare the atmosphere and the experimenters and which ones are the best? Will the aura appear to just one of them or to all of them? What is the order that must be followed, prayers, and so on. What must be done after the aura appears and how will everybody return to his normal position? Must the room be totally dark? What else is needed?

I end my letter before you become terribly angry with me.

Sending you my best regards and my love,
Ilias Katsiampas

NOTE: The above letter never reached Master Nikolaos A. Margiori's hands, because it got lost in the post. Consequently, there was never a reply to it. Of course, the writer, during a face-to-face meeting with his Master, presented the questions of the letter to him, receiving the expected answers. However, wishing to keep the original order and 'language' of his Master's letters, he preferred not to intervene by conveying the answers he had received orally.

2ND NOTE: The above correspondence is just **the beginning** of an important, close, spiritual teaching relationship -it lasted many years and was deep, unique, and extraordinary- that developed between the modern Greek Mystic, **Nikolaos Margioris** and his student, **Ilias Katsiampas.**

A special and close teaching relationship that was built on strong, healthy foundations of profound, transcendental knowledge; major unfathomable experiences; endless respect; conscious discipline; and real, honest love from both sides. People rarely have the chance to experience such things, to know such joy, to surpass themselves, if possible, and maybe take up the part of consciously and decisively imparting all of the above concepts, in order to form a panorama of outer, inner, and spiritual life, validated in the act of this world's everyday life.

Giving meaning to life and its upward evolution is directly connected to the **Great –and the only True- Ideals of humanity's MYSTICS**, ideals which originate from a **Higher-Inner-Transcendental-Intellectual Education**, the only one capable of **CORRECTLY** illuminating and directing humans-seekers-students towards their True Destinies, towards the road of their Improvement, and Divine Realization.

If the main parts of this higher, divine, close, and year-long teaching relationship that followed the above correspondence within the special circle of Margioris' students were to be outlined, it would take several books to properly and respectfully describe it in a way capable of thoroughly informing the reader of a variety of indefinite existential, ontogenical, cosmogonical, and eschatological issues, but also of the true practical means of educating themselves and applying this knowledge in their pursuit of personal evolution, and, therefore, the gradual positive evolution of society itself.

A brief synopsis would barely be able to provide the essential information about the wholesome spiritual values hidden in the soul of everyone and the ways they could unfurl in their lives, gifting true-divine harmony to every human on Earth.

PART TWO

ESSAYS

PREFACE

All the works that follow were created as a result of a strong impulse I had to gather the main metaphysical questions-answers-details that may occupy any seeker-student and to make them accessible to whoever may wish to explore the deepest meaning of his life. At the same time, I show the way in which one can re-orientate and reprogram oneself so as to follow the path of self-knowledge, self-surpassing, self-perfection.

All these studies were composed in the form of letters within a period of about three years, between December 1988 and October 1991, and were sent to my Master Nikolaos A. Margioris who commented favorably on them. The purpose of this presentation is to give as representative and holistic a picture as possible concerning the issues addressed.

The letters examine a broad range of esoteric matters, such as the comparison between the latest scientific and metaphysical discoveries and the Mystical Truth delivered by the great spirits. Some essays on Karma and on the correct teaching of esoteric enlightenment follow, while in other letters the object and the methods of Esoteric Therapy as well as the methods of Esoteric Truth are examined. In general, a great effort was made to present, summarize and elaborate on as many aspects and details of the Esoteric Truth as possible so that everyone concerned may be given the opportunity to form a full and clear conception of metaphysical matters and to walk the esoteric path not only with fewer inhibitions but more steadily, securely and with greater certainty.

1st Essay

Yugoslavia, December 19, 1988

Dear Master,

First of all, I send you my best wishes for your name day and for your birthday. I also wish you a prosperous and creative new year, full of health and joy.

This time I am not going to ask you any questions. I am just sending you an essay of mine of about 20 pages. Certainly, in reality it is a long answer to the expressed speculations of a friend of mine, with whom we have had similar discussions of a Metaphysical nature. However, it is in fact, a deep analysis of esoteric matters and the conception of these matters, in a representative presentation. Of course, I do not know if this analysis will bring about (my friend's) change or acceptance but definitely, these efforts – apart from anything else – will help me to conceive and to condense as well as possible, more simply and comprehensively, the speculations and the subjects that must occupy any seriously thinking and speculative man.

Perhaps I overemphasize certain points, or I do not develop some others as much as I should. Also, concerning some other points 'I do not faithfully follow the references of your books', e.g. I omit the intermediate 'play' of the Intellect - as you will read - and I project the soul more. That is, I made some deliberate 'omissions', in order not to complicate matters and to make them more understandable.

I would like you to assess my work and to correct the points which you think are not right, giving me the proper guidance and direction. Thank you for your attention and for your help.

With much love,
Your student
Ilias Katsiampas

Below, I present the letter, exactly as I sent it to my friend:

Written on November 3, 1988
Let us change the climate of our discussions and let us address the speculations that preoccupied you in your letter and about which you ask my opinion. Your doubts concern, whether you realize it or not, ontological questions. You ask about life, its meaning and its values.

I shall analyze and develop this matter as well as possible in a letter, through my own knowledge and experiences and beliefs. The information I shall give you is based on the philosophical interpretation of everything (and there may not be another one, as you will see below). It is an approximate interpretation, as the words are nothing more than symbols and word forms and cannot render the real meaning (Truth), but only the relative one. So, dear Christos, I shall try to explain to you my own way of perceiving life and its meaning. For me, life, true life, is not only hope, entertainment, joy, happiness, dreams, socialization, friendships, families, children, ambitions or, on the other hand, illnesses, unhappiness, sorrow, pain, misery, pessimism and so on.

What we live every day is nothing more than a mere reflection or a mere badly-made replica of the True and Unique Life. I steadfastly believe that True Life is something superior and higher than everything known and comprehensible to us. It is what we symbolically call GOD-TRUTH-UNIVERSAL CONSCIOUSNESS-THE UNIT-THE SPIRIT-THE REAL BEING-THE ABSOLUTE-THE UNCHANGEABLE-THE PERFECT-SUPREME SUBSTANCE OF THE WORLDS-CONSCIOUSNESS- COSMIC INTELLIGENCE-THESIS INTO THE ANTITHESIS-EVERYTHING-ETERNAL HAPPINESS-BRAHMAN and so on...

Its nature contains three states, that is, it is three-dimensional. I give you the following comparative examples:

1) ESOTERICISM or METAPHYSICS: Infinite Existence (Life), Infinite Knowledge (Wisdom) and Infinite Bliss (Happiness).

2) CHRISTIANITY: Father-Son-Holy Spirit.

3) NICODEMUS of the HOLY MOUNTAIN: Substance - Existence - Energy.

4) HINDUISM: Brahma (Creator) - Vishnu (Preserver) - Shiva (Catalyst).

5) EGYPTIAN RELIGION: Osiris - Horus - Isis.

6) CHINESE RELIGION: Yin - Yang - Tao.

7) OCCULTISM: Power or Will - Love or Wisdom - Intelligence.

8) SCIENCE: Matter - Energy - Dynamic Area.

9) THE COSMOGONIC PHILOSOPHY: (Principles of Energetics - Principles of Passivity - Principles of Equilibrity).

10) JEWISH RELIGION (KABBALAH): Strictness - Mercy - Meekness.

We see this reflection of the Divine Three-Hypostases in nature and in ourselves:

Universe - Anti-universe - Super-universe (Esoteric Dimensions).

Matter - Anti-matter - Super-matter (Esoteric matter).

Terrestrial Beings - Extra-terrestrial Beings – Ultra-terrestrial Beings (Angels).

God - Archetype - Man (Psychology-Metaphysics).

Spirit - Soul - Body (Religion - Esotericism).

Solid - Liquid – Gas (Material - visible nature, Physical world).

Positive - Negative - Neutral (Electricity - Physics).

Faith (Will) - Hope - Love (Apostle Paul).

Will (Faith) - Imagination - Thought (Consciousness).

Conscious - Subconscious - Hyperconscious (Mind).

I write you all this so that you may be able to ascertain for yourself that something is indeed happening, something that is not at all random. All the above combinations come from the four cardinal directions, from different time periods and basically (except for some exceptions) more than 2.000 years before our time. They all talk about the same thing but express it in their own conceptual way.

All our knowledge, any knowledge is based on experience. So, even scientists, in their own, have results that come from experimentation and verification, that is, experience. And their outcomes (conclusions) become known and recognized when they can be replicated experimentally and become a common experience for all people. Now, the question is: Does Religion that has nursed and nurses us have such a basis (experience) or not?

The answer to this question has two sides: one positive and one negative. Religion, as is generally taught in the world, is supposed to be based on faith and belief and on the example. In most cases, it consists only of a series of theories. That is why we see one fighting against the other. These theories are based on faith. Each one asks you to believe and to adopt its favorite ideas (Religion) based only on the authenticity of their allegations. The educated people, in this situation, reject them as a bunch of theories that fanaticize man. However, all of this Universal Faith for Religion does not exist without a reason (where there is smoke, there is fire).

Looking back to their foundations, we see that all Religions are similarly based on Universal experiences. The Christians ask you to believe in a God, in a soul and in a better future for this soul. But if you ask them why, they will answer that they believe in these and that they consider them to be true. However, if you go back to the source of Christianity, you will find that it is based on experience. Jesus Christ said that He saw God. His students and the Saints said the same thing. Similarly, in Buddhism there is the experience of Buddha (God). Also Hindus, Risis or the Sage declared that they experienced some truths that they proclaimed in their scripture and so on. It is therefore evident that the Religions of the world were built on this unique universal foundation of the totality of Knowledge. The direct experience.

All masters saw God, Truth and proclaimed It. If there was ever one and only experience in this world, in any branch of Knowledge, the obvious conclusion is that since this experience was possible in the past, it will be repeated eternally.

Uniformity is a strict law of nature and what happens once may happen always. Masters of the science of Yoga rightly claim that nobody is really Pious unless he himself has had the same conceptions (experiences). Yoga is the practical Science teaching us how to obtain these conceptions. There is no point in talking about Religion, if one has not felt nor experienced it.

To be more specific, Yoga means the scientific (perfect) union of our soul with the spirit (God), or of the inferior with the superior self or of the Conscious with the Hyperconscious. It is the search for and the attainment of Truth. Yoga has many paths and methods of approaching this Truth (There are as many paths to Truth as there are human breaths – Arabic).

The major paths that suit most idiosyncrasies are:

a) Raja Yoga: Scientific elevation from the conscious to the hyperconscious.

b) Jnani Yoga: Through the philosophical search for Truth.

c) Karma Yoga: It is the Yoga of action and work, of the unselfish service or the Yoga of morality.

d) Bhakti Yoga: Through the religious elevation of the believer (worship, love).

There are also Sapta Yoga, Mantra Yoga, Kriya Yoga and Hatha Yoga. The last one is the lowest spiritually.

Truth is accessible only as a personal-individual experience. It requires special preparation and special training that is offered by Yoga. Here are some examples from the New Testament and from our ancestors:

"I and the Father are one", "Know the truth, and the truth shall make you free", "For the kingdom of heaven is within you". "Know Thyself" was the maxim outside the Delphic oracle and outside the school that Pythagoras established in Crotone of Southern Italy. And so that you can understand, Raja Yoga that is the most appropriate system of ascension 'is completed' with three years of training.

During the first year, the student learns how to control his Mind through its three properties, THOUGHT, WILL, IMAGINATION.

In the second year, the student learns the techniques of

the Awakening Energy, Kundalini, elevation (it is the solidified fire that is found in our simulated etheric body, at the base of our spine and that constitutes a most powerful energy that if it awakens, man is able to dominate everything and to work any kind of miracle).

In the third year, an effort is made to merge the two brains (etheric and physical), so that their complete control and cooperation are restored. All this takes place so that the Mind may recognize and attain its transcendence or the Hyperconscious state that is GOD - BEING - TRUTH - UNIVERSAL CONSCIOUSNESS - OMNIKNOWLEDGE - THE ETERNAL PRESENT - THE WHOLE - SELF and so on, and to see its true self (soul) and its immortality. Then it is transformed into a little Word of God and teaches the Truth, it becomes a true AUTHORITY - SAGE - SAINT - PROPHET - MASTER - MYSTIC and so on, who guides the people towards real evolution and true Knowledge (experience).

The rungs of Raja Yoga elevation (royal or psychological-intellectual union from Mind to Supermind or Hyperconsciousness, are 8 + 1 = 9:

1) YAMA: It has 5 restraints (abstinence).

2) NIYAMA: It has 5 observations (discipline).

3) ASANA: Position-posture of the body.

4) PRANAYAMA: In its simple meaning, rhythmical breathing and in the deeper meaning, control of the omni-energy.

5) PRATYAHARA: In its simple form, it means calming down or relaxing and in the deeper form, cutting the Mind off the sensation centers, withdrawing the senses.

6) DHARANA: Concentration, Thought (super-concentration).

7) DHYANA: Meditation (identification, supervision, peeling of the target).

8) SAMADHI: Theosis, Likeness, Union, Universal Con-

sciousness, Ecstasy (we all belong to God), Enlightenment, Fourth Dimension (Etheric, Stellar and lower Intellectual world), Samprajnata Samadhi (bearing seed), the Holy Ghost descends in the form of fiery tongues, the beginning of Salvation (redemption) of the soul.

9) KAIVALYA: Redemption or Deliverance from the bonds of Karma, Liberation (Salvation) of the soul in life, Asamprajnata Samadhi (seedless). These cases are minimal and very rare.

Raja Yoga applies transcendental meditation, for which all people are not ready or rather they do not decide to practice it easily, perhaps from fear of the unknown (ignorance). However, there is also the lower level meditation that can be used by almost anyone after training and that can help man with any problem in his life and with his fellow-men. Also, through meditation one can self-heal or even heal others either from near or from afar, from the simplest to the most cursed diseases. This is on condition that the Esoteric therapist or the meditating individual is knowledgeable about Esotericism and understands the real causes of every illness. On the other hand, he can experiment with hypnotism or spiritualism, to cure the demonic, the mad, the insane, the psychopathic and so on.

I must tell you that at this moment, I am attending the courses of the 2nd year of Raja Yoga. My master is 76 years old. He is one of the few Guru-Masters existing in the Greek and the universal sector. He is an expert, an open encyclopedia, a man accessible to anybody with problems, a source of bottomless Esoteric Knowledge in combination with incredible self-discipline and self-control which constitute unique qualities, making him worthy of physical and metaphysical exemplification. He applies all kinds of therapies. He cured many ailing people who had been condemned by science. A few days ago, he healed a great Greek woman psychologist who sent him a thank you card, saying: "You gave me the sun again." He is a Mystic, a truly accomplished and perfect man.

The steps of lower level meditation leading to identification, are:

1) ATTENTION
2) ATTACHMENT
3) CONCENTRATION
4) SELF-CONCENTRATION or SUPER-CONCENTRATION
5) IDENTIFICATION (PEELING OFF)
6) ECSTASY
7) SAMADHI - THEOSIS

Under the right conditions, lower level meditation progresses and becomes superior, approaching Samadhi. In order for one to succeed in meditating, one must concentrate on one sole thought-target-point-matter-aim (concentration 12') without any other thoughts intervening. Then, he opens a channel that 'peels-off' all matter and sees beyond it to its etheric substance (identification or peeling 144').

It is here that most inferior mediums, spiritualists, therapists, self-hypnotists, intermediates, experimenters in parapsychology, anastenarians(fire-walkers) and so on, operate and in the first stages of ecstasy that fluctuate between 144' (or 2') to 1884' (or 31', 4'), which is Samadhi or Theosis.

But let us return to our subject. Almost all the scriptures of the world religions talk about a fall, about a descent, about a drop (original sin) from the Divine and Perfect world of Beauty and Grace (Paradise), where man once lived. In reality, in an Esoteric sense, there are more of these descents. This fall brought man to the physical three-dimensional World, in the 13th outer Dimension. Although he used to be in the Etheric World - fourth Dimension - Paradise - Kingdom of Heavens or even higher, he suddenly fell and sank to our low physical Dimension.

Creation, from the Source (God) to our etheric-physical world (13th Dimension, has constructed 13 Founding Rays - Paths, each of which has 13 Dimensions. We are in the 13th Dimension of the 7th Founding Ray with its 13 Dimensions, each of which has 7 subdivisions-sublevels. So, our present location is on the 13th outer Physical etheric Dimension, that has 7 sublevels, three in the physical world, solid 1/7, liquid 1/7, gaseous 1/7 (1/7 + 1/7 + 1/7 = 3/7), and four in the Etheric world (fourth Dimension). The sub-etheric 1/7, the anti-etheric 1/7, the etheric 1/7, and the hyper-etheric 1/7, total 4/7.

Our world - Dimension (13th) is Physical etheric, 7/7. The 4/7 of its etheric state is not visible because it escapes the perceptual abilities of our senses. It is beyond the spectrum of visible radiation. Here, we need the hypersenses- hyperconsciousness that is awakened through Meditation.

Our Etheric World becomes perceptible through its qualities and its derivatives that are: Magnetism, electricity, gravity, nuclear power and so on.

Every natural matter-manifestation has etheric matter-substance behind it. The difference between physical and etheric matter (energy) is in the speed of the vibrations. The vibratory speed of our physical matter is in apparent immobility. But inside it everything is agitated - running - moving at incredible speeds. The faster the different waves-vibrations run-move, the faster our world becomes etheric (invisible - immaterialized) and we approach the more delicate (fine) matter states, in more Etheric Worlds. Here we remember Heraclitus who said that 'everything flows, nothing stands still.'

Our natural matter, our physical world is an emanation of these vibrations (energy - spirit) and more precisely in Scientific – Metaphysical terms, it is the extreme vibration of energy or the crystallization - cooling - condensation of energy (Prana - Spirit). That is what we call Matter and the Physical World.

In fact, every physical object has its etheric replica behind it.

This etheric is the creative beginning, it is the standard, it is the mold, it is the reason why each object, plant, man and so on, exists, is preserved and lives, since it immerses it in and provides it with perfection (Aristotle - Basil the Great), Prana (Hindus), Prima Materia or First Matter (Alchemists - Occultists), Ever-living Fire (Heraclitus), Holy Ghost (Christians), Energy (Scientists), Kind and Form (Pythagoras), Spiritual Activation, Rosicrucian Fire (Rosicrucians), Orgone (Wilhelm Reich), Animal Magnetism (Franz Anton Mesmer), Odic Force (Reichenbach), Greek Life Power or Life Substance.

This Life Substance or Universal Energy or Prana and so on... comes from His Seat, from the Source of All (God) and vivifies all the lengths and the widths of all the Worlds - Galaxies and so on. I'm referring to the Holy Ghost. The omnipresent and omnipotent. The Substance of Hypersubstance. It exists in everything and it is the Root of every Existence. Every man contains within him this spark of existence, the Spirit, the Life Substance. He is created in His Likeness (we are all in God and we live and move and exist in Him).

All of us have a small piece of the Divine Hypersubstance, God, within us and we struggle to bring it out, to recognize it and to comprehend its (our) nature. This spirit, substance, is our real Self, our real immortal existence (life), which is deeply buried within us.

This has as its delegator, as its vessel, as its wrapping,

as its means, the so-called soul that takes the staff from the spirit and at the same time inherits the Divine Qualities. That is the Eternal-Infinite Existence (Life), the Eternal-Infinite Knowledge and the Eternal-Infinite Bliss (Prosperity). So, the soul undertakes its difficult mission: the revelation and the accumulation of the experience of the outer Dimensions. But when the soul enters-falls from the etheric world (fourth Dimension or Paradise), to the physical World it is automatically put aside, it remains in the margin, it becomes neutral and leaves in its place the human Mind - a guide, a connection that is called Intellect. Now, the Intellect undertakes the difficult work of mediating and conveying the messages (experiences)and instructions between the soul and the human Mind. The Mind is a construction-creation of Nature (matter) and is inevitably mortal. The Intellect is composed of the finest and most perfect substance of matter and is a 'perfect' organ whose only privilege is to serve the soul and to help the Mind recover. The Soul is substance, it is immortal and eternal. When someone achieves contact with it, it is transformed and changes into a perfect being, into an infinite source of Knowledge, of Happiness and so on.

The matter we mention so often and that we love so much, whether we want to or not, whether we like it or not, is perishable, as our body is a perishable bearer – a diving-suit - cover - deep vessel of the soul. Despite this, we become attached to Nature (Matter), to our exterior self, to the external objects and we identify with them, because of wrong influences and wrong criteria. We forget that these are not the Truth, but crude and stained replicas of Divine Perfection. We do not take into consideration that we are in the world of oppositions, of lies (untruth), in the world of relativity, in the world where everything is only appearances that one day will burst and disappear like soap bubbles, in the world of non-existent permanence, in the world of imperfection, of ignorance and of deceit, of lowly sentiments, of evil, of hate and jealousy, of injustice, of pain, of misery and of vanity.

We do not know that matter is the means for and not the aim of our ascent. Thus, what we are simply doing is building castles in the sand, either with our thoughts or with our actions. So, looking at things objectively, we find ourselves in a continual and perpetual vicious circle, repeating the same mistakes, from which, under present conditions, we cannot escape, as we have been guided and formed since we were little children in this external, shallow way of expression and life. Society, family, our friends themselves and so on, contribute to this situation. All this is due to our true IGNORANCE. I will give you two-three more examples from the New Testament: 'My kingdom does not belong to this world', 'That which is born of the flesh is flesh, and that which is born of the Spirit, is spirit.'

On the other hand, we have the intellect as mediator-transmitter between the Mind and the soul, caring about the right guidance of the Mind from the soul and the acquisition of the correct experiences. Man, due to his continual extroverted mania and to his permanent external course, is attached and yields, without a fight, to the phenomena and the objects, to the form and, generally, to the known (visible) objects, because he perceives only this and because he thinks that he will find joy, happiness and perfection only there.

Therefore, he is left at the mercy of influences and instigations of every kind, he becomes a pawn and a victim of exploitation, and loses the most important guide in the labyrinth of his life. He loses the 'voice of his conscience', the 'the daemon of Socrates', his 'Guardian Angel', his very soul. His extroverted fury and the little information he transmits to the soul, compel the soul to retire temporarily (it is neutralized), he deliberately shuts its mouth and he, himself remains blind and alone in the deceit, the entrapments and the dangers of life.

Then we see man becoming a prey of nature and trying to become like it, due to his unceasing extroverted course. That is, as we say 'a fine appearance on the outside but inside nothing-a void.' Unfortunately, this is the state characterizing us and guiding us to the continuous proliferation of our desires.

Buddha, being enlightened, declared that every attachment (desire) is equivalent to a suffering (unhappiness). Thus we rush into the shameless pursuit of our desires (that are only ours in appearance), into the acquisition of riches of any kind, into ambition, egoism, jealousy, evilness and so on. Man's attachment to his exterior-inferior self (mortal-false-apparent) is total. Consequently, he continues living what we call 'life', without any measure and without any real interest in his true self and his essential nature (life). He goes adrift (without a soul adviser) and is carried away wherever the different currents (the status quo-continuous suggestions-his abnormal formation, and any other influences) pull him. The results and the consequences of all the above are tragic for his health (corporal and intellectual).

Under these conditions, sooner or later (overtly or covertly), man is condemned to fall prey to some terrible disease. From the simplest to the most cursed illness. He either goes mad or he gets depressed or goes insane (this is not a disease of the soul, as we ignorantly believe, but of the Mind).

In fact, man becomes neurotic to the point of becoming schizophrenic. We are talking about illnesses and abnormalities of consciousness (Mind = conscious - subconscious - hyperconscious).

More or less, in the present state of our 'rotting' society

that has no high ideals, all of us are mentally disturbed (insane - neurasthenic) to varying degrees. Psychology, as well as psychiatry, accepts this. Also, man is subject to psychopathy (Mind disease) that is an illness of the subconscious. Or he falls victim to the plague of cancer and of AIDS. And he is tortured because all these are the results of his deeds and of his karma that he himself created. They are the results of the causes he set in motion, of his shameless extroverted desires that left his soul unprotected and created the logical consequences. (Karma = the Law of Retributive Justice, of cause and effect).

I remind you the relevant examples from the New Testament:

'For whatsoever a man soweth, that shall he also reap,' and 'Peter, put your sword back into its place; for all those who take up the sword shall perish by it.'

And all these are caused by man's essential ignorance of his real nature and of his true aim and the meaning of his existence. Man becomes dazzled by whatever he sees (visible - nature) and is drawn to his self-destruction, remaining neutral and unmoved by what he does not see (invisible - true), but may feel or rather sense. If we exclude the existent proof of Science. In spite of all this, man is completely free (Law of the Freedom of the Will) from Creation, his spirit-soul (God), to choose and to follow what he, in his backward Mind and with his limited senses regards as correct or necessary (irrespective of the fact that it is not). That's why he is attached to the apparent, because he sees only what is perceptible and because he thinks that this is his world (life), and this only until he has acquired the necessary experience, until he understands the essential imperfection and vanity of this world. And until he gradually changes and turns within himself (introspection - Know Thyself), to his soul inside, that will give him vast Knowledge, joys, experiences, that will elevate him and will guide him to Immortality and that will acquaint him with and bring him into communion with the Eternal Truth (God).

But I wrote you a very long letter and it is time for me to end. What I have written you was not at all the most essential of what I should have written. That's why, I am afraid that there may be a few misinterpretations. Because, through a letter, one cannot convey the essence of such a matter, without being misunderstood. I expressed in the most general terms what I believe and what I am trying to put into action (experience). I should tell you that the whole time that I've been researching these subjects (as you know very well), I have not found anything else with such a sound philosophical basis and a better way to interpret everything comparatively, wholly and yet separately. Every day, I find explanations for everything through Metaphysical Philosophy and every day I find verification in all sectors, branches and interpretations. And not only this: if one so wishes, he can also find the way-method to leap into other Dimensions, to learn many incredible things, to become the ruler of his destiny (Karma). To get in touch with his soul that will always advise him wisely about every difficulty, obstacle, impasse, that will appear in his form life. To be able to self-heal and to heal others with the aid of his soul, to be in a position to rule the natural elements, and on the day he 'dies', to be aware of the future possibilities, to have insight and to simultaneously see, the physical world and the etheric world, that is, the causes of the present world. To predict, if necessary, as well as many other abilities and Powers, but in the service of the Divine Plan.

Everything, even Science itself (Nuclear Physics - Cosmology - Biology - Medicine - Psychology - Orgonomics -

Parapsychology - Spiritualism - Religion - Esotericism and so on), gives evidence that all the above are completely true and proven. Here are some relative examples from the New Testament:

'He who has ears to hear, let him hear' and 'if you have faith as a grain of mustard seed, then you will know Truth, because you will have been Truth.'

Certainly, it was not by chance nor for no reason that I wrote you this letter. Deep inside me, I felt the need to give you the stimuli, the little but substantial Knowledge through such a letter. I did this to inform you as validly and substantially as possible, about our world (its meaning) and about the opportunities we have to take the reins of our personality in our hands and to perform real miracles or simply through Meditation to harmonize our life here to the utmost and to have strong tools that will aid us in every difficult moment of our life. And why not, perhaps you can start interpreting and explaining the 'strange facts of life' on your own? Of course, you may doubt many of these points, you may misunderstand or misconstrue some other points or you may even consider me to be disturbed or mad. I assure you that I have never had problems of mental instability. On the contrary, I know exactly where I am, what I am asking for and where I'm heading. For a long time now, I have full awareness within me of my true ideals. How sure are you about where you are, what you are, what you are asking for, what your real ideals are and your substantial pursuits? And do they satisfy you completely?

I did not write you the above to scare you or to make you think hard and negatively, for you probably have enough problems in your life (we will have problems in our whole life). I wrote you this because I believe that they will broaden your horizons and that you will be able to see more clearly and to distinguish between what you must or what you think you must do. I also did it so that you could have some kind of measure for comparison and interpretation of the phenomena-states around you. The rejection of some ideas without thoroughly examining them is a fatal mistake. However, it will greatly distress me if you lose this letter, irrespective of whether you use it or plan to use it. Who knows? Perhaps one day, you will need to turn to it in order to find an explanation for something very important to you or to the people around you. But when... one day, you truly fathom its contents, it will be a source of joy and of happiness for you. If and when you wish to become more substantially informed about subjects-branches, such as Scientific Spiritualism, Meditation, Esoteric Therapeutics, Desymbolism, Astrology-Astrosophy, Esoteric Initiation, Hypnotism-Orthopsychism, Occultism - Mysticism or generally about Esotericism-Metaphysics or about relevant books, you may write to me about the matters interesting you and I shall reply. Or, if you want, you may pass by or order some books-essays-journals on the subjects we mentioned above, You may also obtain theoretical as well as practical instruction at the following address:

OMAKOIO OF ATHENS
NIKOLAS MARGIORIS
17 Spyr. Trikoupi street
10683, EXARCHIA
ATHENS
(01) 3608365

Awaiting your news, your ideas and any questions.

Yours very truly,
Your friend
Ilias

P.S.: What's more, we always want to criticize others. And as a whole, we believe that we are judging them fairly (as a rule, we undermine them with our criticism). In my opinion, a fair and just criticism exists only when one judges the other according to the other's ideals and pursuits and not according to his own. To achieve this, first of all you must learn about and relate to the other's ideals as he, himself considers them. Only in this way can one's criticism be correct.

Dear Master, this was my letter-essay. Awaiting your thoughts and views on it, as well as your news in general, in Yugoslavia, at the usual address (I'm rewriting it):

ILIAS KATSIAMPAS
UL: NAHOREVSKA
71000 SARAJEVO
YUGOSLAVIA

I apologize for having tired you.
I send you my best regards
and wishes,
Ilias Katsiampas

2nd Essay

Yugoslavia, September 19, 1989

Dear Master,

I hope my letter finds you with renewed strength and in excellent health, ready for your activities of the new year. All of us, me especially, are anxiously awaiting every new edition of one of your books or essays as well as news of every one of your activities that will offer us a deeper and a greater understanding of Metaphysical matters, on our real position and attitude in and towards life and especially on the techniques and methods that will give us the power and the ability to break out of our intellectual prison and to perceive all matters in the real, correct and complete form they are in. That is, as they really are.

Last year, I happened to come across some of the most recent books translated in Greek of the most noteworthy nuclear scientists of our times: Stephen Hawking, Arthur Koestler, Feynman, Paul Davies, Atkinson and others.

I studied many of these books thoroughly. Certainly, at the beginning it was very difficult for me to comprehend them, due to their specialized terminology. But little by little, after having studied the small glossaries they had and after many repetitions, I understood their terminology as well as their meaning, to a great extent. At the same time, after having read some similar books of scientific content and after having studied all your books, especially *Birth and Death of the Worlds*, the *Three-dimensional and the Four-dimensional world* and so on, I tried to compare, to reject and, in general, to create a little composition and to transfer my personal conclusions, in a somewhat simplified manner, on paper. The subjects I touch on are the vital matter of the basic identification points of the pre-existent Esoteric Philosophy (Metaphysics) with the temporary and passing Exoteric Science (Quantum Physics), in its present form that reaches the point of completely verifying and fully agreeing with the beliefs, the theories and the Philosophies of Esotericism derived from the people who had the ability to communicate with the Invisible Creation and with the causes of every natural phenomenon; the people who had rejected all evil, selfishness and meanness and who loved man and every being truly. They were real Saints.

These books urged me to focus my Mind on them, resulting in the production of the following little essay, which I send to you so that you may tell me your opinion on the way I handled this difficult matter and to what extent I managed to provide a general, simplified picture of reality. It was written on March 25th, 1989.

Mind (consciousness), science, positivism, philosophy, logic, rationality, cannot conceive-understand the world, nature, Creation, everything. That is, it cannot wholly perceive everything as a TOTALITY - UNITY.

For, in essence, Nuclear - Quantum Physics, as well as Cosmology, discusses and proves that the Plane (formerly etheric) from which everything comes and is surrounded by, is found on all the points of place-time simultaneously. Reference is also made to the place-time or to the Fourth Dimension, where there is no time as we know it. There, the past, present and future constitute a unique and indivisible whole. Also, there we also find the Abnormalities or the Extremes (black or white holes in Space), through which one passes to the fourth Dimension, to the Timeless and to the Eternal element, to the Being of the philosophers.

What is the famous 'Spontaneous symmetry breaking of the universe (Creation)' that destroyed the symmetry and the harmony and what nuclear physicists call the 'void', not in the meaning of 'empty' but as something Whole? In this void everything constitutes a unified state, where nothing can be distinguished from the other.

How do physicists perceive 'The Grand Unified Theory', which unifies all the known powers of nature, in order to approach the Mystery of Creation, of Symmetry, of Truth and of the Absolute?

Everything agrees and is orientated to the unification and to the Union of All. Besides, only a well-formulated theory containing everything, could explain all the mysteries and the riddles of Creation.

Of course, this is where a great and tragic mistake is made by all relevant persons and especially by the scientists. It concerns the greatest contradiction. All of them are waiting and persistently searching for the beginning of everything, for the explanation of everything through a unified theory of all the physical powers (* see the end of the essay). I do not deny that this may be attainable within the context of verbal expression (Theory) that will be formulated by means of the terrible as well as expensive experiments with Accelerators and Cyclotrons and the partial interpretations of scientists, who may one day unite and form a 'Symbolic and Physically Relevant Solution' of THE WHOLE, of the Absolute Truth - Harmony - Unity of All Things. This interpretation will concern the explanation of the Absolute Truth, through the conventionality and the relativity of verbal expression. And this is because Consciousness has been formed by external space, by nature-matter-form, by the visible, three-dimensional world surrounding us.

Our logic, science, rationality, is a result of forming matter and every thought, conclusion, theory, word, is the result of the external stimuli we have received and continue to receive. Of course, science and especially the two great beacons of Cosmogony and Nuclear Physics have long ago entered, in their own way, superior vibrations, other Dimensions. They have drawn the intellectual curtain of the conscious functioning of the Mind, not in their Mind but out of it, with the assistance and experimentation on their huge special machines. With these machines, they get a first taste of Eternity and of the Unity of the Universe (God). And because of the strong and intense attachment to the NEW MATTERS that they conceive with their equipment, very few of the scientists manage to penetrate the deeper and more plentiful in Knowledge subconscious and to become enlightened, to feel the inspiration that will give them a more comprehensible theory in logic.

These sciences have long ago left materialism and the superficially irrefutable Laws of our physical Universe behind. They have entered other, 'non-physical' vibrations, they have entered the realm of Religion or rather, Metaphysics.

They have gone through the physical and are investigating, in one way or another, the totally metaphysical areas. For this reason, they boast that they are approaching the Ultimate Truth.

But it is not possible for any material construction to conceive the Absolute Truth. The Ultimate Truth cannot be perceived by man's Mind and Consciousness which are made to operate on one sole vibration, on one sole pulse, and that is our physical world. How can we then define the Truth, the Limitless, the Infinite and the Eternal? As soon as they are defined, automatically the limitless becomes limited to our own measures and weights. It enters a mold. The mold of words, thoughts and of our famous logic - inside of which so many generations have rotted - that is formed from the information we have gathered from our natural world and that is insufficient and imperfect. And it is impossible for them to express anything that is 'completely beyond' our physical world and the trivial limits of our sensory organs that supply us with messages and impressions and form our Consciousness, thoughts, reasoning, and expression, the word, which is descriptive, detached, a simple form of communication in the vibrations of our physical world - Universe. It is a necessary means for the conciliation and the transmission of many experiences in the natural vibrations of our matter.

Our natural speech is not Truth itself, it is only one Truth. The Truth of the representation of form around us. There are other reasons that exist within the other Worlds, in the other Dimensions (fourth Dimension and so on) and which the present form of Science is studying through the underworld of atoms, particles, subatomic particles and so on.

Religions call this other word the Divine Word - Spirit and so on. Metaphysics uses its own terms for all this and having its origins in the beginnings of Creation, has given the most complete interpretation of Creation, of our world, of man, of the Ultimate Truth (God). In simple, comprehensible and direct words, it explains to anyone who is interested first through the written or the oral word, then through the intellect and logic, what exists beyond our world, why we exist, what is the aim and the substance of life, the causes of Creation and of the Creator Himself. Once he has understood with his thoughts all these theorems of word, i.e. the Symbols, which will give him NEW IDEAS and a completely new orientation and a meaning in his life (as he will understand, even with his logic, that the approach to Truth is and will remain a personal experience for everyone) then he will begin, with special Mind exercises, to tear away the veils of logic and to awaken the superior and higher state of

Mind, the Hyperintellectual or Hyperconscious, and to perceive, through the new and more numerous Hypersenses of a new kind, the vibrations and pulses that will offer him the AUTHENTIC LIFE of those Superior and high-frequency Dimensions, that he has now entered with his Hyperintellect, his Hyperconsciousness. And they will prove to him the existence of the soul (God), the immortality of the soul, the unraveling of all the mysteries, of consciousness at least. And when he returns, he will bring with him the most superior form of enlightenment with new symbols so that it may be partially understood by the conscious function of our Mind as well.

In order for the physical function of our Mind, of our consciousness (logic - orthology - positivism, science and so on), to conceive as completely and as comprehensively as possible the appearances, facts, events, problems, matters, states, theories and so on, it is forced by its own nature, to become fragmented and to analyze as deeply as possible the matters occupying it. It uses the multi-dimensional method of perception.

It separates, divides, cuts into pieces, counts, colors, simplifies, names, enumerates, classifies, files, composes, decomposes, compares, distinguishes, forms every thesis and antithesis, cause and effect, perfect and imperfect, worthy and unworthy, techniques, scales, systems, ways, methods, words, parts, members, theories, ideologies, philosophies, religions, sciences, parties, symbols, parables, allegories, poems, arts, paradoxes, similes, metaphors, enigmas, the occult, mysteries, strange miracles, the incomprehensible, the bizarre and so on.

All of the above are created from the inability of our Mind (consciousness) to conceive of all things in a whole and unified way, in one and only being. Its function is such that it conceives every kind of phenomenon and event only partially and separately. However, the more the Mind tries to attach and to unite all the pieces together in order to draw complete and certain conclusions, the more difficult and impossible this becomes. Because some contradictory elements appear that cause terrible inconsistencies and absurdities and go beyond the common experience the Mind has of the physical world, because the logical sequence and coherence of events is lost and because everything turns upside-down and goes backwards. And literally, the Mind cannot understand and explain why it finds itself in an Abyss, face to face with the absurd, the impossible and the imaginary. And usually, it withdraws, it is afraid, it trembles and makes a disorderly retreat in order to seal itself within the shell of its daily routine once again.

More rarely, it advances on, perhaps more than it must and 'it gets lost' - unprepared - in the labyrinths of its Supermind. And then, we characterize it as mad, paranoid. In reality, it is trapped between two worlds, without being able to live in either.

Certainly, in some very rare cases, it enters the planes of the Supermind and manages to return, bearing presents and fruit that will give it the characterization of the Healer, the Sage, the Saint and so on.

Then man becomes really CONSCIOUS and CONSCIENTIOUS because he succeeds in bringing the three states of his Mind: CONSCIOUSNESS, SUBCONSCIOUSNESS and HYPERCONSCIOUSNESS into harmony and cooperation. That is, his Mind operates to perfection. Hyperconsciousness is the highest function of our Mind, but is in a lethargic or rather an Unconscious and non- functioning state for the average man. This is what can conceive Everything unitedly and totally, giving man answers that even the boldest imagination cannot apprehend or understand. For as we've already said, our Mind and its operations work through division, with a very indiscernible tendency towards composition that renders it able to correspond only to the duties and to the necessities of life.

The Supermind gives us the solutions to the paradoxes, the contradictions, the wonders, the good or bad things that happen to us, diseases, creation, the soul (God) and, in general, to everything. This happens because the Supermind comes into contact with and touches the etheric (hidden) reality of the world we live in. That is, the invisible reality that affects us all the time without us realizing it. It is beyond the limited spectrum of the frequencies that the five senses perceive. It is found in the innermost and in the most esoteric point of our physical world, of our physical matter. It is the underworld of the atoms and of the particles. It is literally another dimension that we are unable to access with our poor senses. It is the fourth dimension that we mentioned in the beginning. In it the causes of our existence and of the creation of our physical world are found. There, everything composes ONE and our Supermind conceives it as such, because it is able to communicate with the invisible but primordial and original side of our natural world. And this is where, man's true enlightenment begins, the one that transforms him and changes him into the highest and the most perfect being, representative example on Earth (Christ-Buddha). Here lies the great contradiction we mentioned at the beginning. Like the child playing in the sand, we want to fit the Ultimate Truth of the sea in the small bucket of our consciousness. Only out of Mind - consciousness, by using other means of the transcendental functioning of our Mind are we able to conceive the Unity of All Things, the Truth itself that is GOD whose Rays shine down on the physical three-dimensional world to give LIGHT and LIFE so that consciousness can operate. They represent the apparently individualized single Egos. While in reality, the essence hidden in all the phenomena is the Universal Ego (the Karmic Mind – the Universal Consciousness), God to whom we are everything existent or manifest (visible) or non-existent - unmanifest (invisible).

This is my essay, dear Master. After that, whatever I do, I find big voids. Thanking you for your attention and hoping we will meet soon, I remain

With great love,
Yours faithfully,
Ilias Katsiampas

3rd Essay

Trikala, August 2, 1991

Dear Basil,

I am sending you my best wishes for spirituality and peace. I decided to write you a letter for many different reasons.

The first and most important reason is that in recent years, we nearly lost touch completely. Most of our rare meetings have been almost accidental and momentary, resulting in our losing the old close relationship and communication we had.

This is due to my studies, to your military service, but also to your pursuits of a professional nature (in Germany and on some Greek islands). So, even last year, though there was plenty of opportunity for frequent contact, it was very brief and very rare. As a result, we lost touch apparently and each followed his 'path'.

However, during this whole period, so many things took place on my part, that it is impossible for me, as much as I may want to, to succeed in conveying them to you in any way (oral or written), unless a very specific and lengthy method of teaching and training precedes.

The Tools and the Experience I have obtained are so numerous and great and after immense practical training in its application, I consider it my obligation to inform you and to let you know about it, even by letter, so that you may become involved yourself, provided you want to, within the limits of your own knowledge and capacity.

But let us get directly to the point and let us try to outline the real image of the world. In fact, there is a substantial element within man, that we call the soul – the spirit – the spark – the superior self – the representative of God in the body and so on!

From the very ancient years until our times, everything has been advocating and proving the apparent truth of this fact. From the Scriptures to the Saints, the Wise, the Healers, the Prophets, the Yogi Masters, who, unfortunately or fortunately for us, even today walk close to us and who are the living examples of their teachings, for those who are lucky enough to be able to detect them and to recognize them, 'For many are called, but few are chosen.'

For they are not perceptible and they are unnoticed by most people who do not have the Metaphysical background or education, or the respective criteria to acknowledge and learn from them. That is, to be able to accept the spiritual gifts, guidance, advice, teachings, training, to the degree one wishes and to apply them to one's daily life, for help, improvement, therapy, knowledge and potential spiritual evolution (substantial), that will give one many other transcendental and hyperphysical benefits. But above all, they will bring one nearer and closer to their inner souls and to the guidance and urgings that it continuously sends but that the average Mind of man rejects.

Because the soul can and does send its spiritual radiations - auras - information - infinite details - hyperknowledge - hyperphysical Powers and so on, but the Mind, as a material construction is not able, through consciousness, its operating organ, (Mind = conscious - subconscious - hyperconscious), to conceive and to interpret the spiritual radiations of the soul.

Perhaps, through the subconscious and through prophetic and other dreams, some flares or flickers of concealed information and guidelines come to the Mind, again from the soul that the Mind (the conscious) is not able to perceive and to interpret. But these flares and flickers function only partially and unconsciously in the form of instinct and so on, as a brake to its immeasurable, unbridled, aimless, dangerous and quite irresponsible behaviour and actions in life and toward one's fellow-men.

And where do you think all the diseases, the pain, the unhappiness, the destruction and the suffering come from to man (individually) and to humanity (collectively)? These are the results not only of individual activity and energy in life, but also of the collective one (racial - state - social - national), which unfortunately for all of us, due to the fact that the only guide and counsellor in our life is the Mind (consciousness), which, by nature, is insufficient, very limited, imperfect, sensory (it is guided only by the 5 senses – sources of information). It maintains the full authority over man's body and his activities - choices (Freedom of Will, the first higher law in our world).

So, due to man's material structure and to his totally materialistic formation, without any sign of spiritual guidance, not even in the form of information - advice, the most tragic event befalls him and his like. His entire materialistic formation - instruction - knowledge - experience, guides him towards pursuits - choices - thoughts - knowledge - actions - activities, which are unbeneficial and hinder whatever potential for evolution he might have.

Because all his functions and activities create a horizontal course in our world, which has our individuality - the ego, consciousness, the personality - as its leading principle around which everything must revolve, and which we must worship, admire, envy, hate, dislike, seek to surpass its attempts at exploitation and its cunning manipulations (and then we talk about humanity and evolution), instead of repelling it and making an example of it, advising it through our own life and actions, directly or indirectly offering instruction wherever possible.

This ego - consciousness - personality is what creates, with its egocentric attitude towards life, – in the name of so-called comfort, well-being, acquisition of riches, enjoyment of goods, having everything - all the suffering, as much for itself - personality, as for humanity. This is the source of all the hardships, such as violence, wickedness, vengeance, murder, envy, hate, opposition, disputes, disagreements, confrontations, controversies, hypocrisies, exploitation, pain, disease, crimes of passion, lies, every kind and form of vain labors, vain pursuits and vain practices, that in our times more than ever before are reaching their peak.

And this is where Karma is produced, from the Free Will and the acts of every person who forms causes (seeds) that lead to results (fruits) that unfortunately, for most people will be the worst and the most tragic, because when the untrained and ignorant Mind (consciousness) guides man, the consequences are only negative. We need not go far to find the black magician; he is beside us, he is within almost every one of our fellow-men who due to ignorance and the complete surrender to matter (Satan – the devil - Lucifer), is willing to do anything for his so-called profit and for his acquired rights, using completely ego-centric behaviour that explains the mud and the gutter we find ourselves in, and how from angels, we became human beings. And from human beings, instead of trying to change into hyper-human beings, we are doing everything in our power to become sub-human beings, inferior creatures, without any value and dignity in life and without any orientation.

So, these are the results, this is the society we have created (a jungle society). We are in a swamp which the average man cannot imagine and fathom. Our every thought - action - relationship - activity - creates karma (a debt, a cause).

Everything that is happening to us is our own crimes which we committed in the past and for which we are now paying the price but at the same time, it is our purification, our cleansing from the karmic bonds, that we created in the past, their dissolution and the opportunity for a New Path. But we, as unfortunate, blind, foolish beings, think that when we suffer something, when something unexpected and inexplicable for our conscious limits happens to us, it is accidental and that our suffering is unfair and wrongful. And we allow our thoughts to create new causes (karma) and conditions, by cursing and swearing and asking, "why me and not him, why should I suffer, become ill", and we curse everybody and everything, even God Himself.

So, we make the pit we are in deeper and deeper, instead of trying to close it and to heal our wounds. We turn against our own interest (our real and not our apparent interest).

We do all this because man is ignorant of Creation and its Laws and he is not guided by his soul, which he keeps jailed within himself.

In fact, in everything that happens 'accidentally and unexpectedly' to us, we must see the opportunity to erase the debts that we ourselves and nobody else has created. And we must endure our hardships submissively, for only in this way will we be able to reach the surface of the well in order to see where the sun (light - soul) is shining from and to follow our path.

This is the success of man's hyperconscious functioning that conceives of all invisible Creation and its Laws, those laws that are ineffable for consciousness, and manages to commune with the soul that is everything and gives solutions and guidance, knowledge and powers to overcome all the difficulties - obstacles - dangers and so on.

Hyperconsciousness may begin to function, only when man erases a part of his karmic obligation, and because he lacks communion and the ability to commune with his soul, it is necessary he have his external Master-Guru, the only being that can guide him, direct him, advise him, teach and train him for this purpose. Above all, he must accept him as his student, which automatically means, that he himself will take on and pay off a great part of his karma, of the debts the student has accumulated over thousands of lives, and leave him with the karma of 'three lives', that will provide him with Knowledge and the experience needed for transcendence, because he will consciously pay off his debts now, without accruing new ones.

The Master is the All for every human soul, whether it marches directly or indirectly, or not at all on the esoteric path, but even when it needs some advice, and so on.

For as long as the body and Mind are not guided by a

Guru or by man's spirit-soul even if it is a small consciously and voluntarily inclination, the body-Mind remains 'a useless organ', without any substance, aim, hope. It drifts here and there and continually and permanently suffers from horrible and unbeneficial actions that destroy it in the abyss of loss, of oblivion, of pain, of illness, of conflict (external and internal), of disappointment and of humiliation - vanity - depravity. It remains permanently in the dark, in ignorance, in fear and it suffers endlessly without understanding why.

Here is Hades; here is the hell for the uninitiated. How differently the initiated man accepts this for himself! Smiling and feeling an internal joy and thanking the Lord, he accepts whatever fate - Karma (Free Will - action = Retributive Justice) brings; any 'caprice', obstacle, illness, bad luck and so on, without any anxiety – or as little as possible - showing instead an understanding and awareness that it is a final and irrevocable payment of a specific debt forever.

It means that he is paying off his debts; he is cutting himself off completely and is gradually detaching himself from the weights that are keeping him at the bottom of the well-sea-matter. Then the rising water begins to lift him up, bring him to the surface, perfect him.

Evolution exists and is understood only in this way. Any other proposed form of evolution is fake, false, untrue and without purpose. It buries man in the depths of matter, so that he rarely has the opportunity to detach himself and rid himself of the bonds, because he no longer wants nor seeks it, as his identification with matter is integral and complete and all his actions are guided - defined by it (matter - consciousness). And, of course, it is impossible for him to comprehend, to conceive things (Metaphysics) that have no relation to his experiences and his limited - wholly materialistic - formation and construction. It is difficult for him to conceive them, let alone believe in them or wish to follow or investigate them, even though there is currently a lot of substantial scientific evidence and many discoveries concerning the matter.

Do you understand where we are exactly? Do you realize the tragedy and the wretchedness of our dead-end situation? And we want, in appearance only, to form a society created by very few 'visionaries', intuitive 'minds' (intellectually, not spiritually), who formulate theories that become parties, in order to create a society where people have equal rights and opportunities and possibilities! And then stop... nothing! Because, very simply, nothing will take root, as long as man remains the worst and the most wicked being of all living and nonliving life. And "as long as society does not yield to the Truth, it will die" (Vivekananda). Because Truth is the spiritual elevation of man, the path to perfection in which only a few people are interested. The rest of the people are swept along by their karmic debts. It is karma that puts the brake on the foolish actions of the uninitiated, and it is karma that can affect man and one day... bring him to his senses, so that he can see the light.

On the other hand, it is a tragic karmic error for man to perceive, yet not follow the path – to the best of his abilities - or to be content with his future or, even worse, to leave it completely. And it's here that the Gurus - great and small Masters - make their appearance. Certainly, they are few but they exist wherever people need them.

They are the ones that can offer man all the tools he needs to be able to overcome everything. They are the ones that truly help all people, especially their disciples, day and night. With their piety, knowledge, experience and so on, they enter as karmic catalysts. They suffer hardships in order to lighten the karmic burden of humanity, to avert any natural catastrophes, earthquakes and so on, and to give more souls the opportunity to walk, each one at its own pace and its own potential always a master of its self, the esoteric course, the spiritual path. The only solution to the impasse of the human-mind. Visibly and invisibly, they continuously help, assist, lessen the debts, teach, instruct, heal, they literally provide man with everything, as long as he takes it. But man, being blind, foolish and attached to matter, is scared of losing his possessions and his wickedness, things he will definitely lose either because of an unexpected illness - accident and so on, or because it is the natural end awaiting all of us, that is, death. Nobody escaped death and nobody took anything with him. All of us should take this into consideration and should sincerely and deeply contemplate matters so as to find the solutions and the answers, perhaps also the absolute certainty of the experience of death in life.

But why am I saying all this and who is listening to me? You are listening to me, you understand me, but what are you doing? How do you benefit from all this? What does it mean 'to benefit'? Do you make it reality for yourself and for others? Many times, I have had Metaphysical conversations and have sent you, as well as others, long letters with rare esoteric details. We agree on almost everything and we have all accepted the necessity for Metaphysical instruction and training, the necessity for the Esoteric reformation of man. How can all this be achieved?

a) With substantiated Metaphysical discussions that require Knowledge and experience. Whenever there is a shimmer of interest in esoteric matters on the part of others, we should reinforce this interest, as much as possible, with discussions and cultivate it using the correct dialectic method (questions-answers).

If none of the people we are conversing with show an inclination towards esoteric matters, he ought to try to kindle their interest but always without any fanaticism or dogmatism. Later, one could offer them a Metaphysical book that suits their idiosyncrasy and their background. In Greece, the only books that are genuine, responsibly written, serious and able to explain to man all that he can understand, are those of my Master Nikolaos A. Margioris. Only these books, because of the unique Knowledge they offer, can form man's character and put him on the path to perfection. They place him at the right place in his life and provide him with Knowledge and numerous means to this end. There are books of a scientific, religious, moral, therapeutic, archaeological, philosophical, metaphysical and other nature.

b) By establishing Esoteric Schools. Hence, my longstanding desire to open a school in Trikala. For the time being, and according to my estimations, in the beginning I would like this school, rented solely in my name, to have the form of a home-place-apartment and to be used as a venue for our meetings and for classes on Esoteric matters and so on.

To put it more simply, the second alternative requires a gathering place where all interested parties can meet and where a specialized and experienced Esotericist will provide a thorough and extensive presentation of Esoteric-Metaphysical Philosophy which will be followed by a question period for participants. I cannot now explain to you what an important role philosophy can play. Put simply, an education in Metaphysics will be made accessible. Here again, books are absolutely necessary and should accompany all form of study and consolidation.

c) The third and most important part is interrelated with the previous one and is subsequent to it. It concerns the full theoretical development in all the techniques and methods of the esoteric culture and the awakening of the internal Powers - abilities of man. I shall briefly mention the branches where the potential and the foundations of the above may be instructed: Hypnotism - Orthopsychism, Astrology - Astrosophy, Scientific Spiritualism, Esoteric Therapeutics, Meditation, Desymbolism, Karma Yoga, Raja Yoga, Jnani Yoga, Bhakti Yoga, Kriya Yoga, Atmoliquefaction (Weight Loss), other systems of self-knowledge, and other therapeutic systems that can be applied by anybody.

All the above will convince any person, whether they are distrustful or well-intentioned, because they will be able to apply them on themselves. Each will choose what he wishes. In the beginning, our school will operate with a close circle of acquaintances - and perhaps a few other people, who will be deemed suitable to follow the practical part as well. Karma does not often give such opportunities. My objective purpose is to create, from those of you who will seek deeper, the future executives and my future assistants, because we will soon establish a therapeutic center as we did in Lamia and we will apply these therapies. However, one needs knowledge and experience to do so. Are you ready? Are you willing to work? Have you distinguished the real from the false? The permanent from the temporary? The truth from the lie?

What does all this mean? It means that without any 'sacrifice' nothing can be done. It means that without determination, a strong will and hard work, everything is a mistake. We must adapt (redirect) our apparent personal needs and our professional activities according to where they will really be beneficial, primarily for us and then for those who may appear on our path. Because at some point one must become activated and lend a helping hand to our diseased and slithering humanity, for a better future and for more substantial prospects.

Everything else- theories, ideologies and so on – are shameful lies, inabilities, weaknesses and personal interests, 'karmic attributions' - results of the higher levels of the intellectual range of Consciousness and more rarely of subconsciousness, but not of Hyperconsciousness. Only by struggling in life and with ourselves and with an education in Metaphysics, can we hope that we and the other people will recover our sight; otherwise, we had better hide in a cave, for we do not deserve to be characterized as human beings, to bear this title (of the higher-being). Where are the values of civility, dignity, mutual help, assistance, justice, morality?

We only worship the trifling profit and have an absurd desire for glory; we know nothing else. I must tell you that my description – and I say this with certainty- concerning our qualities is quite mild and lenient because, in reality, by the way we function we are truly 'zero', if not even less than zero. And if this does not bring even the few persons who have developed some Metaphysical knowledge to their senses, does not move and does not activate them, then as a human being, I dare not say anything else, neither about us, nor about the future of humanity. I shall stop here with a clear conscience that I have done and shall continue to do my duty. May God grant enlightenment to everybody...

I await your own views. I apologize for having tired and overwhelmed you with this letter. I would like to have said much more but that was impossible. I look forward to hearing your points of view in Trikala, at my address.

**In peace and light,
Ilias Katsiampas**

4th Essay

Trikala, January 22, 1991

Dear Argyris,

I just received your letter with the enclosed printed material for the electronic acupuncture apparatus you have bought. And after I called you and we talked a bit, I thought I should write you my opinion about the whole matter, as much about the therapy as for the illness. I would also like to recommend some books-essays and some therapeutic methods.

To begin with, I must tell you that the apparatus you have bought will surely offer some help, perhaps even a cure without medicine, though it is a machine. Certainly it is important because it is based on the energetic (pranic) essence of man and tries to restore his equilibrium. However, it is still a mechanical tool.

I shall try to briefly explain the essence – it won't even be a summary – of this great problem of man, illness. But first of all, I shall enumerate some, about 20, of the systems of Esoteric Therapeutics without medicine that I have studied thoroughly. I have even applied 5-6 of them practically, with unexpected and very satisfactory results.

1) Therapeutic suggestion and autosuggestion.
2) Hypnotism - Orthopsychism, three integral systems.
3) With religious emotional prayer.
4) Color therapy.
5) Creative visualization.
6) Iconoplastic therapy - from far or near (N. Margioris' invention).
7) Static therapeutics with the hands - palms.
8) Kinetic therapeutics with the hands - palms.

9) Ancient Greek - Asclepian massage (revived by N. A. Margioris).

10) Kriya Yoga, a body-spiritual therapeutic method (universal level revived by N. A. Margioris).

11) Mantramotherapeutics (with power words).

12) Reflexology - reflex zone therapy.

13) Finger-Vibrations - Finger Tapping (an invention of N. A. Margioris).

14) Chinese Acupuncture.

15) Japanese Shiatsu - Finger pressure (systematization of Shiatsu by my Master N. A. Margioris).

16) Kundalinotherapy by Kundalini exhalations or also by its awakening (Tantra Yoga).

17) Raja Yoga 8 stages – types of therapy.

18) Psychoanalysis - clinical psychology.

19) Glossotherapy (an invention of N. A. Margioris).

20) Exorcisms.

21) A combination of many of the above systems.

The above are some of the most important and most effective therapeutic systems, some of which are scientifically substantiated and are taught in the universities of foreign countries.

But what is health and what is illness and how are they caused?

Health is the harmonious balance and co-existence of the two opposite but complementary systems of the organism, the sympathetic (positive magnetism, made up of 55% of positive energy, that prevails at the back of the body and that has an exit-observer on our forehead), and the parasympathetic (negative magnetism, made up of 45% of negative energy that prevails at the front of man and has as an observer-exit at the back along the nape of the neck).

When this analogy of the power - prana - energy is maintained at the percentages of 55% positive magnetism and of 45% negative magnetism, then there is health, power and life. When these percentages are disturbed or when one exceeds the other to a great degree, then we become ill. Whatever name we may give this illness, it is always a disturbance of the balanced analogy of the life substance, of prana, that revives us and keeps us in life. This imbalance of the analogous and decreed by nature powers may be due to many causes, natural (visible) and unnatural (invisible).

For example, they may be due to bad eating habits (wrong, excessive or too little), to external colds, to viruses, to hardships, to malnutrition, to irregular ingestion of foods in the organism resulting in the retention of toxic substances, to autosuggestion or to heterosuggestion, to improper or incorrect medicinal treatment, to the continuous antagonism itself between the two great energy systems of our organism. Also, most diseases are caused by the overwhelming sentimental burdens and psychical (mental) troubles provoking indefinite redistributions and reshufflings in the energy essence of man, resulting in the disturbance of the balanced analogy of the power-energies within us.

In the same way, an even deeper explanation is that every irregularity in our physical body comes from the flood tide (the excessive intake of the Life Substance) or the ebb-tide (an insufficient intake of the Life Substance). So, this flood tide of the etheric powers - prana that enter our organism continuously, creates the phenomenon either of the overbalance of prana in the organism (flood tide) or of the deficiency of prana in the organism (ebb-tide).

I believe that asthma belongs to the organism overbalance category, with a very increased percentage of prana.

Certainly, as you may suspect, the internal reason of the illness and of everything else in life, is our personal karma that we ourselves set in motion, thus we must suffer it patiently, ceasing to create new karmas with our new activities and thoughts, even about our illness.

Definitely, our probable therapy with some of the aforementioned methods of esoteric therapy is the counter-weight that will deliver us from the specific karma of an illness. Note that a cure is not always attained, even though the rate of success is high (70%-80%), there are always failures or incomplete therapies.

However, besides Karma, we should regard our own soul (spirit) as responsible, for it knows exactly all the necessary karmic counter-balances of Mind and body experiences (sufferings). It is our soul that supervises and directs the entrance of the power-energy flow within us, according to our real necessities and not to our apparent ones!

Therefore, we must learn how to coexist with our problems, with the obstacles, diseases, wickedness of other people and society, and to try, by instructing ourselves, to evolve through what happens to us. The techniques and the therapeutic methods, along with the aid of a therapist and the cooperation of the patient are extremely helpful in closing old karmic accounts. If the healer is attained (enlightened), which means that he is working completely consciously, and if the patient is also cooperative, the therapy will succeed. If the therapist is not attained but works 'unconsciously', using the same techniques with sincerity and self-denial, he can also offer important services to his fellow-men. But almost everything depends on the receptiveness and on the cooperation of the patient towards his healer. If this does not exist, the results will be poor. If it exists, even an unattained therapist can work 'miracles' (we see again that karma itself allows someone to cooperate with or resist one's healer - the karmic elements always exist).

Anyway, I would like to point out that all the esoteric therapeutic methods, besides Yoga perhaps, are not panaceas. But they are the only real help that may be given from man to man, they are true HUMANISM. Of course, what we call 'miracle' does not exist in these therapies, and if, perhaps, it happens somewhere and sometimes only by attained therapists, it is because they decide to carry the burdens of one of their fellow-men. Perhaps in order to enlighten him, perhaps for thousands of other reasons that we, the common mortal beings cannot detect and verify.

However, a miracle does not replace spirituality, nor do the cures we mentioned above. For, as many times as we can cure somebody, he will immediately form thousands of other diseases due to the wrong course he has taken, to his unbridled behaviour and activity which is detrimental to himself and to others and of course, due to the absolute lack of contact and communication with his soul, of which he is continually an adversary and prisoner (its enemy).

Only when we get in touch with our soul, even a little, can we really be cured. Only then will we learn our real nature - self and obtain, by right, all our real Powers and abilities. In a nutshell, all our remedies, all our teachings, all our efforts should direct us to become able to stand on our own two feet, to obtain the first aim, which is to Know Thyself, the knowledge of our existence-Life itself.

This is what all masters try to teach and convey to us. They try to give us the possibility to cure ourselves, to re-orientate and to reprogram ourselves towards the direction of our perfection, and most important, to walk towards it on our own two feet. It is not enough to simply listen to the other people who walked on the same path before us. We, too, must walk the path, even at our own pace, but we should walk on... I would like to discuss many more things but the time is not right; perhaps when we meet, we will talk a bit. Now back to you. As we said, there are preconditions and in your case, the results are certainly positive. You may, any day you like, visit the Master and tell him that it is I who sent you to him. Otherwise, if this is not possible, come to Larissa at the first opportunity you get so that we may make this attempt together. I recommend you read the following books and essays:

The Chiroplastic Therapeutics of Shiatsu, Volumes A and B.
Psychotherapeutics without medicine.
Therapeutics without medicine.
Therapeutics by hypnotism.
Therapeutics for psychopathy.
Kriya Yoga (practical method of psychosomatic therapeutics).
Raja Yoga.

I also, I recommend you read my Master N. A. Margiori's masterpiece, the *Esoteric Key* - 11 triads Esoteric Therapeutics. I strongly advise you to buy the first and the second book. Especially the first book of Shiatsu contains all the theory with a full practical guide, with numerous plans for therapeutic application of at least 186 diseases that have been, for the first time, classified by the Master into 23 groups.

With this book alone, nearly anyone who is interested could apply therapies successfully. If you're in Athens, do buy them, otherwise, you can place an order.

In the beginning of October, a new school of Metaphysics-Therapeutics, where students of the Master teach, opened in Lamia.

There, my Master urged me to lay the ground and foster the climate for a similar school in Trikala. I have already done some preliminary work in this direction. At present, I have promised myself to open a school immediately after I am discharged, with the assistance of some friends. Already, there are more than 15 candidates and I believe that when we start, we will have a great turnout. The school will include almost everything, all the main specializations. On the other hand, different therapies will take place and all my associates will be trained in them. I hope you will be by my side.

Besides all the above, I am thinking of editing an informative journal about radio emissions, as this has been going on in Lamia for one year now, and I may also manage to publish a book in the future. Many of these plans are already in the making.

To end, I would like to go into some aspects, from an esoteric point of view, of the Persian Gulf War.

I strongly believe that it is due to an indescribable web of karmic causes that finds its outlet through this war and that came from the previous (past) actions - activities of these peoples.

To put it more simply, this is the last mass settling of Karmic accounts on our planet, its redemption from the burdens it bore, in order to enter a new period of spiritual evolution and of maturity. We will most probably have more such events before 2000.

I want to believe that as extensive as they may become, they will not constitute any direct danger for the human race itself. Because now is the time, souls are given the time and new possibilities are afforded for a spiritual evolution. According to the Divine Plan, it is a period of settlement and cleansing of people in preparation for their reconstruction.

Therefore, we must work very hard so that all of our old debts - individual, racial and national - may be washed off, and that our personal and consequently, our collective evolution may be precipitated.

Yours sincerely,
Ilias Katsiampas

5th Essay

Melissotopos, May 29, 1991

Dearest Master,

I hope my letter finds you in full peace and happiness.

I was very sorry not to have been able to come to Thessaloniki to attend the Anastenarians. I imagine it would have been a great experience for me. Please, write me about it in great detail. I phoned you but I could not get hold of you.

I feel much better concerning my problem and I am now trying to expel it.

In several discussions, many friends of mine expressed interest in opening a Yonga school with me and they suggested that you undertake to teach every 15 days.

For this reason, please come for a visit so that we may be able to reach an agreement and to work out a schedule. I hope that you will find some free time.

We will make every effort to establish a school where a natural lifestyle and harmony will be taught and where, at the same time, we will develop the Rose Cross Philosophies and so on.

I send you my regards and I wish you peace in your life.

Sincerely and fraternally yours,
Argyris

P.S.: Awaiting your news as soon as possible.

Trikala, June 1, 1991

Dear brother and fellow student on the common path, I greet you and I wish you spirituality and peace.

I just received your letter through a friend of yours and it made me very glad.

First of all, I would like to inform you that I am not a Master, as none of us are. We are fellow students and travelers on the common path of the spiritual quest and of man's perfection. Of course, it is true that I am knowledgeable about some key theories and practices, which are very concrete and thus invaluable, but also very ambiguous and completely unknown to the uninitiated. These can significantly help every well-intentioned person who may wish to try and apply them.

So, I may be a little more advanced today than some others who, may tomorrow surpass me and become my 'Masters' themselves, provided, of course, that they work actively and energetically on themselves, which is not only self-evident but also indispensable. Anyway, it is true that all of us, more or less, are at the same time students and masters. We are students in relation to those who are ahead of us and masters in relation to those who follow us. However, the creation of a school that will be exclusively guided by you (with the assistance and advice of your Guru - with the phrase 'by you' I mean an expert in Esotericism), is something very different and quite responsible, certainly not only towards society and the natural laws of the state-religion-government, but toward your Master, your God and, of course, the human souls which you automatically become responsible for and which you are called upon to account for, at the place where everybody accounts for their acts.

This undertaking needs and requires a particular sensitivity, great tolerance-acceptance, patience, persistence, effort, impeccable teaching-orientation methods, personal as well as collective sacrifices, avoidance of the numerous pitfalls, real esoteric knowledge and a certain degree of experience; otherwise tragic and dangerous errors will be made (de facto), bearing results that I cannot express. And certainly, as a guide, you will bear the integral responsibility, not only for your own actions, but also for the whole and for every individual separately. Because you shape human souls and not only Minds and based on the culture you offer them, you will have the respective results from them, which, in their temporary life, will be expressed as individual actions. And if the seeds you sow do not correspond to (if they deviate from) Esoteric Knowledge and are constructions of your own Mind, then you start straying from your initial course-target and if you are open to negative influences, you become vulnerable and you affect your students with wrong assessments and with mistaken courses that will bring you the respective results.

For such a guide many dangers, traps, reactions, enticements, sufferings, diseases, pains, disappointments, persecutions by the uninitiated, physical and Metaphysical hardships and pitfalls lie in wait. He is literally on a tightrope and must continuously make great efforts to find a balance for himself as well as for the others.

Of course, this does not mean that a good guide does not make errors; however, he definitely learns from them and he corrects them so quickly that they are not perceived by other people nor do they affect them.

However, in order for this to be 'integrally' achieved, it

means that the prospective Master's Knowledge of Esoteric matters (Esotericism - Esoteric Philosophy - Yoga - Esoteric Therapeutics) is real and thorough, that he has received practical instruction (he has passed many hardships with success) and that he has learnt how to serve the Divine Plan, in close cooperation with his Guru-Master.

However, as you may realize, such a man as described above, fulfilling all the requirements and the criteria I mentioned to you earlier, rarely appears. It is obvious that a large number of those who appear and advertise themselves in their schools do not fulfill most requirements and are guided by erroneous motives (even when these motives appear pure and moral) that an experienced eye recognizes at once.

I wrote you all this in order to give you a personal view of how particular and what a great responsibility such a fine attempt is. Most people undertake such endeavors motivated by an enthusiasm without any substantial background (knowledge - experience - application - cooperation with a Guru - Master) and few people fulfill some of the requirements, while even fewer possess all the prerequisite qualifications, and when this happens it is an exception.

In your letter, you mention a Yoga school and you spell it y-o–n-g-a (putting an unnecessary *n* between *o* and *g*). You have to know that the pronunciation of the *n* character is a mistake and even an insult in the Sanskrit language, whether we use it in written or in oral form. The correct pronunciation is the dry yoga, without any *n* in-between. We must use this, otherwise we are wrong and we offend, whether others realize it or not.

You write me that you had some discussions with some of your friends who were interested in a Yoga school and you suggested I come teach there. Yes, it might be possible for me to come 1 or 2 times per month. I may come for a visit to make their acquaintance. But a Yoga school is a school of psychology, research, pursuit, spiritual education-awakening and of live action-application (responsible guidance). And the main requirements for its operation is the existence of souls that are ready to listen - to learn sublime teachings and perhaps, to apply them, something which is also rare, as most people have 'pre-conceived views' which they insert and impose in discussions, believing them to be the only correct ones. In reality, these views have no relation to the conceptual level of everyone separately, which is limited to the five senses and definitely ignorant of Esoteric knowledge and they occupy only a grain of sand which they consider to be the only truth (for example, religious – dogmatic, scientific, partisan, moral, philosophical, realistic survivalist, social, cultural, moral, traditional and so on) and with this small grain of truth they organize their life, their acts and their beliefs and they try to impose it on those they know or don't know, using fanaticism and violence and without taking into consideration or respecting the Freedom of Will – the choice of their fellow-man.

So, we enter a vicious circle of dispute - conflict - contradiction that is a daily living example, wherever we may look. All this simply confirms, for those who have a more open Mind, that all views have a touch of Truth, even if they appear to be contradictory and controversial. We lack the key of Esotericism - Metaphysics that would allow us to comprehend, to connect and to unite them as seen fit internally and externally, to see them as parts of the One Truth that are expressed as they are conceived by limited human Minds. I state all this to you in order to point out that a superficial curiosity or an incidental enthusiasm of a would-be student are not enough. Apart from these, some internal concerns, deep questions must exist (if they do not exist, we ought to provoke - create them) that distinguish those who have an innate inclination for the beyond and for Metaphysics.

With those who are interested, we have to bring forth these questions-concerns by means of sound and undogmatic Metaphysical argumentation through lengthy conversations (that need Metaphysical Knowledge - experience) and by recommending the appropriate Metaphysical works (books), such as my Master N. A. Margiori's books. We recommend the respective works according to each person's idiosyncrasy.

That is, it is essential we start with a first encounter with the Esoteric Circle of Knowledge, in the form of dialectical discussions (questions-answers), as well as a dissipation of certain doubts, so that a certain familiarity may be attained by the seeker-candidate student and then, according to the evolution of his soul-spirit, he will either drop out, or continue or ask to interrupt and start again, whether on a theoretical level only or wishing to pursue the field more deeply.

So, since you tell me that you are preparing some individuals and you suggest a school with me as supervisor-instructor, you must also become aware of the objective and certain difficulties of your decision. But since you think that you are ready to prepare these souls without any fanaticism, I will happily inform you about the general plans you must definitely follow (we will certainly discuss it more when I visit you - soon I hope).

I believe that you can offer many things and I trust that you will succeed. But you need to work hard with the interested persons (conversations) and with yourself (self-critical introspection), to recommend them the proper books of Esotericism, to answer their questions and to orientate them Metaphysically, so that they may be in a position to follow the educational lectures that I will present when I visit you.

Also, at the same time, you must work on yourself, certainly not only by following the instructions you have been taught in the past and that are few and of limited content, even if they do touch upon Metaphysics, but by reading other books of superior spiritual value, such as those by my Master, which I recommend you unreservedly and which you may recommend in turn to other interested parties. You need much work. You must be ready to work simultaneously for yourself, for these individuals and for your own daily bread. Try. I am sure that despite all the difficulties, you will reap the respective fruits (physical and metaphysical) that are only for those who know how to give without expecting a reward.

Because it is crucial that this be done by people who are not afraid and who do not hesitate to accept the responsibilities of their acts, even of their errors, since they themselves are on a perfect line of orientation.

It is the time for us to rule over what creates obstacles. What is needed is resoluteness, will, effort, organization and responsibility to ourselves, to others and to God.

You also write, at the end of your letter, that we will try to establish a school for natural life and harmony and at the same time advance the Rose Cross philosophies, whereas before that you mention a Yoga school where you invite me to teach. Your proposal greatly honors me, but I am obliged to clarify that since you invite me to teach in a Yoga school that may be - for you - at the same time a school of health and harmony and Rosicrucian inquiries, I must warn you that you have taken a wrong approach. Because, since you invite me to teach there, you allow me to express what I know, what I have been instructed in and have experienced completely freely. Otherwise, it would be meaningless for me to undertake the duty of esoteric guidance. Now, if my experience allows me - and if there are relevant queries, I may touch upon other systems for purely informative purposes, I agree. But my substantial teaching and practice will cover only what I know well and what I have experienced and lived, otherwise, we are walking in the wrong direction. Certainly, Comparative Philosophy will be taught, but the primary role will be held by Esoteric Philosophy which is the only philosophy that can explain Metaphysics, Creation, Man, God, Truth, with sound and logical arguments in terms that anybody can conceive, comprehend and apply, if he so desires. When I come there, we shall discuss all this.

In peace and in light,
Ilias Katsiampas

6th Essay

Trikala, October 2, 1991
To Mr. Katsiampas

Dear Sirs,

I would like with this letter, to convey my support and my participation in your holy purpose. Please, also accept my written request to become an active member of your school the OMAKOIO OF ATHENS. I wish you personal well-being and success in your high mission.

Yours truly
Panos

Trikala, October 13, 1991
To Panos

Dear Panos,

Thank you very much for your sincere desire to assist and participate, as well as for your warm wishes for the work that I have undertaken. Of course, your request for membership in our school has been gladly accepted. But, as a formality, in due time, you will be called upon, as all new students are, to complete a special application form that will be accompanied by an analytical prospectus, e.g. on Raja Yoga or any other existing branch that you may wish to attend. For informative purposes, I briefly mention the general plan toward the creation of the following branches of Yoga: Raja Yoga, Kriya Yoga, Esoteric Philosophy, Esoteric Therapeutics with all the sound approaches both within and without Yoga. What's more, a therapeutic center which will undertake to treat 'all kinds' of diseases will begin operation, under certain conditions which we can discuss when we meet.

That's all for now as a beginning but we must not rule out the activation also of other methods or departments or the substitution of already existing ones by others.

I must confess that the primary aim of this school is to educate the already 'ready' persons, those who have already done some searching and cultivation in the field of Metaphysics - Esotericism. So, these few lucky people will get all the Esoteric Knowledge, experience, practice and tools they need, depending on their individual thirst for Knowledge and absorption − assimilation of esotericism.

I ought to tell you that such knowledge, and especially

the practical and technical methods, are taught only by very few people and sparingly either because, first of all, they do not know, and secondly, the few things they do know they keep for themselves, to maintain a superior position over other people. Those few who are able to teach in the right way – since they themselves have been educated correctly and by genuine experts (Guru, Masters, Enlightened Ones), certainly teach with prudence and fully aware of the responsibility towards the souls (men) which they undertake to instruct and to guide on the esoteric course, hiding nothing, saying everything.

Many times, the level of the apprentices is too low for them to be able to grasp all the afore-said. To reach the appropriate level one needs time, effort, work and sacrifice. With time, a gradual expected change occurs in the student as he goes from exoteric (intellectual) to esoteric (hyper-intellectual) knowledge, which must correspond directly to his everyday actions and behaviour in life and with his fellow-men. When this takes longer than it should or rather when it is never accomplished because the student fails to respond to and apply the theory and the practice of Yoga, and possibly due to a hypocritical and clearly self-interested handling of these matters, then there is immediate danger. Firstly, for this essentially uninitiated apprentice who is still unchanged, without any progress and secondly, for the rest of the group which advances with pride and leaps gradually into deeper strata of consciousness, but which continually accepts consciously or completely unconsciously, the inhibitive influence of this individual that, at all time, disturbs the harmonious evolution of the group. So, double harm is done. As regards the non-progressing student, it is dangerous for his mental state, because he forms and creates for himself and for others, the most hazardous and absolutely negative karma.

Thus, these individuals are gently distanced from the group, because on the one hand, they are not ready, and on the other hand, they are dangerous for themselves as well as for the others. As you understand, these are deep karmic matters that only a few can follow today. For this reason, a lot of time will be, consumed, along with the other lessons, on the karmic matters that all Esotericists must know in depth and extensively.

Metaphysics, Esotericism, Yoga, Mysticism and so on, are Truth, Perfection, God themselves, and when somebody approaches or - more rarely - touches these transcendental states, he need not fear anything or anybody. He teaches without fear or passion and under abundant light, all that can be expressed in common terms -respective approaches- on transcendental conceptions (Creation, Laws, Truth), in order for them to be initially understood by our logic - consciousness, to be cultivated and to constitute a permanent pole of attraction and research subject, that is the ONLY ESCAPE from the dead end not only of contemporary man but of the man of all times as well. Afterwards, the special practices and the personal struggle (the correct struggle) in life follow that will lead every genuine seeker to the peak of esoteric experience, Enlightenment, Truth, and that will transform him into one of its humble vessels on earth. Is all this easy? The answer is no. Can many people attain this? No, very few and very rarely can one attain this in its totality. Must everybody (whether ready or not) be trained in the above? OF COURSE and DEFINITELY. It is absolutely necessary that everybody receive the Metaphysical incentives and the Esoteric education best suited to one's abilities and level in order to be able to organize one's life on the right bases, to realize more or less the meaning and the destination of one's life, and, in accordance with one's level of comprehension and experience, to undertake one's personal and social responsibilities. Only Mysticism, Yoga can provide the teaching of the Indefinite Truth. Because it is Perfection and every man's real destination and it is taught in abundant light, far and wide, so that everyone can take what suits him and ascend at least one step higher.

Occultism, magic, brotherhoods, the Freemasons and, in general, all closed-membership societies – though the latter have lately become more inclusive, have no relationship with the truth per se, but with particular truths, relative truths. They delve into some parts of the invisible creation, of our neighbouring dimension, where illusions lurk, and are subjective, not objective, states of truth; or they train in the desymbolism of various esoteric symbols and in a deeper understanding of esoteric meanings.

To put it simply, there is a smattering of knowledge, imperfections, and, at times, selfishness. Moreover, as with everything in life and in every field, people from the above-mentioned areas are driven by opportunistic motives, ambition, pride, passions, grudges, hatred, revenge, calumnies, and personal advancement.

To put it mildly, they aren't much different from the rest of the world. Some of them act against and not, as they should, in favour of the whole. Thus, they spread negative karma, and, sooner or later, they will get what they deserve. Because self-interest, selfishness, negative passions, serving one's own interests, the hunger for power, and the supposed absolute truth they alone possess, is against the truth itself. A truth that can't be revealed by words; it can only be experienced in one's soul. It is the complete opposite of such human weaknesses, which are living proof of a reality for anyone who has lived near or has met people of such occult circles.

Of course, this does not mean the condemnation of all occult groups, alas! On the contrary, there are healthy occult circles - groups that have or ought to have a Mystical aim; however, they do distinctive work in one part of the dimension next to ours, while, at the same time, they try to evolve esoterically. But these tasks are destined for those few people who have especially developed and versatile Minds and nerves of steel. For the path of occultism is so turbulent and dangerous that only a few people can bear it. However, that which is the most important is that it does not lead to absolute Truth, but to partial and secondary truths that, most times, lead to a very negative and loaded karma for those who partake in them without any limits, standards, a moral basis and so on, because these are rarely or incompletely provided in preparation for the path into the occult. And the consequences and the prerequisites are probably defective and deficient from the beginning. Therefore, the results will also be of similar quality. For this reason, greater attention and greater discretion are needed when dealing with the occult.

On the contrary, in Yoga there is an order to everything; each person evolves and matures at a normal pace, from whatever stage he's at, and no matter how high or low the step he comes from. Because he is dealing with the same Truth that ALL of us have trapped within us and that we are called upon to approach according to our personal potential and limits (karma). And after a hard struggle to awaken it, to bring it to light and to let it be our luminous guide for every difficulty, obstacle, impasse of our life on Earth but also in the other Dimensions and for the people who would like to precipitate their evolution and who will decide to learn in order for them to serve in turn, gradually breaking the karmic bonds.

Only in this way can we hope for a better society and a better and more enlightened humanity that will be perfectly balanced, fulfilling its purpose on earth, in harmonious cooperation with its souls and in full consciousness of its personal and social responsibilities.

I considered it important to state all the above, after having touched upon these topics the two times we met. Certainly, it is not possible for us to cover all the matters that must be dealt with, for that requires hard work on both our parts. I hope that I have somehow outlined the general plans of these matters. I am willing to discuss and clarify any questions you may have. I can also give you some of my Metaphysical essays that contain esoteric truths in a more condensed form.

Now, concerning the school and the modules that will be taught, my wish and desire is that you take and use all those elements that will help and will complete, reinforce and elevate the course of your own work, so that you can continually broaden what you offer to others, giving them answers, solutions, techniques, methods, lessons that will be complete and adapted to their needs and to their idiosyncrasy. It is a really difficult mission, requiring particular sensitivity and discretion.

Your experience and your complementary knowledge and training in Yoga will help you not only to handle every case with ease but also to teach many ways of dealing with every case, as you handle it personally.

Sincerely wishing you the best,

Yours very truly
Ilias Katsiampas

7th Essay

Trikala

Dear Mr. X,

I have received your letter with the accompanying prospectus in Greek as well as your book on Agnihotra.

Thank you very much for your letter as well as for your interest. I send you the prospectuses of the OMAKOIO OF TRIKALA departments currently in operation (Raja Yoga, Kriya Yoga, Atmoliquefaction) translated in English.

I also enclose herewith the Esoteric Key prospectus and the curriculum of the branches of Esoteric studies offered as a correspondence course (only in Greek, at present). Finally, I enclose the only book, just 50 pages, translated in English and which refers to the common ancestors of Greeks and Indians and, in extension, to the common origin-descent of Yoga that the first Greeks (the Pre-Hellenic Greeks) of the Aegean Sea, the Dravidians possessed and first used. All the above are based on new archaeological findings and the discovery of the two most ancient cities in the world, dated 8.000-12.000 before Christ, Mohenjo Daro and el Harrapa.

The discoveries proved the migration of a pre-existing civilization from the Hinterland of the Mediterranean Sea and Hellenic area to India, and at the same time, the discovered statuettes in Yogi postures and other such findings confirm the knowledge and the use-origin of Yoga, specifically by the Dravidians who lived in the Mediterranean area before 12.000 BC.

Briefly, I will refer to the work of the Omakoio of Trikala of which I am in charge. The following departments are in operation: The first one is of Raja Yoga (and Tantra), for the first time in a Greek province, in full format and in gradually ascending order.

The second one is Kriya Yoga that is a method of body-soul therapeutics (edification) and now the unique and necessary guide-prerequisite for the initiation of the student in Raja Yoga.

Then, we have the third department that is focused on Yoga techniques and weight loss by natural Atmoliquefaction.

The fourth department is Esoteric Philosophy taught in depth with lectures on all the sections-branches of Metaphysics and with dialectical discussions - answers.

The fifth department is Esoteric Therapeutics (therapeutics without medicine). Therapies are made with all the means and the methods we have been taught by my Master, for all diseases and illnesses, whether corporal or psychical (intellectual). Finally, many Seminars on different Esoteric matters are organized.

According to the Esoteric Philosophy of Blavatsky, in the 5th Root Race where we are now, Mahayoga, the codified Raja Yoga of Patanjali will become activated and prevail universally. And it will give man the highest achievement-conquest: hyperconscious actualization.

Alice Bailey supports exactly this view in her book *The Light of the Soul* in which she analyzes Patanjali's aphorisms and says that Raja Yoga will rule over the 5th evolutionary phase of humanity (5th Root Race).

But also Vivekananda who was the first to introduce Yoga to the West, in his book *The Yoga systems: Karma, Bhakti and Raja* considers Raja as the apex of all the other types of Yoga, that, as he himself says, will rule over the 5th Root Race. On the other hand, it is not by chance that he makes a deep analysis and interpretation of Patanjali's aphorisms that concern the gradual ascension of Raja Yoga.

Yogananda first introduced and spread Kriya yoga in the West through his famous book *Autobiography of a Yogi*, without however referring to any practical details. It is my Master who wrote the first textbook in the world, exclusively on Kriya Yoga, with sketches of the poses (Asanas - movements – breaths) and with a full analysis - explanation for all the phases of every exercise separately. He also wrote the book *Raja Yoga* that is the only published edition with such an extended and detailed analysis. There is still Vivekananda's above-mentioned book, which refers only briefly to Raja Yoga.

Concerning titles, names, clothing, rhetorical forms, grandiose salutes, secretiveness and so on, I quite comprehend that all these are external expressions – presentations, which as a rule, have no relation to the esoteric quality or accomplishment.

Certainly, all Esoteric Schools offer something and do spiritual work. The difference lies in the degree and quality of what is offered by every School and every Guru, where there is one. Nobody can represent Truth. Truth is within us and only if we receive the right stimulations can we start awakening and emitting it. And it is exactly for this reason that a proper and responsible man is needed, a man-Master, sent by the Divine Plan who can offer a proper and rounded education or who can reshape - revive - restore the already existing but strangely unmanifest one, as well as offer the most important personal contact-stimuli with him (visible and invisible). Such men are rare indeed.

So, on the one hand it is the School - Master and on the other it is the man himself – the seeker – the student, who as low or high as he may be intellectually and socially, what he finds depends on what he is looking for. If he asks for bodily health, he will have it; if he asks for emotional balance, the same; if he is seeking to develop his mental health, he will find it; if he seeks all three, he will attain them. But if, apart from these, he seeks (even on a theoretical level if not a practical one) recognition - self-revelation of Truth - God - Perfection - Transcendence and so on, then only he can be considered a true student on the spiritual path and no matter how small his steps may be, his ascending evolution is the last ring of the chain of Truth, the only sincere and responsible bearer-vessel outwards. Because his apprenticeship and his training come from the direct contact and cooperation with, submission to, struggle, sacrifice and guidance of a Guru with a mission and free of karma. Basically, we're talking about Avatar and it is they who are 'hidden' more than all the others and who never promote themselves but only follow their students' initiative. People know very few things about them and this only at a price of a karmic burden to their students for any revelations. I should point out that these 'men' are 'inside the world but not of this world', which means that they live - pass through – dress like - maybe also behave like all of us: they get married, bear children, perhaps they dwell beside us but they are difficult to recognize and approach. This is because, first of all, they are modest and, secondly, because they agree to keep only those who have pure motives and a powerful will for evolution - knowledge – education by their side. For the others, they will become known in the far future, when they will have already departed, but they will have left them their seal which is a new radical foundation and restructuring of all the values - ideals and esoteric educational systems - methods via contemporary words (written and oral) and capable members who will put them into practice.

At any given moment, they teach and make an example of their own way. For those who know them, they are simply considered perfect as men, for those who are their students, they are perfect gods and for those who are in their service indeed they are 'perfect men and perfect gods', because their teachings, their revelations and their justice are perfect as concerns the human and perfect as concerns the spiritual. They are the excellent expressers - bearers - revealers of 'transcendental Truth, using human words, and with a complete education and serving as examples on all levels, to all those who respond and are truly interested in advancing and in approaching the supreme Truths, first externally and then internally. I do not mention all this in a subjective, casual and arbitrary way. It is the result of my apprenticeship in different schools of Esotericism and from year-long studies, knowledge and experience-practice beside an AVATAR, without my wanting or being interested in creating any impressions or receiving special treatment. I always say and teach all that I verify and experience personally, because I am interested in the Truth, in all its expressions-manifestations, and I am only trying to be its advocate. And I have a 'holy obligation' to transmit and to teach all that I know wisely, under any conditions and in any way.

Of course, I have neither the time nor is it the place to mention more details about all that I touched upon. We can discuss whatever else you wish. Also for further details about Kriya and Raja Yoga, do not hesitate to write me.

Yours very sincerely,
In the light existing within us,
Ilias Katsiampas

PART THREE

GLOSSARY OF SANSKRIT

(ANALYTICAL PHILOSOPHICAL
DICTIONARY OF 400 WORDS)

PREFACE

The reason for which this glossary of Sanskrit was written was my agonizing and continual effort, during my esoteric course-apprenticeship to grasp every spiritual meaning and to separate-clarify and classify it in my mind, in order to form a clear personal understanding of every presented term which is found codified in every language including Sanskrit.

Therefore, I was driven to undertake a personal quest and I came into contact with thousands of metaphysical terms (some of which were in Sanskrit) which I codified within me in a substantial and sound way. I was greatly and catalytically helped in this by my Spiritual Master Nikolaos A. Margioris who offered me a truly Panoramic Spiritual Banquet and Exaltation, while at the same time he offered me an incomparably complete method on how to apply the whole Esoteric Philosophy, on the basis of which I continue my esoteric course while at the same time, I convey it in turn with full responsibility, wisely and with guidance, to any person who is really interested in knowing the Causes of his Existence, the deepest meaning of Life and how to gain the power of his Being, and become a true ruler of Himself.

So, looking back on my personal course, I realized and confirmed the awful and continual distress and confusion I suffered, in order to be able to grasp and clarify the metaphysical concepts within me (Sanskrit or not). But this seems to be a common course for anyone wishing to truly and more responsibly penetrate, explore and probe this unexplored and unclassified area and learn the correct terminology of Metaphysical Science.

Therefore, seeing the immense void that exists and causes man to form insufficient personal appraisals and thoughts, that eventually cause greater confusion and suffering to the world, I initially decided, because of all the above reasons, to write a complete Metaphysical Work which I would call "The Most Complete and Thorough Guide –Encyclopedia of Metaphysical Terms", where I would clearly and thoroughly clarify any spiritual confusion or terminology which is more or less familiar.

So, I started by tirelessly collecting metaphysical terms of every kind, which resulted in my gathering an immense amount of material (more than a thousand metaphysical concepts), which is, of course, quite representative and able to substantially enlighten any well-intentioned seeker-student on every esoteric matter-question that might arise during his esoteric course and to give him a stable, certain and truly meaningful answer-concept-guide, which will orientate him nearly wholly toward the metaphysical Truth.

But unfortunately, the development and the thorough analysis of such a metaphysical guide is not a work which one can finish in one or two days. Time and labor are needed to complete such an undertaking. So, while I was progressing with my first book under the title *From the Master's Mouth to the Student's Ear*, I was simultaneously preparing a skeleton analytical guide of metaphysical concepts and their sporadic development.

During the course of my work and after having prepared the analysis of the Sanskrit meanings which co-exist with many other metaphysical words, I thought it would be a good idea to separate them and include them in my first work which was to be published so that any interested person may benefit at least from the Sanskrit terminology, of which there is a substantial lack of in the form of Greek published data and which hinders quite a few people who search to find answers and interpretations. Moreover, at the same time, I thought it would be excellent supplementary material for the present book. So that's what I did. I separated the Sanskrit terms from the rest of the metaphysical ones, giving the readers the opportunity to come into contact with the Sanskrit terminology-semantics. The Sanskrit glossary is closely bound to the rest of the work of the writer which is being written and is going to be published in the future and which will constitute a *Complete Dictionary-Guide of Metaphysical Terms*. The glossary will be included in it, along with any necessary supplementaries.

In addition, I would like to stress and make clear that every spiritual activity I take part in, has the Perfect Mystical Conception of the Truth of My Master Nikolaos A. Margioris, as well as the year-long apprenticeship and experience near him (it is 100% Margioritic) as its springboard.

I emphasize this because irrespective of any other research I've conducted and knowledge I have gained from anything I have come into contact with and studied, it was only due to the relationship which I developed with my Master (the biographical details about Nikolaos A. Margioris can be found at the end of this book) that I succeeded in finalizing and firmly piecing together, theoretically and practically, the puzzle of the Mystery of Creation; that is, in reassembling the shattered thousand – piece mirror.

I consider it necessary to point out the above so that one may grasp the colossal and unsurpassable work of the Greek Mystic Nikolaos A. Margioris which includes 34 books (and more unpublished ones), 34 essays, 49 issues of a 100%-metaphysical journal, correspondence courses, personal tireless teachings (thousands of tapes with his speeches, lectures, seminars, excursions).

Throughout this exquisite work of unprecedented revelations of my Master, there is substantial unity and connection, an unbreakable bond-cohesion-succession and interaction toward the common objective of the transcendental Seat-Source.

With his unique gift of explaining things in layman's terms and his sound metaphysical basis and knowledge, he addresses an immense range-variety of subjects such as History, Archaeology, Science, as well as matters of Therapy without Medication, Psychotherapy, Self-therapy, Religion-Theology, Self-Knowledge, Yoga, Esotericism (Occultism and Mysticism). His work leans toward the One and Unique convergence of infallible Unity that gives evidence of His incomparable worldly quality and stature.

I baptized the third part of the book 'Glossary of Sanskrit', meaning (depending on the analysis of each word) the simple interpretation or the essential meaning of every term. The sole purpose of this glossary is to transmit a part of my personal knowledge and experience. Therefore, without paying attention to matters such as the gender of the word, I focus instead on the substance, the meaning and the spiritual message of every concept.

At this point, I will allow the reader to skim through, and later study more deeply, this glossary that is well worth reading, which he may use at any time during his esoteric course, and which will, in my opinion, point him, in the right direction.

GLOSSARY OF SANSKRIT

A

Acharya: Spiritual (religious) Master.

Adhama: It is the inferior form of pranayama - breath (inhalation 12″ - holding in 48″ - expiration 24″), of the Sri-Ganesha method. The other two forms are Madhyama (middle) and Uttama (superior). The presence and the guidance of an expert on the matter, of an Instructor of Esotericism, is considered a prerequisite for the safe practice of pranayama and yoga generally.

Abhava Yoga: The other side of Raja Yoga. Yoga that does not believe in any superior power, in any God but it believes in Zero, in non-existence. An atheistic yoga.

Advaita: Non-duality. The Absolute Unit (Nirguna Brahman). It refers to the non-Dualistic school of Vedanta which teaches the unity of God, the soul and the universe. Its principal interpreter was Shankarachary or Shankaracharya (788-820 A. D.).
There is one and only reality. It is God, beyond and above every category and every form. It is Brahman of Upanishad, Sat Chit Ananda, the absolute Existence - Consciousness - Prosperity.
Advaita considers the whole existent world to be unreal, but it does not consider it to be non-existent. The exis-

tence of the world is likened to the snake we think that we see in the semi-darkness, while in reality it is only a piece of rope. As long as the place is dark we consider the snake to be absolutely real, but as soon as there is light, we realize our mistake. Exactly the same happens with the 'conceptions' we have formed about the world around us, using our limited senses and our consciousness as our only means.

In the last century, the Advaita Monk who gave the supreme initiation (Nirguna Samadhi) to Ramakrishna, the last great saint of India, was monk Totapuri.

Agama: It is one of the two systems of spiritual orientation that belongs to the Dravidians. In the Tantric and Puranic tradition, it contains some internal soul-spiritual states, unknown to the second nature-loving system of Nigama. Also Agama contains within it our known Yoga.

Agami Karma: Karma that is created in the present life and that will bear fruit in the future.

Agni: Fire.

Agni Yoga: Yoga of fire.

Ahamkara: The ego, the sense of self-consciousness. Ahamkara, the sentiment of ego, the element of individualism is developed from Buddhi.

Ahimsa: Non-violence in thought, in words and in actions. It is the 5th commandment-abstinence of Yama. (Yama is the first of the eight steps of Raja yoga). With the practice of non-violence, Mahatma Gandhi managed to free India from English occupation.

Non-violence not only in relation to our fellow-men, to the animal kingdom and to non-living creation, but also to ourselves and the speed of our personal education and evolution on our esoteric course, that must always be within the limits of a free, natural, gradual spiritual development and maturity.

Aitareya Upanishad: At Master Aitareya's feet.

Ajna Chakra: Ajna means 'commandment'. It is the center from which man gives orders to himself and to others. For this reason, it is also called 'Guru' or 'Guru Seat' or 'Guru Chakra' or 'Esoteric Guru'. It is the so-called Third Eye and is found in the interior of the forehead between the two eyebrows (Jnana yoga). It has the sixth sense and Akasha.

Its lotus has two petals. It reflects and supplies the epiphysis with life and it is the soul seat. The colored prana corresponding to it when it enters from Sutratma, is milky-stellar, while the color corresponding to it when Prana comes from Antahkarana is white or colorless. It has 7 thirdcenters-thirdstations-satellites. (The Ajna Chakra has 7 sub-centers which constantly move around it like satellites)

Ajnana: Non-knowledge, ignorance.

Akasha: A derivative of Prana. It is the first-born material substance in an etheric state (first matter) that, under Pranic influence, shapes the worlds of representational form.

Akashic Records: The famous archives we mention here are in the eighth (8th) Dimension from outwards going inward, from our own 13th Dimension to the 7th (13th, 12th, 11th, 10th, 9th, 8th, 7th). The Mystics and the Initiates of earthly times come to take the information that is encoded in these archival forms of all Things and of all times. The internal elements of the eighth Dimension concerning the seven external worlds or skies or dimensions, contain within them every piece of information and every fact that will happen in these universes - dimensions, as much during their formation and their life duration, as during the time of their absorption from the eternal and great Architect.

Their division contains three wings or three repository centers of what is to be.

The first repository contains the creation of every dimension and of every universe or of every sky-world. Even, if needed, the construction of a 14th dimension that will play the role of a kindergarten or a preparatory school for our own 13th dimension.

In the second wing, there are the archives and the Molds, the First Ideas, of all forms that are to be present in all the seven universes-dimensions-worlds of the infinite.

In the third wing, there are the tragic archives of the shrinking and of the folding (End of Times) of the world-dimensions. In order for a soul to be able to approach the difficult task of reading these holy archives, it needs the corresponding evolution and higher and supreme enlightenment, as well as an internal disposition of the human soul to be able to enter the sacred mysteries of Omnicreation (see the books *Birth and Death of the Worlds*, *Posthumous Life*, *The Two-Volume Metaphysical Encyclopaedia*, *Omakoio Journal*, *Branches of Study of the Esoteric Key*, and others by Nikolaos A. Margioris).

Ambrosia: A life (omnitherapeutic) and immortality hormone (it helps in the awakening of Kundalini) that is secreted from the Yogi's palate, after special and painful exercises (e.g. Kechari Mudra). It is the ambrosia of the ancient Greeks or Amrita of the Indians. It is also called Soma or in Greek 'Salari', which means saliva.

Amrita: Ambrosia.

Amritabindu Upanishad: A Drop of Ambrosia. It is a clearly theoretical text explaining different spiritual subjects and terms.

Amritanada Upanishad: The Immortal Sound. Amritanada Upanishad teaches us the mystery of sound that is immortal because it is exactly Brahman itself, in word form. In order for the student to be able to attain the knowledge of the Immortal Sound, he must use Om and the exercises in Yoga, according to the sequence given in the present Upanishad.

Annamaya Kosha: It is our physical body which depends on food (anna) for its existence and sustenance in life,

Ananda: Divine Prosperity - Bliss - Happiness.

Anandamaya Kosha: The sheath of bliss. It is called so because it is nearest to Atman.

Anahata Chakra: Ana means endless. Hata means limit. Anahata is the infinite, the endless state of consciousness. Anahata is also called Chintamani: Chinta is the thought and Mani is the jewel-gem and means that all thoughts can be expressed in fine words. Anahata Chakra is the center of the Heart and corresponds to the thymus gland (Raja yoga). It has air and touch under its authority. It belongs to the 2nd ray (Love - Wisdom), to the Buddhic. The lotus of Anahata has 12 petals. The color emanating from Sutratma is a deep golden mat and the color coming from Antahkarana is a bright gold or deep fire red. It has eight stations - satellites.

Anga: Members, parts, humps, e.g. Ashta-anga yoga = eight-member yoga.

Antahkarana: It is the internal organ that is composed of Buddhi = Intellect, of Manas = Mind, of Ahamkara = Ego, self-consciousness and of Chitta (brain or mind).

Antesha: Divine commandment.

Apana Vayu: It is the second vayu of the first five. It is situated in the coccyx. It governs the elimination of all substances from the body.

Aparigraha: It is the first of the five restraints of Yama (Yama is the first of the eight limbs of Raja Yoga). Aparigraha means the non-acceptance of gifts, because our conscious is in danger of becoming dependent (bribery) through the acceptance of presents that are offered with the purpose of buying us off - consciously or unconsciously – together with the obligation that derives from the reciprocation of any gift.

Apta: Attained. Of course, to be attained, one has to reach ecstasy, by all means. He is an enlightened man whose words may be regarded as 'infallible', because they reflect the rendition of Truth in matter - form.

Aranyakas: Aranyakas are the forest texts which emphasize the spiritual meaning of the religious rites and which were studied by those who had withdrawn from life and lived in the forests.

Artha: Meaning.

Arya: Aryans.

Ardha Matsyendrasana: Twisting asana. Anti-diabetic and anti-asthmatic exercise. It exercises the waist and the organs of the abdominal area. It induces the pancreas to secrete insulin and opens up the respiratory system thus fighting against asthma.

Technique: We sit straight with legs stretched out in front of us. We bend the right leg and we bring it over the knee of the bent left leg. We bring our right hand behind the back and then forward, fingers reaching the inner thigh. And the left hand rests on the toes of the right foot. Of course, the head turns toward the right. The same is repeated on the left side, in combination with appropriate breathing exercises (see the book *Kriya Yoga* by Nikolaos A. Margioris).

Arjuna: Arjuna is the central hero of Bhagavad Gita (the Song of Songs or the ballad of the beloved or of the adored) who, during an impending battle against his relatives that had usurped his kingdom, is overcome by doubts as to whether he should war against his cousins and his uncles, and so he retreats.

The Bhagavad Gita book is the documentation of the long discussion and the serious arguments set forth by Krishna, Avatar of God Vishnu, whose deep internal moral and spiritual answers help him and succeed in dissuading him.

Arhat: An enlightened and recently liberated person from the cycle of reincarnations. More simply, it is a person who has managed to enter the 6th Intellectual level of the Dimension and is now, free from Karma and from obligatory rebirth. He chooses to be reincarnated as a delegate so as to facilitate the precipitation of the evolution of the souls that will approach him, and to bear his own Divine Gifts.

Asamprajnata Samadhi: Seedless samadhi. It is the first liberating samadhi that now has no seed of rebirth in the life of representations and that takes place as soon as the initiated enters the 5th step of the seven steps of the superior Intellectual world of the 11th Dimension. This happens after meditation within the Mind itself, expelling every incoming thought, gradually creating a Void that will cause the destruction of the seeds-waves-samskara within us, and that will free man from every material bond - dependence – karma, thus giving him the right to progress, now liberated, to a higher evolution in more spiritual dimensions until he attains Perfection (see Nikolaos A. Margioris' books *Karma, Reincarnation, Posthumous Life, Birth and Death of the Worlds, Mystical Teachings - 3rd Volume, Raja Yoga*). Another word that defines the same state of emancipation is the word 'Kaivalya' (see glossary). When the soul manages to attain Asamprajnata Samadhi, it no longer wants to come back and we see that the soul remains in these transcendental and holy states for many years, due to the incomparable bliss, fullness and emancipation it feels.

Asana: Position, pose, stance, figure (therapeutic treatment). It is the third of the eight steps of Raja yoga and contains within it all the kinds of Hatha and Kriya Yoga positions that ascend from 4 - 88.000 asanas or (posture variations) each of which serves different purposes.

Asana aims to train and to gradually bring stability and immobility to the physical body, so that a restorative procedure of the damaged organs of the organism to their initial normal state can begin. So that a normal distribution of the internal pranic energies (vayu) going through our body may return and finally, through the stability of the body it may be able to give a message of immobility to the Mind which by mimicking the body will gradually begin to become still and thus peaceful and unburdened of the irrepressible, annoying thoughts that consume its Life Essence (prana).

However, the basic element that is crucial in training for higher Yoga (Raja Yoga) is to find the appropriate pose that you can hold for a long period of time so that you can practise concentrating (Dharana). The following poses are considered appropriate according to the case: Singhasana or Sukhasana, and certainly, above all, Stira Souka or otherwise Padmasana (see the books *Hatha Yoga*, *Kriya Yoga*, *Raja Yoga*, *The Two-Volume Metaphysical Encyclopaedia*, *Omakoio Journal*, *Esoteric Key-Meditation Branch*, by Nikolaos A. Margioris).

Ashram: Commune, hermitage, learning and holy dwelling of a Master or Guru or Initiate. In extension, in our times, Ashram is any place where systematic esoteric teaching takes place under the guidance and the supervision of a Wise Master or of a real Esoterist. Ashrams were built of different material such as stone, asbestos and mainly clay, which are the best materials to hold in the magnetic waves (fluid).

The Guru or Master forms a magnetic covering with his radiating emanations which surrounds the Ashram. More simply, Ashram is the Antaskaranic (see Antaskarana) bridge of an Initiate just as the silk cocoon is the bridge of a worm from which the chrysalis will emerge. Any student who stays under this spiritual cloak-covering will have the possibility to be changed into a saint, a Sage and probably, into a Master of Divine Wisdom. An ashram is a sanctuary and a therapeutic center for people. From this center of Divine Peace, a Master disperses the Substance of Life in all directions of our earthly sphere. Those who are good recipients and evolved beings come into Intellectual Contact with him. Of course, apart from the natural shelter - commune of the Master, there is also the etheric one that is more important and more glorious. There, the Master talks to and teaches his students, when they leave their half-awakened physical bodies on Earth, for the etheric mission - life.

It is there also that he cooperates with other Masters and superior beings (see Nikolaos A. Margioris' books *The Two-Volume Metaphysical Encyclopaedia, Esoteric Key, Esoteric Initiation Branch, Omakoio Journal*).

Ashtaranga Kumbhaka: Retaining the air (prana) in our organism always with a simultaneous outward projection of the diaphragm while retaining the breath in. The opposite is called Bahiranga.

Ashtanga Yoga: Eight-limb or eight-step Yoga. This is Raja Yoga (see the book *Raja Yoga* by Nikolaos A. Margioris). Its eight clear steps are Yama, Niyama, Asana, Pranayama, Pratyahara, Dharana, Dhyana and Samadhi. And the 9th, the final and 'secret' one, is Kaivalya. In our times, the best preparation for someone to become able and suitable for initiation into Raja Yoga but also to absorb as many of its teachings as possible and to apply them correctly, is to attend the prerequisite somatopsychical school of Kriya Yoga. Of course, this does not exclude the possibility of some souls going directly to instruction in Raja Yoga, if they are truly consumed with a desire for Divine Knowledge and they fulfill the requirements for the necessary introversion that must constitute an inseparable part of their being. Besides, Raja Yoga remains an independent, autonomous and pure system of esoteric development in man (see the books *Hatha Yoga, Kriya Yoga, Raja Yoga, Esoteric Key, Meditation Branch, Theurgy teaches, Mysticism,*

Christocentric and Christocratic Mysticism, The Two-Volume Metaphysical Encyclopaedia, by Nikolaos A. Margioris).

Ashwini Mudra: It is the seal of the Horse (mare). It is a special exercise that is used in combination with others for the awakening of Kundalini. It is based on the rhythmic contraction of the anal sphincter, directing flow upwards, exactly as the mare when it excretes.

Asmita: Egoism.

Astavakra: This is the old Sage with eight humps, Hindu Master of Raja Yoga (perhaps the same Raja Yoga in which Janaka was initiated) who, according to legend, initiated King Janaka in Raja Yoga, in instant actualization (Brahma Jnani, that is the direct knowledge of Brahma). Literally, Astavakra means eight humps (eight-humped) and clearly, the eight humps are the eight steps of Raja Yoga. Astavakra is also called Astavakra Gita.

Asteya: It is the third commandment of Yama (Yama is the first of the eight steps of Raja yoga) and means abstinence from envy and theft.

Atharva Veda: It is the second Veda. Its name is derived from the priest Atharva who is said to have composed this second Veda 'by apocalypse'.
It is composed of 731 hymns making up 6000 verses in total. It contains sorcery, curses, exorcisms, wishes and formulas, in general, for the healing of the ill that the Brahmans used in their rites. Certainly, this Veda is of a different spirit which was formed later and that is the result of the compromising spirit that Vedic Aryans had adopted against the new - for them - Gods whom native Dravidians (conquered by the Aryans) worshipped (see Nikolaos A. Margioris' book *Dravidians, the Ancestors of Greeks*).

Atman: Spirit. It is our real Self, our Divine Self. It is the ever present Omni-universal Spirit. Atman and Brahman is one and the same, without any difference between them.

AUM: AUM is a derivative of the Absolute Unit, of OM and it is the Hindu Triad - the Three Hypostases - Trimurti that is composed of the following three letters: A = Vishnu (preserver), U = Shivas (Catalyst) and M = Brahma (Creator). A is the more open guttural. The letter M is the bilabial consonant and we articulate it through the nose, as our lips are closed. The letter U is pronounced by pushing the sound from the larynx to the lips with the aid of the larynx muscles.

Aurobindo Ghosh: He is the visualizer of the supersoul (Bija Akshara). Sri Aurobindo was born in Calcutta, in 1872. He studied in England, in Cambridge and in Oxford. Apart from ancient Greek and Latin, he also learnt French, German and Italian. When he returned to India, he started studying Sanskrit.

Aurobindo was imprisoned for his revolutionary activities during the national liberation struggle in 1905, during the British Partition of Bengal. During his imprisonment, he had a sudden deeply religious experience that changed his life. As he later narrated, he heard the voice of God telling him to prepare for another mission. So, in 1910, he withdrew completely from all political activity and settled in Pondicherry where he lived until 1950. There, he founded an Ashram, devoted to meditation, to prayer, to philosophical conversations and to good work. From 1914, he started the journal called *Arya*, where he published in sections what was going to be his most important work, the *The Life Divine*. At the same time, he wrote some commentaries about Bhagavad Gita and philosophical essays. In 1926, he retired into seclusion. Since then until his death, he never appeared in public. Only at rare intervals did he meet privately with some followers of the Ashram.

He introduced a strange meaning of the Supersoul ('hyperconsciousness' - Atman) that he considers to be a connecting ring between the world of becoming and of pure being. Aurobindo's theories may be characterized as esoteric. The chasm between the common spirit and the 'supersoul' is completed through yoga that corresponds to Aurobindo's philosophy of Jivanmukti (freedom from rebirth) of Hinduism.

Avatar or Mahavatar: According to the Hindu Philosophy the avatar (or the avatars) is a ray (or rays) of the great One, of the Unit. They represent the descent of the God-Spirit to our three-dimensional physical-ethereal world (13th dimension).

They are Beings with great spiritual powers (men or women). In essence, they are individualized spirit-souls that, through their previous incarnations, have been liberated from Karma and from the wheel of Incarnations. That is they have arrived at the 5th Intellectual step of the 11th Dimension and up to the 7th Dimension, and from the 7th Dimension to the fatherly embrace. (As is evident, there is a scale with many levels, according to the qualitative evolution and perfection of every such Divine Being).

These superior beings are sent with their consent by the Divinity to help and to guide their fellow-men (the primitive or undeveloped spirit-souls) to Truth. Each of them has a special mission. One can only teach, the other can only write, the third can cure covertly or overtly, the fourth can live an exemplary life without offering anything. It is rare for a Teacher of Wisdom or a Mystic (avatar) to actualize more than one task at a time.

They are all endowed with Insight and Intuition and have the right to change people's Karma when and if necessary, in accordance with the esoteric evolution or the change of the spirit-soul facing them. Of course, they sometimes try to exhibit some weakness (absent-mindedness, alleged memory lapses, small defects, a few mistakes) in order not to draw the curiosity or the attention or concern of their friends, acquaintances and relatives. They carefully hide their identity and their Mission so that no autosuggestion is imposed on people who will then lose their Freedom of Will; furthermore, they do not wish to gain assistance and favor in a hypocritical and underhanded way due to the great modesty that distinguishes them.

However, the breadth of their radiance and of the superior vibrations that they continually shed on their fellow-men are in proportion to their work, so that an experienced, formulated and above all mature soul being crossing their path may be able to recognize them and to approach them by placing itself willingly at their well-meaning service that will prove most positive not only for the soul itself but for its surroundings and for every fellow-man it meets on its way (see Nikolaos A. Margiori's books *A Two-Volume Metaphysical Encyclopedia*, *Light in the Dark*, *Birth and Death of the Worlds*, *Posthumous Life*, *The Omakoio Journal*, *Esoteric Key*, *Reincarnation*).

Avatara or Mahavatara: Creature having the greatest spiritual powers. It is a unique and perfected spirit-soul from the human race. Sometimes it is individualized (incarnated) or sends rays to Earth or becomes coordinated and guides liberated beings that he sends in order to withdraw, to re-establish and redefine - reclarify the path of the Spirit to Humanity. This Spirit-soul is the Word that has the single privilege of translating the messages - commandments of the Father for all of Creation and its beings.

Avatiam: the unmanifest state.

Avidya: Ignorance, non-knowledge of the Esoteric Truth (in other words, only the existence of materialistic knowledge).

Ayurveda: It is the ancient science of Ayurvedic medicine. Ayurveda comes from Atharvaveda.

B

Baba: The one (Hindu) Master of my Master's Nikolaos A. Margioris two Masters. His second Master was Krino Adre Salvatore de Castro. This Baba has no relation to the living Satya Sai Baba, who was one of the numerous students whom my Master was charged to supervise and to instruct when he was in India.

Babaji: The Master of Lahiri Mahasaya who, in turn was indirectly Yogananda's Master (see Yogananda's book *A Yogi's Autobiography*).

Bahiranga Kumbhaka: Emptying the air from the organism and holding the air we exhale 'out' of our body. The opposite is Antaranga.

Bandha: It is a technique that aims to direct energy wherever the Mind wishes and desires in order to perform some high mission - work, such as the awakening of Kundalini. Bandha is the Key, the Bond, the Control, the Contraction with retention, the Tightening, the Pulling. Bandhas are more difficult than Mudras. Some examples of technical Bandhas are Mula Bandha, Jalandhara Bandha and so on.

Bhadrasana: The pose that beautifies everything. It helps in sex. Technique: Sit in an upright position with legs bent (sideways), and the soles facing each other - united. The legs and the thighs must touch the floor. And the hands, depending on the exercise phases, squeeze the soles or lean on the knees or are placed forward. The exercise phases are accompanied by the proper breathing techniques (see Nikolaos A. Margiori's book *Kriya Yoga*)

Bhagavan: The beloved, the adorable.

Bhagavad Gita: The first Greek to translate Bhagavad Gita (as well as other Hindu books) from Sanskrit into Greek, was the unforgettable Dimitrios Galanos (1760-1833), who lived in India for 40 years.
Bhagavad Gita is a part of the epic poem Mahabharata and is translated as the Lord's Song or Hymn or as a Sublime Member or as the Song of the Adored. It is written in the form of a dialogue between Avatar Krishna and his student Arjuna. It contains 18 chapters constituting three parts. The first part refers to Karma Yoga, the second part is devoted to Jnani Yoga and the third part to Bhakti Yoga. It holds a high position in Hindu metaphysics, in religion and in morality.

Bhakti or Bhakta Yoga: the Yoga of worship, of the love for the ideal of one's personal God. It is the yogi's unconditional delivery to his Divine ideal and it derives from his absolute devotion to it. In Bhakti Yoga we have the following Yogi categories of worship: Santa Bhava, Dasya Bhava, Sakhya Bhava, Vatsalya Bhava and Madhurya Bhava.

Bhakti Yogi: A student of Bhakti Yoga.

Bhastrika: 'Pera' or the 'Bellows Breath'. It is also called 'the Blacksmith's Blows'. It is an extremely difficult and dangerous respiratory exercise but it is salvation from most of the diseases that the human body bears, provided that there is a Master to teach it. It comes as a knife and beats Kundalini to awaken it.

Bhava: A particular sentimental relationship with devotional feelings that a Bhakti yogi (worshipper) cultivates for his God (personal God). The five principal kinds of relationships (Bhava) are: Santa Bhava, Dasya Bhava, Sakhya Bhava, Vatsalya Bhava and Madhurya Bhava.

Bhoja: A great Indian Philosopher and Master of Yoga, who filled the apparent 'voids' that the father of Patanjali Yoga had left.

Bhujangasana: The Snake pose. It strengthens the blood circulation and the cardiac muscles. It exercises the vertebral column, the chest muscles and the thyroid gland. It fights back and rib pain and headaches, as well.
Technique: Lying on our stomach, we join our legs and stretch our arms forward. We open our legs and arms to the side. Then, we bring our hands forward and leaning on the palms, we raise the body from the waist up, while the legs stretch back in a straight line. The head bends backwards, slowly. In combination with the accompanying breathing techniques (See the book *Kriya Yoga*, by Nikolaos A. Margioris).

Brahma: Creator (M). It is the first person of the Hindu Triad (AUM).

Brahman: The Spirit.

Brahmanas: Brahmanas (1000 - 800 B. C.) compose the

second branch of Vedas and were created when the priests became a professional class and reached the point of regarding religion as belonging exclusively to them. They tried to impose the extreme view that rituals and sacrifices, in particular, should be considered the exclusive means of soul purification and the sole prerequisite for a religious experience.

In Brahmanas, we encounter, for the first time, the division of Hindu life into four stages, Ashramas, which are still respected, at least theoretically, to this day. They are: the period of Brahmacarya, the apprenticeship; of Grihastha, family life; of Vanaprastha, the study of the holy texts; and finally, of Sannyasa, devotion to the search for redemption through seclusion.

During the Brahmana period, the Aryans are separated into three castes (Brahmin, Kshatriya and Vaishya). The fourth caste, Shudra does not contain Aryans. Pariahs are not classified and are called Panchama.

Brahma Jnani: It is the Spiritual Knowledge or Brahman's knowledge. According to the Esoteric Tradition, spiritual knowledge can be transmitted in the twinkling of an eye (from moment to moment), provided that the would-be student is prepared and a suitable vessel to receive it. On the other hand, we should not forget that every man has real communion with the roots of Truth deep within him and if the turn inwards is genuine, its completion will enable him to instantly perceive, transfuse and comprehend the meaning and the significance of Zero-Everything. Brahma Jnani is obtainable through the method of Raja Yoga, as we are very rightly taught by King Janaka's Indian myth about wise Master Astavakra (see glossary).

Brahmacarya: It is the second abstinence of Yama. (Yama is the first of the eight steps of Raja Yoga). Brahmacarya is purity in everything, and it particularly emphasizes abstinence from sex, so that the student of raja yoga does not waste the life force existing within him aimlessly, but that he may use it for his elevation to the third and superior Mind function, the hyperintellectual one.

Brihadharanyaka Upanishad: Famous dialogues in the woods.

Buddhi: Buddhi is on an individual scale what Mahat is on a cosmic scale. It is the personal organ that is enlightened by the Intellect of Purusha. Simply, it is the individual Intellect. It is composed of a pranic substance of manas quality that is much superior to the Mind. It is in a more gaseous state (gases) and it has a positive charge while the Mind (manas) has a negative charge. Buddhi or Intellect plays an immense role in the control and the guidance of man's consciousness. It is this consciousness that mediates and converses with the soul to which it transfers every experience that the Mind (consciousness) transmits and inversely, the soul to the Mind. It is man's controller. When man is ruled by extroversion, he distances the Intellect (the representative of soul) resulting in the loss of his evolution, his burdening with Karma and his total entrapment in the cogwheel of matter and negativity. When man leans toward and cultivates Introversion, then he truly lightens his Karma every day and broadens and expands his spiritual horizons, communicating more substantially with his Intellect that at some future moment will render him able to directly contact his very soul.

C

Carvaka: It is one of the six non-orthodox (non-Vedic) Indian philosophical systems (darsanas).

Cela: Student.

Chakras or Suns: Wheels or disks or lotuses or suns or etheric centers or etheric glands or energy centers or psychical centers or energy vats. These are the seven basic etheric centers: a) Muladhara (Adrenal gland), b) Svadisthana (Seminal glands), c) Manipura (Pancreas), d) Anahata (Thymus gland), e) Vishuddi (Thyroid gland), f) Ajna (hypophysis) and g) Sahasrara (epiphysis). They undertake to store and transform the Cosmic Energy (Prana) from the above etheric glands-centers to the respective physical glands in order to generate the phenomenon of life.
There are also the 21 sub-chakras or sub-centers that are connected with the respective chakras-centers. Then there are 221 third chakras or third centers or third stations or satellites that activate another 220.032 permanently mobile points-centers.

Chandogya Upanishad: The Chandogya Upanishad dogma.

Citta: Cerebrum - brain (memory), solid, north.

D

Darsana: It is the philosophical system - view - aspect. In Hindu Philosophy we have six orthodox Philosophical (Vedic) systems: Nyaya, Vaisheshika, Samkhya, Yoga, Karma, Mimamsa or Purva Mimamsa and Vedanta or Uttara Mimamsa or Brahma Sutra. The above six philosophical systems are bound in pairs. So, Nyaya and Vaisheshika compose the first pair, Samkhya and Yoga become the second pair and Karma Mimamsa with Uttara Mimamsa are the third and last pair. We also have six non-Vedic philosophical systems (six non-orthodox): Carvakas, Jainism, Vaibasikas or Sarvastivada, Sautrantikas, Yogakaras, Madhyamic (see the respective words).

Dasya Bhava: It is one of the numerous relationships that an evolved Bhakti can develop with his God. It means the connection of adoration and obedience of the servant to his master.

Desa: Space or Universe.

Devahan: It is the angelic world, Paradise.

Devadatta Vayu: It is the power of the angel, it is the vayu that supervises our body for the return of the aethers (etheric energy /sub-pranic energy / etheric gases) to their previous position and mission, when they have not correctly performed the work with which they were charged.

Devas: Angels.

Dhananjaya Vayu: This Vayu has the responsibility and the supervision, after death, to first dissolve the etheric body, so that the soul may be able to find its liberation and to depart for the sub-dimension of the stellar or the lower intellectual element where it belongs evolutionarily, and then to dissolve the physical body.

Dhanurasana: The Bow Pose. An anti-diabetic exercise that helps the pancreas to secrete insulin. From the prostrate position, we lift the head and the torso and we bring the hands up and back to take hold of the ankles of the bent legs, thus forming a bow. The body leans on the pelvic bone and on the hips. From this position the body moves to and fro like a swing. In combination with breathing exercises (see the book *Kriya Yoga* by Nikolaos A. Margioris).

Dharana: It is the 6th step of Raja yoga that means Concentration - Thought. Every human activity is based on this extremely significant word. Absolutely nothing can move and function without the concentration factor. The greater the concentration potential in every problem is for man, the greater the results he obtains.

Raja yoga is based exactly on this point and develops it, through studied and tried methods and techniques that were lost in the depths of the past but that have been saved almost intact to this day. They can be used by any well-intentioned person and they can enable him to develop his latent powers to the utmost.

The only difference is that in Raja yoga man must firstly and necessarily direct his concentration to his Internal world in order to be able to approach the secret folds of his Esoteric Being, of Himself.

Concentration is also called Thought, a word that Socrates and his student Platon used, wanting to define the mechanism that is able to activate the transcendental activity of the Mind. Therefore, Dharana means to set a purpose - subject - thought – object, either subjective (invisible-mental-with eyes closed) or objective (visible with eyes open) and to try to keep our thought on it for 12" without another thought slipping in. When this single thought touches the 12" X 12 times = 144", then we say that for the first time in his life, this person has entered the 7th step of Raja,

Meditation (Dhyana) and that his Mind started activating his hyperconsciousness and working on a hyperintellectual level, grasping the Causes of every natural result existing around us or in relation to the concentration-meditation matter.

If we multiply 144" by 12 we have 1728".

So, when we are successful in extending the duration of concentration on the same subject-object to 1728", we automatically enter Samadhi. That is, the full Contemplation - Union - Theosis, where man himself realizes the One Truth and then, nothing can move him or change in the least the Fullness of his Esoteric Experience that classifies him as a completed being in our Esoteric planet - world, a self-ruled, self-sufficient being, an expert of the visible and the invisible mysteries and a holy, a suitable vessel for the transmission - dissemination of the superessential Truths and guidance for any interested person.

The immediately following and higher step is Kaivalya (emancipation). When and only when one... attains it, will one be liberated from Karma and will not be obliged to be reborn in our world – unless on a special mission - and he will continue a true spiritual evolution in the Esoteric Dimensions of Creation (see the books *Hatha Yoga, Kriya Yoga, Raja Yoga, ; Esoteric Key, Meditation, The Two-Volume Metaphysical Encyclopaedia*).

Dharma: Duty. Dharma means Cosmic Law, Cosmic Duty.

Dhyana: Meditation, supervision, contemplation. It constitutes the 7th step of Raja Yoga. At this step, man manages to identify with the object of his meditation, he achieves the first esoteric contact. He dissolves his external attire-covering and he communicates with his etheric base-root.

That is, a two-way relationship is automatically created between him and the object, a state of communication where the knowledge concerning the object is transferred to the Mind of the meditating person and vice versa. In a word, successful meditation means that the meditating person managed to break even the finest elements of resistance of his intellectual prison (the last and most refined inner walls of matter in his Mind) and for the first time in his life he obtains the right to face the other side, the one that is invisible to the physical eye which gives him a first taste of a transcendental perception of things and assures him more than anything else of the seed of Immortality and Eternity he bears within him. This is called Ekatva (superior identification) and begins from Dhyana, gradually giving man the right, after infinite time periods, to regain his real identity, to discover his spiritual status-quality and mission, and to place himself consciously in the service of the Divine Plan and of every animate or inanimate life.

Dhyana-bindu Upanishad: Perfect Concentration. Dhyana-bindu Upanishad presents us with the basic nadis (etheric channels) in our etheric body, as well as the ten main vayu (winds). It also analyzes some Bandhas (Keys) and Mudras (Seals) such as: Mula Bandha, Uddiyana Bandha, Jalandhara Bandha, Kechari Mudra, Mahamudra and so on.

Dijis: Fingers.

Dik: Place.

Djwal Khul or The Tibetan: A great being. He is a Master of Ancient Wisdom, one of the first missionaries sent by the Lord, when the Manasaputras descended on Earth, in the form of sparks. He always remains in the etheric grounds of the Gobi Desert. At certain periods, he is incarnated and is presented in a figure. He teaches the good and charity. He gives lessons in tolerance and patience. He suggests Piety. He advises people to distance themselves from the futile in order to be released from the tragedy of reincarnation. According to Alice Bailey, it was Djwal Khul who telepathically dictated to her the books she wrote. Also, two of his assistants, El Morya and Koot Hoomi helped Helena Petrovna Blavatsky.

Dravidians: The whole matter concerning the Dravidians was stirred up when the lucky Indian archeologist, R.D. Barnerji, discovered the first six engraved stones in 1922 in Pakistan, and informed English archeologist John Marshal about it. Marshal, after having examined these engraved boulders, expressed his doctrine about the existence of a pre-Sumerian civilization. Then, in 1932, young archeologist Child, feeling enthusiastic about Marshal's conclusions, discovered the most deeply-hidden towns in the soil, which had a civilization which was far superior to the towns later built over them.

The first and deepest town, Mohenjo-Daro was built 6.000-8.000 years BC The wealth of its inhabitants, the Dravidians, is obvious from the variety of gold and silver jewelry. Their technique is great because it shows a deep knowledge of anatomy and shows sensitivity and a delicacy that surprise the researcher-observer. Here, many statuettes in yoga poses and other relevant representations have been found.

Therefore, Yoga is a product of the Dravidians who came from Asia Minor and from the islands of the Aegean Sea. At a certain period, they were called Lycians. Greeks called these peoples Termiles. And Herodotus identifies Crete as their country. Indian archeologist S.K. Chatterji, in the chapter "Race Movements and Prehistoric Culture", in the first volume *The Vedic Age* of his work *The History and Culture of the Indian People*, acknowledges the hypothesis of the emigration of Dravidians from Crete and other islands, from Asia Minor, from Continental Greece and in general, from the Mediterranean to India.

The Lelekes and Lycians, Cretans (Eteocretans) as well as the inhabitants of Continental Greece and of all the islands, came from one race and formed the Dravidians, a developed people whose civilization was far superior to our modern one.

Distinguished archeologist and philosopher Biraja Sankar Guha, in his work *Racial Elements in the Population*, London 1945, distinguishes four main racial varieties that are fully merged nowadays. These are: a) Negritos b) Australoids c) Dravidians who are now the basis of all the people of South India and of other regions and d) Arians.

In our times, the substantial spiritual offering of the Dravidians to the Indian Civilization is a well-known fact and the Knowledge of Yoga Science that they have transferred, transmitted and implanted in India is indisputable. Although the Dravidians were captured by the technocratic-materialist Arians, they won at the end and prevailed spiritually.

Today, at least 120.000.000 Indians speak the Dravidian languages and the number is continually increasing, according to new surveys, not due to the population growth but due to the continual discovery of more dialects and to the adoption of the Dravidian language. Here we must point out that there is a great similarity between the pre-Homeric language (in the conjugations and in the cases) and the Sanskrit-Dravidian language.

Another strong factor that advocates the common origin

of the later descendants of the Dravidians, i.e. the Indians, Egyptians and Greeks, is the worship by all these peoples of the bull or the cow. The holy animal of Indians, the Cow, is the symbol of production and reproduction. In Egypt, the same holds for the holy Sarapis or Apis. The Bull is also the holy animal of Cretans. All this together with the holy animal, the Cow of our forefathers the Dravidians, constitute a common form of worship and Religion, a very ancient doctrine for the Supreme Feminine Origin (Matriarchy). Here we must add one more esoteric element which in turn, confirms that Mysticism is born and bred mainly of these three peoples (because they are ruled by old and experienced souls) and flows in their blood. These three peoples gave and continue to give us to this day the greatest Mystics, which is rare in other peoples.

Besides, only a very ancient antediluvian Mediterranean civilization can justify the early maturity of the Egyptian and the Greek civilizations (of the Aegean Sea). Only in this way can it be explained how some objects which were found in Crete and in Egypt had strange symbols on them which were related to the images, meanings, knowledge of the Mind engraved on rocks and on other objects. The disk of Phaistos in Crete, due to its strange symbols, looks like the books made of clay, which were found in Tell Asmar (near Baghdad), just as the Prince of the Lilies (Prince-with the Crest) in Crete looks like one that was found in Mexico a few years ago.

The Dravidians lived in Hinterland, in the district of the Aegean Sea and, according to esoteric tradition, before the cataclysm-flooding, the Mediterranean area was covered by a magnetic veil which, after its destruction, became the Aurora Borealis. There, in the vast areas of Eden on Earth, innumerable herds of cows grazed in the magnetized grass and offered the people of Hinterland, this paradise, the prosperity and incredible longevity with their milk. It is said that this grass was called 'thrav' or 'drav' and that's where the name Dravidian comes from. The destruction of Hinterland resulted from the conflict between the Atlanteans and the Dravidians (both belonged to the 4th Root Race) with their super-weapons. This conflict brought about the sinking of their civilizations (see the books *Dravidians, the Ancestors of Greeks, In the Times of Minos, the Great King of Crete, Desymbolism of Greek Mythology, Pharaohs, Omakoio Journal, Essay: Dravidians, the First Greeks of the Aegean Sea*, and so on, by Nikolaos A. Margioris).

Dvaita: Dualism is one of the three ways of conceiving Truth according to the Philosophy of Vedanta. According to this Dualistic school, God is worshipped in form, that is, in categories, since a form without categories cannot exist. So, according to the Dualistic belief, the Universe, Jiva and God are three separate and eternal entities but the Universe and Jiva belong to God and depend on Him. That is, Dualism conceives of God as an otherworldly Being who rules the living and the nonliving reality.

E

Eka: One.

Eka padasana: The Tree. One-legged pose. It combats nerve weakness and it reinforces the nervous system.
Technique: From a standing position, we unite the palms of the hands at the height of the chest in a prayer pose. At the same time, we bend one leg, its sole leaning on the

inner part of the thigh of the other leg. Then, we stretch our arms and the bent leg sideways, while the body leans on the other leg. Repeat by alternating the legs and with accompanying breathing techniques (see the book *Kriya Yoga* by Nikolaos A. Margioris).

Ekagrata: It is the absolute attention that when applied correctly, under a master's guidance, leads the student of Yoga and Esotericism to Manolaya, the full domination of thought.

Ekatva: Superior Identification. It refers to the recognition of the Mind of the true identity of the individualized Soul it bears in its body, that after year- long, laborious training and constant efforts to make sacrifices, succeeds in experientially touching the 7th step of Raja Yoga and communicating with its real Self, attaining its superior Identification (identity) and the beginning of its Divine Rights.

F

Fohat: Word of Force meaning Light.

G

Gandhi: It refers to the famous Mahatma Gandhi who thanks to the practice of non-violence (ahimsa) managed to liberate India from English occupation.

Ganesha: Indian Teacher of Yoga.

Gata: It refers to Upanishads and means: pot, earthenware jar - Kumbhaka (see glossary).

Gayatri: It is the psalm sound. The repetition of the words of power (mantras).

Gunas: Qualities or categories or attributes or states of Substance. We have three gunas - qualities: Sattva, Rajas and Tamas.

Guru: Guru is an Enlightened Spiritual Master. He is the one who attained Samadhi - Enlightenment and who undertook the responsible role of instructor and guide for any interested person. A Guru may be liberated from Karma but, though enlightened, he may not have fully exhausted all traces of his personal Karma, despite the fact that he has already touched Truth and can wisely and responsibly guide his students along the same path of spiritual completion.

H

Halasana: The Plow pose. A cure-all. It cures indigestion, constipation, colic, the vertebral disorders, liver diseases, rheumatism, arthritis.
Technique: From the supine position we lift and stretch our legs over our head to touch the floor with the toes. The hands are also stretched out until they touch the toes. It is executed in combination with correct breathing. It is not recommended for those who have a weak heart or are suffering from a thyroid gland disorder.

Hamsa: The Swan.

Hamsasana: The Swan pose. It affords the body balance and harmony.
Technique: From the kneeling position (seated on the back part), we spread our thighs; we place our palms on the ground, our fingers turned toward the inner part of the thighs. The torso leans slightly forward. Then, we lift the bent legs back and the body leans on the toes and on the palms. Finally, we bend our arms and our forehead also touches the ground. It is combined with respective breathing exercises (see the book *Kriya Yoga* by Nikolaos A. Margioris).

Hamsa Upanishad: The Migratory Bird. Hamsa Upanishad presents, the act of studying, the practice of Yoga, the Knowledge of the Migratory Bird (Hamsa), that is of the soul that must pass - fly through the six centers, as indispensable equipment.
Upanishad points out that the best exercise for one to reach the fourth state beyond sleep is the repetition of the Bird mantra, which is actually slow and well-regulated breathing together with concentration. Also, it states that the Flight of the Bird is accompanied by a sound similar to the nasal resonance contained in the syllable Om. Every such type of resonance corresponds to a step on the path of Yoga and has the mark of supernatural potential (Siddhis).

Hasta Padangusthasana: Hand and feet pose. For strengthening the Mind and the senses.
Technique: From the standing position, with the torso straight, we lift the leg up and forward until the corresponding hand touches the toes, without the torso leaning in and without the other leg bending. It is repeated with the other leg too and is accompanied by suitable breathing

exercises (see the book *Kriya Yoga*, by Nikolaos A. Margioris).

Hatha Yoga: 'Ha' is the sun and 'Tha' is the moon. The name of Hatha refers to the esoteric matters - mysteries and does not have any substantial relation to the correct practice of Hatha. The word symbolizes the positive and the negative factor, the negative-positive/man-woman dynamic that requires specialized Esoteric Teaching and superior Yoga for it to be desymbolized.

It must be noted that most people in Western countries see all of yoga as in the form of Hatha Yoga (something which is completely untrue) which is nothing more than body exercises and simple breathing techniques for strengthening - coordinating our physical body - vessel. More precisely, Hatha Yoga is substantially a union - attachment to our physical body. Certainly, this had a meaning and a purpose in the olden times (roots, races), when man was incarnated for the first time (according to the Esoteric tradition) and he had not yet obtained control of his natural vessel. So, through these exercises, he had to cultivate and control it. This was successfully accomplished and helped man become coordinated with his natural vessel, so that he may be able to use it constructively.

Some great beings who passed through our planet (Ramakrishna, Vivekananda, Margioris, Blavatsky, Alice Bailey - according to Djwal Khul's dictates), stressed and pointed out that Hatha Yoga in no way serves the modern evolving man and that its teachings are better suited for past times and past needs of man. Nowadays, Hatha Yoga cannot offer anything substantial. On the contrary, it can often create a strong dependence-bond between man and his physical vessel and other extensions and thus make him lose his actual aim - especially when there is no Esoteric Teaching- which, according to Yoga, is the Intellectual Instruction that will bring him to the gates of his actualization as a spiritual being.

Of course, there is also the science of Kriya Yoga that can now replace Hatha Yoga fully. It is the edifying preparation and the completed arrangements for man's spiritual ascent. It starts with corporal self-purification (healing man by applying some Asanas, in combination with breaths, then there is the intellectual purification (therapy) of all the bad and harmful habits, phobias, passions, obsessions and so on, by performing special mental exercises. Finally, after developing a healthy and balanced body and a healthy and balanced Mind, man can fearlessly and confidently move toward the activation of the third and higher part of his Mind, of hyperconsciousness (Raja Yoga) that will bring him to the height of his expected spiritual hyperperception of the Self and of Everything (see the books *Hatha Yoga, Kriya Yoga, Raja Yoga, The Two-Volume Metaphysical Encyclopaedia, Omakoio Journal* and so on, by Nikolaos A. Margioris).

Hatha Yogi: The student of Hatha Yoga.

Himsa: Violence. Hence, the derivative Ahimsa meaning non-violence.

Hrid: Heart.

I

Ida: It corresponds to the left nostril. It is the lunar power or the negative magnetism - dynamism entering from the left etheric nostril (nadis) of man.

Indriyas: The sensory organs.

Instructor or Teacher of Esotericism: A person who apprenticed by the side of an Avatar or a Master of Wisdom or an Initiate or a Mystic or even an ascended student of the above beings for a long time. He receives rigorous instruction in matters of Esoteric Education (Esoteric Philosophy), Yoga, therapeutic techniques without medicine and so on. He undergoes numerous trials and experiences with success and becomes able, through his own experience and will and with his Master's consent and approval, a completed instructor, a link in the chain of Knowledge from which his fellow-men will benefit.

Isa Upanishad: Lord.

Ishvara: Personal God (the form of God). For the student of Bhakti, it expresses his personal ideal of Divinity.

Ishvara Pranidhana: It is the first commandment of Niyama (Niyama is the second ascending step of Raja Yoga) and it is interpreted as the devotion to God.

Iti: This.

J

Jainism: It is one of the six non-orthodox (non-Vedic) Indian philosophical systems (darsanas).

Jalandhara Bandha: 'The contraction of the Bearer's Lakes'. The chin lock. *Jala* means net and *dhara* means pull. So, Jalandhara means pulling the net. In this Key (Bandha) we try to get the chin to rest between the collarbones while at the same time we perform the pranayama technique that corresponds to this exercise and always under an expert Master's guidance, as in all Mudras, Bandhas and Yoga techniques.

Janaka: He was an Indian King who studied the Scriptures and wanted to personally experience their Truth. He had holy readers who read the holy books to him. At one point, while they were reading some texts about instant actualization (Brahma Jnani) that can occur while man is mounting a horse, he interrupted the holy reader and asked him to prove it. The poor reader said that he believed in it but that he did not have the power to prove it. The king imprisoned him and called some other wise men but not even they could prove it in practice. Finally, Master Astavakra came from the jungle and taught him the path to actualization. Only then did Janaka believe in the holy scriptures and became, in turn, a true Master.

Japa: It is the continuous repetition of a Mantra while the Mind concentrates on its esoteric meaning. At the same time, there must be, on behalf of the student, an attitude - relationship of worship to the spiritual ideal representing every Mantra, which means that the Mantra should suit the meditator's idiosyncrasy and ideals.

Jinarajadasa: President of the Theosophical Society in India, who wrote the book *The Occult Evolution of Humanity*.

Jiva: The individual soul.

Jivanmukta: He who attained liberation while he was alive.

Jnana Kanda: The philosophical teachings of Vedas, in opposition with the rituals of Karma Kanda.

Jnana Yoga: It is Yoga of Knowledge - Gnoseology - Philosophical pursuits. The Union through Knowledge based on the Intellect. Jnani contains within it, Raja Yoga, Karma Yoga and Bhakti Yoga. Without Raja, Karma and Bhakti, it cannot complete its great work. Let those who are taught with the help of Jnani find Wisdom and bliss.

The aim of Jnani is to elevate the mortal being to immortality and to enable him to achieve the magnificent connection with his hyperconsciousness, so that he may grasp the messages of the perpetually vibrating Eternal Father. As soon as this happens, the limited Mind becomes One (Yoga) with the eternal and infinite Great Mind.

Jnana Yogi: The student of Jnana yoga.

K

Kaivalya: It is Perfect Isolation, Perfect Rupture, Supreme Meditation, the apotheosis of man, the severing of ties with Karma, Asamprajnata samadhi. The Kaivalya corresponds to the 5th of the seven steps of the 11th Dimension existing in the Intellectual World, which is also the deliverance of man from Karma and its reincarnations.

Kaivalya Upanishad: It is the Upanishad that teaches the liberation from the bonds of the reality of form.

Kakra: See 'Chakra'.

Kala: Time.

Kali: It is the personification of the Feminine side (Kundalini) of Energy (Prana) in our body. In the Indian pantheon it is represented by the Goddess Kali. Ramakrishna, the last saint of India was a worshipper of the goddess Kali. He attained Saguna Samadhi, helped by the personification of Divinity, in the face of goddess Kali. Only when he managed to surpass Kali's image-context did he attain Nirguna Samadhi (the limitless spiritual state).

Kali Yuga: The dark era.

Kalpa: twenty-four hours of Brahma's life (one day and one night). See glossary Yuga.

Kanthasana: The neck exercise. A therapy for neck pain and tension. Salt deposits are dissolved.
Technique: Usually in a standing position. The head bends forward until the chin touches the collar bone. At the same time, we stretch our arms out to the side and then to the front. Then, we bend the head back and bring our hands to the waist. While the head is still bent backwards, we rise on our toes, our hands raised. We return to our initial position. The exercise phases are always performed in combination with the corresponding breathing phases (see the book *Kriya Yoga* by Nikolaos A. Margioris).

Kapalabhati or kapalbhati: *Kapal* means skull - head and *bhati* means shining, illuminating. So, the term Kapalabhati refers to a yoga exercise that makes the head shine and the Mind radiate. Hatha, Kriya and Raja (Tantra) use it as Bhastrika. It is also called 'diaphragmatic breathing'. It is a cleansing of the organism by taking quick exhalations and inhalations only through the nose. It is done in the Sukhasana and Padmasana pose. It is very strong so for this reason one should pay attention during its execution and strictly follow the directions of the Instructor.
Results: It brightens up the face. The pulmonary alveoli are cleansed and oxygenated. It rids the blood of waste and carbon dioxide, the tissues are strengthened and the cells of the organism are rejuvenated. The intestines re-

ceive an internal massage. It cures asthma and diseases of the lungs, pharynx and esophagus. If used carefully, it can even cure liver and kidney disorders as well as diabetes.

Kapalasana or Viparita Karani Mudra: Upside down. The Torch. It cures appendicitis, hernias, stomachaches and chronic stomach diseases. It exercises the muscular and nervous systems. It is not indicative for those who suffer from heart, lung and thyroid gland disorders.

Technique: From the supine position, first bring hands under the hips and raise legs until the body leans only against the upper part of the back, against the neck and the head. It is combined with certain breathing exercises (see the book *Kriya Yoga* by Nikolaos A. Margioris).

Karma: Act - energy - action. The Law of Retributive Justice, of Cause and Effect, of Action and Reaction. It is the total of our positive and negative acts (thoughts, words and actions), for which at a certain moment, we will be called upon to account for by receiving the equivalent reactions, positive or negative. We have three kinds of Karma, Agami Karma, Prarabdha Karma and Sanchita Karma (see glossary).

Actually, Karma is every second of our physical life. Every moment in our life, depending on our activity, we form our good or bad Karma, which we will definitely be called upon to settle at some point.

In order for a person to be released from the bonds of Karma, he needs, above all, the correct Esoteric Education that will enlighten him, an extended apprenticeship in Karma Yoga and many years of struggle. For more information, see the books *Karma, The Law of Retributive Justice, Reincarnation, Light in the Dark, The Two-Volume Metaphysical Encyclopaedia, Omakoio Journal* by Nikolaos A. Margioris.

Karma kanda: The ritual section of Vedas, in opposition with the philosophical Gnana kanda.

Karma Yoga: Union through activity - action. Karma Yoga teaches all the Karmic obligations of man, as well as their consequences, in detail. Thus, one is informed about the inexcusable daily events that are the results of one's thoughts, words and deeds. Man also studies their causes and their results and learns how to face his own Karma with such spiritual strength that he can direct and surpass it.

This is achieved through altruistic deeds - work. So, every work that is done by the student of Yoga whose purpose is not personal gain, without expecting anything in return, leads to the emancipation from Karma.

In order for this holy aim to be obtained, the student of Karma Yoga has humility and non-attachment to the results of his work as his guide, results which he offers to the whole, to Divinity. His effort is to break the chains holding him in the three-dimensional prison, his only means being modesty and activity, the altruistic work (manual, intellectual, spiritual).

Karma Yogi: The student of Karma Yoga.

Katha Upanishad: From the branch of Katha Vedas.

Kechari Mudra: 'The Bird Seal'. It is the key of the tongue (tongue key) and has two ways of being applied: the external, where the tongue is extended outwards and tries to touch the tip of the nose and then it ends at the base of the nose; and the internal, where the tongue rolls back and goes back and up to the pharynx until it finds the two little holes. With this exercise, the hormone Amrita (in Sanskrit) and Ambrosia (in Greek) is secreted.

Kena Upanishad: By whom?

Kirtan: They are the yogic songs containing Mantras that have the ability to relax the mind and to create an agreeable and harmonious atmosphere.

Kleshas: The obstacles - sins obstructing man's liberation are the following five: a) Ignorance (Avidya), b) Egoism (Asmita), c) Desire (Raga), d) Dislike - aversion to good (Dvesa), e) Possessive attachment to - gathering of goods (Abhinivesha).

Konasana: The Angle Pose. It cures liver diseases. It exercises the muscles of the ribs and limbs. It acts upon the vertebral spine, the waist and the abdominal area.
Technique: From the standing position, with legs slightly apart and arms raised, we bend the torso to the right, until the right hand touches the other leg. The left hand follows the inclination of the torso, lifted over the head like a cover. This exercise is also repeated from the left side and is combined with corresponding breathing exercises (see the book *Kriya Yoga* by Nikolaos A. Margioris).

Kosha: It is the sheath, the covering, the wrapping, the layer. According to the Taittiriya Upanishad, Atman is covered with five Koshas that are one within the other. The last one contains the Spirit. Beginning from outside inwards the five Koshas are the following: Anamaya Kosha, Pranamaya Kosha, Manomaya Kosha, Vijnanamaya Kosha and Anandamaya Kosha (see the respective words).

Kumbhaka: Means holding or restraining. It has two phases. The first phase is called Astaranga Kumbhaka and occurs after an inhalation and refers to the holding in of air in our organism while simultaneously projecting the diaphragm outwards. The second phase is called Bahiranga Kumbhaka and occurs after an exhalation and refers to the holding out of air of our organism (the created air pocket). The air held within us (internal holding), is also called Gata or Jar or Pot.

Kundalini: It is the Life Force (Prana) that is found stored in an etheric state at the base of the spine. With responsible guidance and year-long education, this force can be awakened and can ascend through the central channel - nadis of Sushumna activating all the chakras it meets on the way and arriving at the height of the thousand-petal lotus, the Sahasrara chakra where the marriage between Shakti (Wisdom or Kundalini or even Kali) and Shiva (Divinity) will take place and will convert man from mortal to immortal, from imperfect to perfect.

Kundalini is a separate system of activating man's hyperconsciousness which is based on Tantra yoga (SAHAJA Yoga) and Upanishads and it is the second way - method of accessing the hyperconscious.

The main lever for the orthodox ignition of Kundalini is the regulated pranayama with long internal holding of breath (Astaranga Kumbhaka) and with additional support from a combination of physical and intellectual exercises that are called Mudras (seals) or Ekagrata and Manolaya, Bandhas (keys, contractions or Controls) and so on.

Kurmasana: The Tortoise pose. A reviving, longevity exercise. It fights against headaches, stomachaches, salt deposits, rheumatisms, arthritis, spine and neck diseases.

Technique: Seated on the ground, we stretch and spread the legs forward, holding our torso straight. We bend the right leg and we lean the head forward until it touches the bent leg, more specifically, the sole, while the right leg passes under the angle that the bent leg forms. The palm leans against the sole. This exercise is repeated with the left leg, always in combination with the appropriate breaths (see the book Kriya Yoga by Nikolaos A. Margioris).

Kurma Vayu: This Vayu keeps watch over the opening and the closing of the eyes.

Krikara Vayu: It is Vayu that overlooks hunger and thirst.

Krino Andre Salvatore De Castro: One of the two Masters of my Master Nikolaos A. Margioris (see the book *Pharaohs*). The second master is Baba (see glossary).
According to the dedication that my Master included in his book, Count Krino Andre Salvatore de Castro was great from birth. Neither his studies nor his aristocratic family created him. He was an eminent personality. It was not the title of count that distinguished him. It was his whole appearance that made him an eminent being and such an imposing figure to his interlocutors; it was his indisputable radiance. He was a true Sage. He was his Master of Metaphysics and of First Philosophy, which deals with the cause of Everything. He was the beloved maestro whom native Egyptians and foreigners loved and whom his few students adored.
Master Nikolaos A. Margioris was taught Esoteric Philosophy, Archaeology, Egyptology, Harmony, ancient Egyptian, Sanskrit and ancient Hebrew, Esoteric Christian Theology, the phenomenon of Man by Krino.

Krishna: A great envoy (Avatar) of the Indian reality.

Kriya Yoga: Kriya Yoga constitutes one of the branches of the whole of Yoga and its roots are very ancient. It is a method of psychosomatic therapeutics and a preparatory stage for the gradual initiation of every interested person to Raja Yoga. In Greece, it was first taught and established in 1981 by the Master of Yoga, Nikolaos A. Margioris who revived it because it was a lost science.

In Sanskrit, Kriya means act - action and Yoga means union. Through its practice, a harmonious communion - union of the Body, Mind and Soul is achieved. Kriya Yoga addresses and especially benefits the people of our times who are tortured on a daily basis by accumulated problems, stress and pressures and the rapid pace of life. The Kriya system aims at the physical and psychical (mental) health of man and at Mind control. It prevents disease and cures, revives and strengthens the organism. It manages to strengthen the muscles and it contributes to the formation of a shapely body.

The attainment of these aims is achieved through a sequence of exercises that are performed in rhythmical movements, combined with proper breathing exercises. In essence, they are a combination of timed breathing exercises and bodily exercise which are executed with the participation of the Mind (consciousness and hyperconsciousness) in order to balance the nervous and muscular system. The whole exercise program is performed easily and loosely; it does not tire. On the contrary, after the lesson, we notice a revival of the body's muscles and cells, good health and a relaxation of pressure and nerves. We also notice a healing of ailing parts of the body. After the body exercises, the Kriya student proceeds to the special Mind exercises that aim at the edification and the perfection of man's character: at self-knowledge, at the extinction of different psychological problems, bad habits, obsessions, phobias, at concentration and at Mind control. The Kriya program also includes and teaches a relaxation method that renews, detoxifies, calms and reconstructs the entire organism.

It was Yogananda who presented Kriya to us in his very interesting book *A Yogi's Autobiography*. But he mentions no practical details and although he constantly mentions Kriya, he avoids presenting it to us. Master Nikolaos A. Margioris has published the first essay in the world, *A PRACTICAL METHOD OF PSYCHOSOMATIC THERAPEUTICS- KRIYA YOGA* in which for the first time, the lost practices of Kriya Yoga are made known. In this book, numerous representative sketches are presented, as are detailed directions and explanations of the seven-phased poses-movements-breaths. It constitutes a useful and necessary reference book for every student or person interested in Yoga.

Nikolaos A. Margioris revived Kriya Yoga after a Samadhi that concerned this matter.

Ksurika Upanishad: The Knife. It is the concentration of the Spirit which is practiced so that Yoga may be performed, in combination always with the holding of the breath within us.

L

Lahiri Mahasaya: The Master of the parents of Yogananda who was indirectly his master as well.

Laya Yoga: It is the Yoga of absorption, of submersion, of dissolution. It is the loss of the self in an idea or in a matter prevailing within man. It is based on the awakening of Kundalini through the absorption in an obsession that it pursues to realize.

Lila: It is the game of matter, which dazzles us with its continual reproduction into new forms - states, and keeps us within the limits of the intellectual functioning of the Mind, in the three-dimensional prison of matter-form, not allowing us to see beyond it.

Lingam: Phallus.

M

Madhura Bhava: It is one of the numerous relationships that a Bhakti yogi can develop with his God. It is the pure love of the wife to her husband or to her lover, free of sensual desires, but full of eagerness to be united with the ideal.

Madhyam: It is the second (middle) pranayama method, according to Sri Ganesha. It begins with 24 matras/seconds of inhalation, then you hold the air in (prana) for 96" and exhale for 48". For all pranayama techniques, as well as for the responsible and safe practice of Yoga, the presence and guidance of an expert, an instructor (see glossary) of esotericism, is considered indispensable.

Madhyamika Sutra or Mula Madhyamika Sutra: Refers to one of the 6 non-Vedic (non-orthodox) Hindu philosophical systems (darsanas). It is the theory of the Absolute Void by the Indian Sage Nagarjuna. The two great Buddhism schools, Hinayana and Mahayana, each presented us with two branches. In Hinayana we have a) the Vaibhashika school and b) the Sautrantika school. Mahayana that was glorified by Buddha presented us with two schools, a) Yogacara - Vijnanavada and b) Madhyamika.

The Indian philosopher Nagarjuna, who lived in the 2nd century A. D., placed the basis of his inaccessible Mystic system on... nothing, on the... void (Sunyata), which was called 'the philosophy of the Absolute Void'. This Sage greatly influenced the famous Shankara who, in the 8th century expressed the Absolute Oneness, Advaita (Nirguna Brahman).

(See the books *The Two-Volume Metaphysical Encyclopaedia, Omakoio journal, Birth and Death of the Worlds*, by Nikolaos A. Margioris).

Maha: Great or Greatest.

Maha Bandha: The Great Key. 'The Bond of Excellency'. The student puts his left leg on his genitals and holds his right leg with his hands, lowering his head until his chin touches his chest. He always inhales from the nose, he holds his breath as long as possible and then, he exhales. Afterwards, he begins again, reversing the leg positions. The leg he is holding with his hands must be placed over the opposite thigh.

Mahabharata: One of the two great epic poems of India. The second one is Ramayana. Mahabharata (400 BC - 400 AD) is the epic of the Indo-Aryan settlement in India. The work is attributed to Vyasa who pieced together many scattered sections in a huge book of 6 million verses. From these verses, about 90.000 couplets have been saved to this day.

The plot of Mahabharata concerns a long war that took place most probably when the Aryans conquered North India. The events of the war give the writers of the epic cause to express their moral message, which is based on the perceptions of the popular masses, who are of Dravidian origin. This is particularly true for the chapter of Bhagavad Gita, which is one of the most important works of Indian Philosophy and one of the masterpieces of world literature.

Maha Cohan: The position of Maha Cohan and Maha Manu (see glossary) is held by Saint Germain or Count Rakoczi or Malhos. Saint Germain comes from the human race and has evolved into an Ascended Being, after an exemplary and evolutionary course. As Maha Cohan, he is responsible for the formation of the new Root Race of the human species, of the Sixth, that will be influenced by the new merging of the peoples, with the aid of the Masters who will descend to give a new drive - education. But this presence of the New Person has many difficulties, mostly due to the modification - mutation of the etheric body, of the etheric cells and then, to the change of the physical body. It is a time-consuming procedure needing hyperknowledge and Masters who will apply it.

Mahadeva or Mahadevas: Archangel or Archangels.

Maha Manu: According to esoteric tradition, in every race, in every nation or country, the White Hierarchy and the three plus one Lipika (the others being the Karma Masters) designate a responsible Manu. Maha Manu is the leader of all Manus and the one predominantly responsible for the speed of evolution of the whole of humanity on Earth. It is he who regulates and handles the proportionate and necessary reception and use of Prana Life Force Substance from the human or similarly-evolved beings existing on our planet (our physical etheric world). Finally, he is responsible for our mental development. Nowadays, Maha Manu as well as Maha Chohan, is Saint Germain who comes from the human race (see Nikolaos A. Margiori's books *The Two-Volume Metaphysical Encyclopaedia, Omakoio Journal*).

Maha Mudra: 'The Great Seal', the Great Mudra. The Great Mudra is a physical exercise that is executed by pressing the heel on the perineum. This pressure on Apana – the downward flowing energy - starts pushing and redirecting energy back upwards, creating an inversion of the descending flow of Apana currents and in combination with other exercises, awakening and directing Kundalini towards man's elevation and apotheosis.

Maha Purusha: Great Soul - Spirit.

Maha Suhka: Great Happiness - Pleasure.

Mahat: The Great. The Cosmic Intellect (the Cosmic organ that reflects the Intellect of Purusha) according to Samkhya philosophy.

Mahatma: Great Soul - Spirit.

Mahavakya Upanishad: The Great Word. Mahavakya Upanishad teaches the student how to gain the vision of the soul, which will help him become one with the Lord.

Maha Veda: Great Veda. 'The Great Piercing'. A variation of Maha Bandha which involves internal breath retention with the aid of Jalandhara Bandha, 'the chin lock' so that the two channels, Ida and Pingala, may be able to fill up entirely.

Maha Yoga: Great Yoga. There is one and only Great Yoga: Raja Yoga (Royal Yoga).

Maitri Upanishad: It is Brahman's Knowledge, as it exists in all Upanishads and as it has been revealed by wise Maitri.

Makarasana: The crocodile pose. An exercise against insomnia. It rests the body, it frees the Mind from the irrepressible flow of thoughts, it causes natural sleep.

Technique: Lying prone, we stretch our arms forward and we spread our legs slightly. Then, we bring our hands to the sides while we join our legs and lean against our toes. Now, we cross our arms (the right palm holds the left arm and vice versa and the body leans against the elbows. We lift the head and shoulders from the ground. We can also sit on our knees and lift our back to form a vacant space under the belly. The exercises are combined with corresponding breathing exercises (see the book *Kriya Yoga* by Nikolaos A. Margioris).

Manasaputras: The Children of the Spirit or the children of Manas. They are the first spiritual beings that were incarnated in our Dimension in animals, which until that moment, did not have any logic and manas. With their descent, they changed the unreasonable animal into a reasonable man.

Manas: Mind (grey matter - liquids), a mixture of prana and akasha. A substance of superior- quality matter. A negative or feminine charge.

Mandala: The construction of a Mandala is a particular symbol in the tantric rituals. The term Mandala literally means 'circle' or 'center' or 'that which surrounds us'. It refers to a very intricate pattern with unlimited variations. Mandala is simultaneously a picture of the Universe and an expression of Divinity or the vessel of the Gods. On the other hand, it functions as a protective shield against any destructive power.

Mandukya Upanishad: At the feet of Master Mandukya.

Manipura Chakra: Mani means jewel - gem and Pura means a place or a town. Manipura is the jewel city. It is the center of the solar plexus and corresponds to the pancreas (Karma Yoga).

The color of prana coming from Sutratma is deep fire red while the one imported from Antahkarana is yellow fire red. It belongs to the 6th ray (emotion-will), the Stellar, it has 10 petals and is connected to eyesight and fire (flame). It has 8 thirdcenters - stations - satellites in its jurisdiction.

Manolaya: In order to attain Manolaya one must have first been trained in Ekagrata (Absolute Attention). Manolaya means intentness in the pursuit of one sole thought, so that a temporary annulment (dissolution) of the intellect can occur, in order for the hyperintellectual Mind to find free space and to become activated; to give man the knowledge that centuries and millenniums have not given him and will never give him through the conscious perception of things-phenomena. Only with hyperconscious functioning does the hyperperception of all hidden-to-consciousness quintessential truths and self-actualization as a spiritual being on the path of evolution begin for man.

Manomaya Kosha: The Mind sheath (manas). It is the receiver of sensory information and constitutes the place of good or bad desires.

Mantra Yoga: The power words of Yoga. Union through the power words.

Mantra or Mantras: Power word or words that many Gurus use to train their students in concentration. Also, these Power phrases operate as ascending pipelines of the famous Kundalini. The highest Power word is Om, which symbolizes the Absolute, the Divine. There are two ways to utter Mantras. The first one is phonetic, to whisper or say aloud. The second one is internal or mental and is mostly used by the more advanced.

Marga: It is the path, the way.

Marmasthanani: The 16 zones in which yogi have divided our body for the purpose of relaxation, which are the following:
1) Feet, 2) Shins, 3) Knees, 4) Thighs, 5) Abdomen - Diaphragm, 6) Solar Plexus, 7) Chest, 8) Spine, 9) Hands, 10) Forearms, 11) Upper Arms, 12) Neck, 13) Occiput (back of head, 14) Jaw (jawbone), 15 Eyes, 16) Top of skull.

Math: Convent.

Matras: Seconds. (They are also called heartbeats).

Maya: Delusion, hallucination, illusion, deep subjectivity, perception only of the material representation. More simply, it is the error that is formed in our Mind by the limited perception afforded to us solely through the five channels (the 5 senses) through which impressions – experiences enter and not by the total of the soul's senses. The whole of these senses (103 hypersenses) is activated as soon as man manages to activate the superior, hyperintellectual-hyperconscious function of his Mind, when he attains the whole Truth and not a partial or fragmented Truth.

Moksa: Liberation.

Mudra: Seal. It is a technique(s) to practically combine pranayama and asana exercises, whose aim is to quickly and carefully awaken Kundalini, controlling and guiding the pranic powers that are in use through pranayama (pose + breath + Mind + nervous and muscular system). Some examples of different mudra techniques are: Ashwini Mudra, Kechari Mudra, Mahamudra and so on.

Mukti: Emancipation.

Mula Bandha: 'The Root Lock'. Mula is the root. Bandha is the Key, the tightening, the pulling. In Mula we tighten the sphincter and lift it upwards. This exercise is executed in combination with Maha Bandha, with Jalandhara Bandha and with others whose aim it is to help Kundalini awaken.

Muladhara Chakra: Mula means root. Adhara means support. Muladhara is the base root. It is the base center of the spine and corresponds to the adrenals (Kriya yoga). The color that comes from Sutratma is light strawberry while the color coming from Antaskarana is very light pink strawberry. It belongs to the 4th ray (harmony - union through comparison). In physical form, it has 4 petals and is connected to smell and earth. It has 30 third chakras - stations - satellites.

Mundaka Upanishad: At the feet of the Monk.

N

Naam: Word (Logos).

Nadis: Etheric cablings or channels which the Life Force Substance (Prana) goes through, passing from the etheric power centers or Chakras (primary or secondary or tertiary) to the physical centers, to the physical glands. Nadis are also called Photons.

Naga: It is the Serpent sect to which the Advaist monk Totapuri, who initiated Ramakrishna in the Nirguna samadhi, belonged.

Naga Vayu: It is the vayu that protects the diaphragm and controls belching and hiccupping.

Nagarjuna: Nagarjuna is the Indian Sage, who in the 2nd century AD, presented us with the Absolute Void Theory,

Madhyamika Sutra or Mula Madhyamika Sutra (see glossary).

Naukasana: The Boat Pose. It aims to unburden the nervous and the muscular systems, to cleanse the Mind, to fight against amnesia.
Technique: Lying face down, we lift our legs to form an angle of about 45° (degrees) with the rest of the body. At the same time, we join our hands over the spine, while we lift the chest and the head to form an angle of 15° from the ground. From this position, the body sways alternatively toward the left and toward the right, the whole torso, from the shoulders to the knees, touching the ground. It is combined with breathing exercises (see the book *Kriya Yoga* by Nikolaos A. Margioris).

Neti: A Yoga exercise for cleaning the nostrils.

Neti: Means 'not this' and is the opposite of *iti*, which means 'this'.

Nidra: It is relaxation, artificially-induced sleep that is, however, controlled. Learning to relax is deliverance for every person because it rids his organism of toxins and his Mind of different stresses, pressures, strains, phobias, while at the same time, it revives the body and Mind in a very short time. For further information, look up the word 'Pratyahara' in the glossary.

Nigama: It is the second system of the psychical orientation that belongs to the Aryans. It contains the rituals of the Vedic period and the ones formed later on in accordance to the Aryan psychosynthesis.

Nimita: Causality.

Nirguna Samadhi: Samadhi that is done without a context

- image - quality. In this Samadhi the individualized spirit perceives Divinity-Perfection without any barriers-limits-qualities.

Nirvana: It is man's deliverance from pain and from the continual cycle of reincarnations. It is the 'extinction/annihilation', where the student attains a state of endless immobility, overcoming the matter-nature bonds and attaining a state of transcendence and remaining in a 'permanent' paradisiacal state that fulfills and unburdens him of all the hardships he has suffered in the outer dimensions of Omnicreation.
There is a difference between Samadhi and Nirvana. While in nirvana we attain a 'permanent' state of 'immobility' and bliss, in samadhi we have full spiritual activity and participation.

Nirvichara Samadhi: When, in meditation, we go beyond Savicara Samadhi and the sense of time and place disappear and we perceive the fine elements as they are, we have Nirvichara Samadhi.

Nirvikalpa Samadhi: Nirvikalpa Samadhi means the undifferentiated or unchanged samadhi - state - integration. Another name is nirguna samadhi. In this state the individualized spirit realizes Divinity - Perfection without differentiations or limits.

Nirvitarka Samadhi: Unlike Savitarka Samadhi (by questioning), Nirvitarka Samadhi involves no questioning. In this type of meditation, when somebody attempts to place the elements out of time and place and to think of them as they are, we say that we are applying Nirvitarka Samadhi.

Nishtha: One-way street. The devotion to one and sole ideal.

Nitya: Eternity.

Nivritti: Non-involvement or denial or withdrawal. According to the term 'Nivritti' every action is rejected because it implicates man in the cycle of rebirths. The opposite is Pravritti.

Niyama: Niyama means non-death / immortality. It is the second step-level of Raja Yoga and has 5 obligations-rules: a) Devotion to God (Isvarapranindhana), b) Study of books concerning atonement (Svadhyaya), c) Discipline and endurance (Tapas), d) Pleasure from whatever you have (Santosa) and e) Purity of the body and soul (Sauca).

Nyaya: It is the first of the six Orthodox Indian Philosophical Systems (darsanas). Together with the second Philosophical system, Vaisheshika, they form the first pair in Indian Philosophy. The writer of this first philosophical treatise is the sage Gautama (between the 3rd century BC and the 6th century AD). It contains sixteen subjects or categories (padarthas) or realities or pathways to Truth, gathered in five books developed along the lines of the Aristotelian logic concerning the meaning of the written word, and struggles to give, through its own perception, the true and correct way of THINKING.

These 16 categories are:

1) Pramana, meaning proof or cognitive function, 2) Prameya, meaning the object of valid knowledge 3) doubt, 4) purpose 5) example, 6) conclusion, 7) reflection, 8) argumentation, 9) ascertainment 10) debate, 11) disputation, 12) destructive criticism, 13) fallacy, 14) quibbling, 15) refutations and 16) the point of the opponent's defeat.

O

Ojas: They are energy (prana) reserves in an etheric state that are gathered in the back part of the head, behind each ear and are used by the Mind for the function of thought as well as for every conscious and unconscious activity of man.

Om: A holy word. It is considered the strongest power word (mantra) in Sanskrit philosophy. It signifies the One and Only God, Absolute Truth, its expression constitutes the three-dimensional cosmic unit (Vishnu or A, Shiva or U, Brahma or M) and is presented as AUM.

Om Darsana Raja Yoga: It is a mantra and means that the Absolute is comprehended and obtained only through the system of Raja Yoga.

Om Mani Padme Hum: *Om* is God. *Mani* is the gem. *Padme* is the Lotus and the Master's knees and *Hum* means 'kneel' or 'It is I. I bear all this or these within me, as divine qualities.'

Om Raja Yoga: It is a mantra and means that one attains the Absolute only through Raja Yoga.

P

Padahastasana: Hands under Foot pose. It cures the nerves, the lungs, headaches. It exercises the limbs, strengthens the abdominal muscles and helps digestion.

Technique: From the standing position, we bend the torso towards the ground, we straighten the knees, until the palms touch the floor and the head reaches almost to the knees. It is combined with correct breathing (see the book *Kriya Yoga* by Nikolaos A. Margioris).

Padmasana or Lotus Pose or Kamalasana or Stira Sukham: The well-known Lotus pose.
In a sitting position, we straighten the torso and we cross the legs as follows: the right foot is positioned on the left thigh and the left foot on the right thigh. It is considered the perfect pose that brings all the organs of the body to their correct and harmonious position, while at the same time, it allows the pranic energies to circulate in balance (see Nikolaos Margiori's books *Kriya Yoga*, *The Two-Volume Metaphysical Encyclopaedia*).

Pandit: An Indian sage or scholar of the Scriptures.

Para: Supremacy.

Paramahamsa: The Supreme Swan.

Parvatasana: The mountain pose. It strengthens the weak bodies and the lungs.
Technique: From Sukhasana or the Lotus pose, the torso is held straight, the hands are lifted, the palms facing forward, the fingers are stretched out and the thumbs unite. From this position we unite and separate (open and close) the fingers (five times) alternatively upwards and downwards. We repeat the exercise combining it always with breathing exercises (see the book *Kriya Yoga*, by Nikolaos A. Margioris).

Patanjali: Indian Master of Yoga that from the 2nd to 3rd century BC, collected and put together the scattered dictates for the deliverance (Kaivalya) of man. Using what he collected as a basis, he wrote and presented us with the well-known Yoga Sutra, which is Raja Yoga.

Patanjali's Yogic Philosophy is divided into four main parts: 1) Aim and result of Samadhi, 2) Means and method for its accomplishment, 3) Technical analysis of the means used and of the powers (Siddhis) obtained by the Yogi and 4) The exact definition of deliverance and where it aims to guide every man.

Pavanamuktasana: Release of the organism from the ill winds residing within us. It fights against pains, swelling, hypertension, stomach problems and constipation.

Technique: From a supine position, the knees and thighs are pressed against the chest, with the help of the hands that wrap around the knees. In this way they create a pressure on the abdomen. This exercise is combined with correct breathing exercises (see the book *Kriya Yoga* by Nikolaos A. Margioris).

Pingala: It is the right nostril, the solar energy or the positive dynamism-magnetism-prana entering our organism from our right nostril.

Prakriti: Cosmic Matter - Nature.

Pralaya: It is the Great Absence of the Divine Being. Brahman's Cosmic Night.

Prana: It is the Universal Energy that, in the form of a Creative Dynamism, supplies every living and 'nonliving' being, every living and 'nonliving' matter form with life. When, at one point, it stops supplying beings with life, the natural marasmus - death comes to the living or the nonliving matter that loses its life substance. Prana is a seven-composed power-expression. That is it contains seven different vibrations-colors and it is introduced by the etheric apparatus Sutratma that we have in our head.

Pranamaya Kosha: The sheath of Prana, of the Vital Force. It keeps us alive.

Prana Vayu: It is the first vayu and is situated in the heart and is responsible for its operation. It is formed by the input of Prana (Universal Life Substance) within us and overlooks the correct channeling of Prana within our organism.

Pranayama: Prana is the Life Substance, the Universal Energy that exists diffused throughout the entire Universe and its Dimensions, and supplies everything with life. Yama is death. Pranayama means the 'killing' of prana. To put it more simply, with the correct and methodical technique of rhythmical breathing, we gradually capture and control the energy entering our body.

Pranayama contains four basic categories-steps of execution. The first is called 'simple pranayama'. The second is called 'semi-intricate', the third is called 'intricate' and the fourth 'full'. It is always executed with a strictly defined rhythm.

In Pranayama we breathe only through the nose. Breathing from the mouth is strictly prohibited. There is also the breathing through both nostrils at the same time as well as the breathing alternately through the nostrils (we inhale through the right nostril exactly as long as we inhale through the left nostril).

By practicing pranayama regularly, we feel revived and we strengthen our entire organism, our Mind and we even become able to intervene, directing prana as we desire, in the healing of any ailing parts of our organism. Thus, we create not only health but also set the ground for longevity. At the same time, we start stimulating and disturbing the energy sleeping within us, Kundalini, and, in the long run, if we work correctly, we may be able to awaken it.

Prarabdha Karma: Karma that has been accumulated in previous lives and that has started bearing fruit in the present life, where it must be used up.

Prashna Upanishad: Questions.

Pratyahara: Pratyahara is the fifth step of Raja Yoga. Here begins the introversion of man (of his Mind). Pratyahara means 'detaching one's Mind from the sensory centers which exist in the brain'. This means that the student diligently practices the intellectual exercises that will allow him to gradually become detached from his surrounding space-world, in order to relax-become detoxified from the awful intensities and strains of everyday life. At the same time, he opens the only right path and enters and communes with his internal world. So, Pratyahara, in its simple application, is a small or great break from the daily pressures that helps us to regain our strength, while at the same time, for the more evolved beings, it is the path which will lead us to the much sought after Concentration. This detachment of the senses is called withdrawal and its successful execution is called Void of Mind. Natural sleep is not enough to detoxify and to cleanse our organism, nor to replace the life force existing within us nor even to conserve the energy that man will need for higher and more spiritual purposes.

In a truly successful execution of Pratyahara where the Mind remains in the Void for one hour, it is equivalent to four hours of natural sleep. He who has not learnt Pratyahara can never hope to succeed in Dharana-Concentration.

There is an enormous difference between Pratyahara and Hypnotism. In Pratyahara there is awareness of place and time, the perception and the direction of the procedure. On the contrary, in Hypnotism the awareness of place and of time is lost, and we have artificial sleep. This is exactly what makes Pratyahara a superior method and the only suitable one to create the preconditions for the functioning of the hyper-consciousness of man.

The practical way to achieve Pratyahara is through the centripetal or the centrifugal relaxation-withdrawal of every sensation from our body. This is done by following a well-structured program that the student has fixed and that is carried out faithfully, while throughout the whole process of experimentation, a part of our Mind (anti-Mind) follows the execution of the exercise which has been set by the Instructor.

Pratikas: It is the worship of things that constitute the substitutes of God but that can help the worshiper's consciousness gradually attain higher spiritual meanings.

Pratimas: It is the worship of images. Angels (Devas), saints and so on, may be included in this kind of worship.

Pravritti: It means to turn outward. That is, it means the total involvement and participation in the material world. Its opposite is Nivritti.

Puraka: Puraka is a breath phase in Pranayama technique.

Puranas: The term Puranas means all that has survived from the very distant past until now. Puranas are attributed to Vyasa, the writer of Mahabharata. It is the popularization of the philosophical, religious and spiritual theories of Vedism and the Upanishads and the description of the lives of Avatars, saints and kings.

Purusha: According to Samkhya philosophy, it is the cosmic Spirit, a Clear Conscience.

Purva Mimamsa: It is the theoretical foundation of the Vedic sacred rites that took place between the 3rd century BC and the 8th century AD, and constitutes the fifth orthodox Indian philosophical system (darsana) forming a pair with the 6th Vedanta. Mimamsa means a systematic-thorough search. Purva Mimamsa is based on Vedas and on Brahmanas, unlike Uttara Mimamsa (Vedanta) which is mainly based on Upanishads.
This work is attributed to Jaimini (about 300 BC - 200 AD) who is thought to have been the student of Vyasa, the author of Mahabharata. The principal aim of Mimamsa is a) the substantiation of the authenticity of the Vedas as an indisputable source of revealed Truth, and b) the conveyance of their real meaning, especially concerning the holy rituals.

Prithvi: Earth.

R

Raja Yoga: In the 2nd or in the 3rd century BC, Patanjali (most probably a student of Vyasa), codified Raja Yoga into sutras (aphorisms). *Raja* means king and *Yoga* means union. Raja Yoga is the Masculine Beginning, the Queen of all forms of Yoga. For this reason, it is also called Royal Union, as well as spiritual union or psychological union or intellectual union or scientific union. Some other names of Raja Yoga are: Maha Yoga, Raya Yoga, Ashtanga Yoga, Astavakra and Yoga Sutra.

The aim of Raja Yoga is to bring the harmony of the elements that constitute it to man's Mind and to promote the unhindered operation of his three levels of consciousness (conscious, subconscious, hyperconscious), without one interfering with the rights of the other. It is the harmonious relationship between the operational procedures of the separate parts of the Mind.

The entire ancient (Dravidian) educational system of the Mind aims to discipline the unruly intellectual workings of the Mind and bring them under control; to teach the Mind to control itself. By controlling our wild intellectual Mind, we control the subtler and nobler part of nature-matter, which will allow us to hope that we can control many vibrations of matter operating in our physical body as well as a few of the others surrounding it.

The aim of Raja Yoga is the harmonious coexistence of man's three levels of consciousness, as we mentioned above. This automatically brings the Mind to its normal balance, offering the student physical, mental and spiritual purity.

Finally, by improving and gaining a deeper understanding of the exercises of the Mind (Mind training) the Mind is refined to such a high degree of vibrations, of spiritual purity and peace that the first flicker of hope that one may be ready to spark the functioning of one's Hyperconsciousness is created.

Then, the lucky and blessed student of Raja Yoga will be flooded with the prosperity and wisdom that Divine Nature granted man during the blessed moment of creation.

The eight steps of Maha Yoga (Raja Yoga) are the following: Yama, Niyama, Asana, Pranayama, Pratyahara, Dharana, Dhyana and Samadhi. There is also the 9th step which liberates the enlightened Yogi-Guru. It is Kaivalya or Asamprajnata Samadhi.

RAJA YOGA, by Nikolaos A. Margioris is the ideal book for those who want to learn Raja Yoga because it is unique in its development and detail. Of course, we also have Vivekananda's book that simply touches upon the topic, but nonetheless offers an introduction to the whole matter.

Raja Yogi: The student of Raja Yoga.

Rajas: Activity, mobility, impulsiveness, dynamism, progressiveness.

Ramakrishna: Ramakrishna is the last real Saint of the East. He was initiated into nirguna samadhi with the guidance of his Master, monk Totapuri of the Naga Sect. Sometime before, he had received instruction in Bhakti yoga by the Brahmana nun Bhairavi Brahmani. For six full months, he remained in a state of nirguna samadhi, while his body had fallen into a state of hypofunction and it was his nephew Hriday who took care of it. During this period, he conceived the unlimited and unrestrained Supreme Truth of Everything, visible and invisible, the very essence of Unique-Divine and he returned as an ascended Master, as a conscious Avatar and as an initiate, to teach his students and the other people the whole truth, as far as the Karma and Free Will of each individual allowed and as much as it was possible for a man who had actualized and changed the truth in our physical dimension to express it in simple words.

One of Ramakrishna's greatest students, and after being initiated and enlightened, a conscious Avatar, was Vivekananda, who, in soul and in body delivered himself to the Work, to the Divine Work, in absolute self-sacrifice, ignoring any obstacle and danger, to serve, as his Master did - Truth, Man, the One Life. (See the books: *Ramakrishna, the Madman of God*, Spiritual Sun editions, *Sri Ramakrishna's Gospel*, Konidaris editions, *Ramakrishna, the Demi-God, Vivekananda the Sage*, Divrys editions, *Mystical Teachings, 3rd Volume* Nikolaos A. Margioris, Athens Omakoio editions, *The Two-Volume Metaphysical Encyclopaedia*, Nikolaos A. Margioris, Athens Omakoio editions).

Ramayana: One of the two great epic poems of India. The other one is Mahabharata. Ramayana (400 BC - 400 AD) is the epic of the arrival of the Aryans to the Indian South. It is much shorter than Mahabharata (it has 24.000 couplets versus the 90.000 of Mahabharata) and is attributed to the writer Valmiki. The central theme of Ramayana is the exaltation of honor and truth as the only correct path leading to God.

Raya Yoga: It is a variation of the term Raja Yoga.

Rechaka: Exhalation through the nose during the execution of pranayama techniques. Depending on the exercise, it could be through one or both nostrils.

Rig Veda: The oldest Veda is Rig Veda. It has 1028 hymns with which gods are invoked to the sacred ceremonies. These hymns also contain prayers, references to mythology that attest to the customs of litanies. Because of Rig Veda, we have a clearer picture of what and how Indo-Aryans worshipped.

Risi: A Sage.

Rupa: Figure.

S

Saguna Samadhi: It is the samadhi with limits-images-properties. There are two kinds of Saguna: the small pre-liberating Saguna and the big, pre-perfect Saguna. Nirguna Samadhi or Nirvikalpa Samadhi which has no limits - borders - qualities is superior to Saguna Samadhi. In Saguna Samadhi, although the soul was liberated long before - by Asamprajnata or by Kaivalya Samadhi - from Karma and from Reincarnation, it perceives Perfection - Divinity within limits - borders depending on every person's personal evolutionary course and the spiritual standards - ideals, which he has cultivated and tried to approach as perfect reflections of the Divine Mind - Perfection.

Sakhya Bhava: It is one of the numerous relationships that a Bhakti Yogi can develop with his God. It is the friendly relationship involving a friend's love for his dear friend.

Samadhi: It is Union - Theosis - Likeness – Rising up (spiritual elevation) - Enlightenment. The subject and the object stop existing. The man who achieves this communicates with the WHOLE TRUTH and is automatically changed into a Divine being, into a Light and Truth bearer.

A loose interpretation of Samadhi is as follows: *Sam* means union of all the elements of man's personality, which when united, address (a) his internal aim - purpose; that is man's deeper being, (Dhi). This is attained when the meditating person succeeds in holding his Mind focused on only one thought for 1728". Then, he develops such internal strength that he automatically enters the Samadhi state.

The main types of Samadhi, in ascending order, are:
1) Samprajnata, 2) Savitarka, 3) Nirvitarka, 4) Savicara, 5) Nirvichara, 6) Sananda, 7) Sasmita, 8) Asamprajnata or Kaivalya, 9) Savikalpa or Saguna, 10) Nirvikalpa or Nirguna.

These Samadhis can take the form of the following categories: 1) Simple Samadhis, that last a few seconds, 2) Long Samadhis, lasting a long period, 3) continual Samadhis, that come, end and begin again, a few or many times a day or night, 4) Permanent Samadhis that last for many months, uninterruptedly and without return to conscious life. Finally, they are blessed, that is fatal.

The Soul is set free and enters immortality or the cycle of reincarnation, depending on its evolution. The Intellect (Buddhi) can follow until the Asamprajnata Samadhi. Then the soul starts a direct dialogue with the Mind, without the interference of the Intellect, which becomes unaware of and neutral to what the Mind converses with the soul.

Samana Vayu: It is the vayu residing in the navel-solar plexus. It is responsible for the digestion of food.

Sama Veda: The Sama Veda is one of the four Vedas and contains instructions on how the psalms used in the Vedic sacrifices, must be sung. Most psalms are borrowed from Rig Veda. It also contains sacerdotal songs that accompany the preparations for and the actual offering of the sacrifice.

Savasana: Corpse Pose. It cures arteriosclerosis and hypertension. It combats insomnias, nerves, stress, asthma. From this position, true relaxation is achieved, that is, Pratyahara (Mind withdrawal from the sensory centers). It is basically the supine position, with hands lightly separated from the body, the palms facing upward and the legs also slightly separated. The eyes are closed while the muscles and the nerves are relaxed.

Savicara Samadhi: When meditation goes a little higher than Nirvitarka Samadhi and focuses on the Tanmatras, thinking about them in time and space, then the Samadhi is called Savicara, which means with discretion. Immediately after that, Nirvichara Samadhi follows (see glossary).

Savikalpa Samadhi: It is samadhi in a select or differentiated state - union - absorption (it is also called Saguna Samadhi). Superior to it is Nirvikalpa Samadhi. In this samadhi, the spirit-soul partly perceives Divinity-Perfection, through the personal ideal it worships.

Savitarka Samadhi: It is a samadhi that is executed with a question (see Samprajnata Samadhi). We ask the object of meditation to deliver us its Substance and its Powers. There are two kinds of objects for meditation in the 25 categories of Samkhya: 1) the 24 imperceptible categories of nature and 2) the one perceptible Purusha. This type of meditation, whose objects are the crude external elements, is called Savitarka.

Knowledge is power and as soon as we start knowing something, we exercise power over it. The immediately superior type of meditation is called Nirvitarka (see glossary).

Samasti: Universal, generality. Its opposite is Viasti.

Samhitas: The four Vedas are also called Samhitas, which is a collection of hymns (see Vedas in glossary).

Samkhya: It is Counting - Classification. It constitutes the third Orthodox Indian Philosophical System and forms a pair with Yoga, being the fourth Orthodox Philosophical System. The founder of Samkhya (8th century BC) is the famous philosopher Kapila, who wrote the Samkhya Pravachana Sutra. This work affected Buddha very much. Another work that appeared as Kapila's work, Samkhya Karika, was written after a long time, by Kapila's capable student, Ishvara Krishna.

Samkhya Pravachana Sutra presents us a covert atheism or a covert infidelity. In contrast, Samkhya Karika presents, in its more formal philosophical way, absolute atheism and absolute Dualism.

Samkhya places its system on two basic and permanent principles from the cooperation of which everything comes and derives. These two principles are Purusha (Soul-s) and Prakriti (the Material and Physical World Substance). Purusha is a kind of spiritual existence or a spiritual element and is not a principle or an authority or even an independent or pre-eternal Mind. On the contrary, in a perhaps unconscious state, there are countless similar Purushas (individual souls). When the cooperation of Purusha with Prakriti is interrupted, dissolution follows (Pralaya) or Prakriti is abandoned in a wholly non-existent state. Samkhya unwillingly lets us conceive of the existence of a peculiar principle-entity that carefully avoids deification.

Certainly, this principle is Purusha. A second need is man's unchangeable tendency to be emancipated. At this very point, Samkhya and Yoga withdrew and formed Kaivalya (liberation) because the co-existence and the cooperation between Purusha and Prakriti resembled, according to Gaudapada, the cooperation between the blind and the paralytic. So, somehow, Samkhya Purusha corresponds to the Atman of Oneness of the Upanishads.

The Universe, as we see it, according to Samkhya, is the

result of the disturbance of three qualities, Gunas, which exist from the very beginning in Prakriti.
1) SATTVA (SATTVA) = Luminous quality.
2) TAMAS = Dark or inactive quality.
3) RAZAS = The tendency to disrupt, the dynamic - energetic element of Prakriti.

The Prakriti scale, for its presentation as a perceptible and, of course, as a conscious world, under the influence of Purusha, shows us the twenty-five forms or elements or vibrations (Tattvas) in which it exists. We set Purusha aside, as it is located outside the psycho-material reality or Prakriti and we present the 25 Tattvas:

PURUSHA: Cosmic Spirit
Spiritual individual unit.

1st) PRAKRITI: Cosmic Substance.
The material and psychical world substance. Here we should add that under the continual influence of Purusha on Prakriti, the latter retreats into the soul of the universe (Mahat) and then it is expressed in three derivative elements, whose total is called Antahkarana.

2nd) MAHAT: Cosmic Intellect.
Here we have the spiritual view of the world reflecting spiritual Purusha.

ANTAHKARANA
Not counted. It is man, Mahat, as a spiritual phenomenon. The interior organ.

3rd) BUDDHI
Individualization of the spiritual person, of the above-mentioned Mahat.

4th) AHAMKARA: Cosmic Ego.
The self-consciousness of the Ego itself.

5th) MANAS: Cosmic Mind.
The Ego as the indicator of the content of the senses. Ma-

nas is found where there is spirit, according to the other Indian philosophical schools.

6th - 10th) they include the five known organs of our senses in relation to Ahamkara that is, as we said, the self-consciousness of the Ego itself. 6) Tsrotra = Hearing, 7) Tvak = Touch, 8) Caksus = Eyesight, 9) Rasana = Taste, 10) Ghrana - Smell.

11th - 15th) TANMATRAS

They are the defining factors of the five elements (etheric elements) of nature. 1) Sabda = sound, 2) Sparsa = Touch, 3) Rupa = form, 4) Rasa = taste, 5) Gandha = smell.

16th -20th) AHAMKARA, formed. The five organs of action in their relationship with Ahamkara 1) Vak = word, 2) Pani = function, 3) Pada = movement, 4) Payu = thought, 5) Upastha = reproduction.

21st - 25th) TANMATRAS, derivatives. The five basic elements that take their characteristics from the five TANMATRAS: 1) Akasha = Ether (Emptiness), 2) Vayu = air (movement - pressure), 3) Tejas = fire (Luminosity-dilatation), 4) Apas = water (Fluidity - contraction) and 5) Prithivi = earth (solidity - cohesionl). (See *Omakoio Journal* and *The Two-Volume Metaphysical Encyclopaedia* by Nikolaos A. Margioris).

Samprajnata Samadhi: A seeded samadhi. It is the samadhi still containing the rebirth seed for the spirit-soul that has attained it and it is located mainly between the 1st and the 4th of the seven steps of the Intellectual Dimension. Although it is the guide of the Asamprajnata Samadhi (liberating), it does not free the soul. A person may obtain all the control powers of nature but may still fall again. This danger exists until the soul passes beyond nature, surpasses the 4th step of the Intellectual World and enters the 5th step as a winner.

Samprajnata Samadhi has six categories: Savitarka Samadhi, Nirvitarka Samadhi, Savicara Samadhi, Nirvichara Samadhi, Sananda Samadhi and Sasmita Samadhi.

Samsara: Rebirth, reincarnation, cycle of rebirth (See Nikolaos A. Margiori's books *Reincarnation*, *The Two-Volume Metaphysical Encyclopaedia*, *Omakoio Journal*).

Samskara: It is the impression, the stimulus, the information, the waves and so on, that we receive by our surrounding environment-world, through the five senses or even the one that rises as a repressed image from the thirteen channels of the instincts existing within us (see the book *Raja Yoga* by Nikolaos A. Margioris).

Samtosa (or Samtosha or Santosha or Santosa): It is the fourth obligation of Niyama (Niyama is the second ascending step of Raja Yoga) and it means the pleasure of what exists.

Samyama: When the last three steps of Raja Yoga (Dharana, Dhyana and Samadhi) are executed together as a unity, then we say that we apply Samyama or Meditation or some type of Samadhi. There are many types of Samyama that a trained Yogi can perform. For example, he can apply Samyama to every visible or invisible matter-object, animate or inanimate, to the body itself, to his Mind, to Chakras, to Vayu, to his Master or to some higher Entity, to Karma, to his pre-incarnations, to the past-present-future and so on. Every separate Samyama he performs brings him, apart from the knowledge on the matter of which he is meditating, abilities and powers that are completely unknown to the average man (see Siddhis in glossary).

Sadhana: The spiritual exercise or the spiritual practices (disciplines) that are used on the path of ascension in Bhakti Yoga.

Sahaja Yoga: Everlasting Union. Those who attain it are called Sahajis because they are in continual touch and communication with the Father - Perfection. In Sahaja, they teach a combination of Raja Yoga (Patanjali - single molecule) and Tantra Yoga (Kundalini).

Sahasrara Chakra: Sahasrara means 'thousands' or 'infinity'. It is also called the one-thousand-petal lotus. It is the heart center on the head and corresponds to the epiphysis gland (Bhakti yoga). The color of prana emitted from Sutratma is celestial white, while Antahkarana is colorless or - let's say - emits a warmth of inconceivable color. It belongs to the 1st ray (Divine Will), to the Unique and it is the seat of the Spirit.

Sananda Samadhi: The step following Nirvichara Samadhi is when the crude as well as the delicate elements are abandoned, and the object of meditation is the internal organ, the thinking organ. So, when the thinking organ is considered to be released from qualities of activity and indolence, it is called Sananda Samadhi, Blissful Samadhi. Next on the hierarchy, on a somewhat higher level, we have Sasmita Samadhi.

Sanchita Karma: It is Karma that was created in previous lives and waits to bear fruit in future lives.

Sandi: Peace.

Sannyasa: Hermit, monk, renouncer.

Sanskrita: Sanskrit, the perfect, the noble language.

Sarpa: Snake, reptile.

Sat Chit Ananda: Existence - Consciousness - Prosperity.

Satori: It is a samadhi of Jainism.

Sattva: Balance, harmony, rhythm, order, light, goodness.

Satya: Truth. The word Satya constitutes the fourth abstinence or restraint of Yama. Yama is the first of the eight ascending steps of Raja Yoga and it means Truthfulness.

Satya Sai Baba: A great Indian Master of Yoga who is considered to be a modern Avatar. At a very young age, he was the student of my Master Nikolaos A. Margioris who, for 13 years lived in India (he spent two or two and half of these 13 years in Tibet). Margioris was also charged by his Guru to supervise and train a group of young students, among whom was Satya Sai Baba.

Sarvam: The Whole.

Sasmita Samadhi: It is the broadest Samadhi. When the Mind itself is the object of meditation, when meditation is very mature and focused, when all the ideas of the crude and fine matter are abandoned, when only a Sattvic (Sattvas) state of the Ego remains, differentiated from all the other objects, then it is called Sasmita Samadhi.

The person who attains this is –as they say in the Vedas – 'released from the body.' He can conceive of himself without his crude body but may continue to require a finer superior body (an etheric body). Those who find themselves in this state in the world without having managed to reach the end, are called Prakritilayas. But those who do not stop there and arrive at the end attain freedom (see Asamprajnata Samadhi).

Sauca: It is the fifth and last obligation of Niyama (Niyama is the second ascending step of Raja Yoga) and means the purity of the body and soul.

Sautrantikas: It is one of the 6 non-orthodox (non-Vedic) Indian philosophical systems (darsanas). The school of Sautrantikas, of Relative Realism (supreme aphorisms) was established in the 2nd century AD, by Kumaralata.

Shabd Yoga or Logo Yoga or Surat Shabd Yoga: It is Yoga of the Celestial Rolling Sound Current, Sound-Word Yoga. It was Kirpal Singh who undertook to transmit it – after the death of his Master Baba Sawan Sing. It is a system that differs from the well-known basis of Yoga as set down by the codifier and classifier Patanjali.

Here, the Channels passing through the universe and every physical body, as well as our own, are sought. A substance finer than Prana passes through these Channels and is discerned in light, sound and other unknown subtler qualities. The student of Shabd Yoga communicates with this substance and his being is filled with multi-knowledge, while he feels the Heavenly Kingdom within him.

Although it may seem an easy form of Yoga, suitable for people of all ages, it is actually destined for the prepared Mystics and not for simple seekers or students.

Shakti-a: It is Life force (prana) in its feminine form, situated within man, at the height of the coccyx (Kundalini).

Shamballa: Etheric channel. Such etheric passages-channels are found in the Gobi desert, in Crete, in Samos and so on. They open and close at regular and different time intervals.

Shankara: He is the hermit-Advaitist saint who lived between the 8th and the 9th century AD and presented us with the Nirguna Brahman. He has written many commentaries on the Vedanta Sutras, on the Bhagavad Gita, and on the Upanishads as well.

Shankaracharya or Sankaracharya: See Shankara in glossary.

Shanta Bhava: It is one of the numerous personal relationships that a Bhakti follower can develop during his ascending course towards his God. It is a calm relationship, a love without passion or extremes but with respect and peace towards God (see Bhava).

Shiva-s: Catalyst or destroyer (U). He is the third person of the Indian Triad (AUM). He is a God of Dravidian origin passed down to our days.

Siddhasana: The Accomplished pose. It is an alternative to the Sukhasana and the Padmasana.

Siddhis: Supernatural powers that, on the one hand, function as road markers and as direct proof for the evolving Yogi but, at the same time, they still constitute dangerous trials - obstacles hindering the elevation of the prospective Yogi - Guru, if there is an attachment or a demonstration of these powers (they are also called Vibhuti). According to the aphorisms of Patanjali, eight of them are the most important:
1) reduction (anima), that is to willingly become as small as an atom (the ability to enter all objects, even an atom of matter, to be able to see its internal substance), 2) expansion (mahima), to voluntarily expand (it is the ability to see everything in space, 3) weightlessness (laghima) is to willingly neutralize gravity (here we often use the phenomenon of levitation that some Yogis present), 4) approach (prapti) to achieve everything or to voluntarily arrive at a place, 5) fulfillment (prakamya) of every desire, 6) ownership (istva), to control the energies of nature, 7) self-control (vastva), to have self-possession, to command

all creatures and all powers of nature and to be free from influences, 8) control of desire (kamavasayita), to voluntarily stop all desires.

By exercising self-concentration (Samyama) and the beginning of self-control - self-possession, other achievements of secondary value also appear for Yogi. They are: 1) to understand the language of birds, animals and plants, 2) to know previous reincarnations and when you will die, 3) to read the thoughts of others, 4) to be able to know about secret matters and things that concern other planets and stars, 5) to predict the future, 6) to carry oneself to any place in the world, 7) to cure by touch, and 8) to attain physical grace and harmony.

Here we ought to point out that a true Esoterist - and much more a Master - rarely if ever shows or publicizes these Powers – whether he possesses all or some of them. He simply mentions them in his teachings so that the apprentice may have the fore-knowledge of what he is likely to encounter and how to use it to continue his evolution and as an invisible tool to help his fellow-men.

The aim of every serious student of Esotericism is Spiritual completion and Spiritual Omnipotence, which is incomparable. All the other powers are substitutes, practical proof of progress and useful equipment for the ascension of the apprentice.

Simhasana: The Lion Pose. It cures voice and throat related disorders. It helps the senses of sight and hearing function as well as the throat. It solves problems with chewing and swallowing.

Technique: From the Siddhasana (Diamond) pose; that is on our knees and seated on our heels, we separate the thighs and we place our hands against the knees. The eyes are opened wide and the tongue is stretched out of the mouth. Then, the mouth closes and the head and the torso bend slightly backwards. Return to the vertical-straight position and repeat in combination always with the appropriate breathing exercises (see the book *Kriya Yoga* by Nikolaos A. Margioris).

Sitali: 'Cool', refreshing breath. Sitali means 'catapult', he who cuts. It is a technique which involves inhaling from the mouth, through the circular shape the tongue has taken for this exercise. Hold in the air and then exhale through the two nostrils simultaneously. It cures bile disorders, stomach diseases, atrophy and infectious fever, as well as relieves thirst. It is an important stimulus for the awakening of Kundalini.

Smriti: It is one of the two categories of Hindu Holy Scriptures. They are considered traditional works. The second category is Sruti.

Soham: It is I.

Soma: The Divine Drink - Nectar or Water of Life or Spiritual Water.

Sri: It is the title 'mister' that is often used before the names of distinguished Indians, especially in written form.

Srisi: Evolution.

Sruti: It refers to one of the two categories of written holy texts of Hinduism. They are considered to be the Revelation texts. The other category is Smriti.

Sthira Sukha: Steady - Comfortable pose. It is another name for Padmasana or otherwise the Lotus pose.

Sukhasana: The easy pose. The simple position. It involves sitting cross-legged, with the left leg under the right leg, when performing Raja Yoga; while, when we practice Kriya Yoga, the right leg is positioned under the left leg. The head and the torso are held in a vertical straight line, the hands press against the knees.

Supta Vajrasana: With this exercise, we exercise the lower muscles of the hips.
Technique: Seated on our backside, we stretch our legs forward. We bend the right leg and we place it under our backside and then we do the same with the left leg, forming the Diamond (Siddhasana) position. We cross our hands behind our head and we bend the torso backwards until our back touches the floor. Then, we lift the torso forming a right angle, our legs remaining folded. It is always combined with the appropriate breathing exercises (see the book *Kriya Yoga* by Nikolaos A. Margioris).

Surya: The Sun.

Surya Namaskar: Exercise to salute the sun. It contains a series of poses- Asanas in combination with breathing exercises (see Nikolaos A. Margiori's book, *Kriya Yoga*).

Sushumna or Susumna: The greatest and most central etheric channel (Nadis) through which Kundalini will pass when it awakens. It lies lengthwise along our vertebral column and is surrounded on the left and on the right by semicircles of two other great channels - nadis that are called Ida and Pingala. However, the structure of these three channels reminds us of the Sermon of Hermes and the symbol that physicians have adopted (see *Omakoio Journal*, *The Two-Volume Metaphysical Encyclopaedia*, by Nikolaos A. Margioris).

Sutra: Aphorism.

Sutras: Sutras were created by the priests who, due to the fact that texts weren't committed to paper, were obliged to develop mnemonic strategies which helped them retrieve entire extracts of a holy text from memory by using a few key words. The collections they had for this purpose were called Sutras of aphorisms.
Sutras do not constitute a part of Vedas nor are they the revealed truth (Sruti). But they are considered to be closely connected with Vedas, so they are characterized as 'members' (Vedangas). Sutras are the six Darsanas, that is, the six orthodox Indian philosophical systems.

Sutratma: Sutratma is an etheric Life Substance (Prana) conductor that looks like an upside-down mushroom and is located on the top of our head in an etheric state. It functions throughout all of humanity and introduces the prana of seven composites, seven colors, seven qualities to our etheric body; the prana that, upon entering our being, splits into three vibrations and is distributed in three different parts. One part goes to the back of our head, behind the ears and creates the remarkable Ojas (reserves of etheric life force). The second seven-composite part of prana is distributed proportionately in the 7 etheric energy deposits (chakras) and every chakra or cakra takes its corresponding vibration color-form. Finally, the third part descends the Muladhara chakra, at the height of the coccyx, in the Kunda membrane and is stored, forming the well-known Kundalini (accumulated energy).
When ....one day... man is enlightened, Sutratma automatically withers away and then, we see Antahkarana, which is superior in conception and height of vibrations with three receptive antennas flourishing and honors only Initi-

ates - Avatars and those who were recently released from Karma. Of course, Sutratma is also the valve that regulates man's life on earth. When this valve closes, death comes to the physical body (see *Omakoio journal*, *The Two-Volume Metaphysical Encyclopaedia*, by Nikolaos A. Margioris).

Svadhyaya: It is the second obligation of Niyama (Niyama is the second ascending step of Raja Yoga) and means the study of books that deal with the freedom of the soul.

Svadisthana Chakra: It is the center of the genitals and corresponds to the seminal glands (Hatha yoga). Prana coming from Sutratma has an orange or a deep pink color while the one belonging to the 3rd ray (reproduction), to the etheric, is connected with taste and water, has 6 petals and 8 stations - satellites.

Svetasvatara Upanishad: The Svetasvatara Upanishad analyses the way to practise Yoga and gives us the arithmetical limits of pranayama, on the basis of which the student should be trained for long periods throughout the four phases of the day.

Swami or Suami: Literally it means Master, he who manages to control or to dominate himself. It is also the title that the monks of the Vedantic Philosophy use.

Swamiji: It is the diminutive of Swami.

T

Taittiriya Upanishad: From the Taittiriya section of Vedas.

Talasana: The Phoenix pose. It gives height, it cures spine disorders. It exercises the limbs, the belly and the pulmonary muscles.

Technique: From the standing position, with our feet together we lift ourselves on our toes, raising our hands while stretching and straightening our torso. It is combined with the appropriate breathing exercises (see the book *Kriya Yoga* by Nikolaos A. Margioris).

Tamas: Indolence, inactivity, staticity, passivity, darkness.

Tantra Yoga: It is Bibliology, the language of the Upanishads (Dravidian system). Tantra (from 500 AD and on) is the weaving together and means the gathering-attainment of Knowledge for the perfection of man. Tantra Yoga (Kundalini Yoga) is the Feminine Principle and constitutes the second great course, the path to the attainment of superior Mind functioning through breathing techniques (pranayama) using inhalation (Astaranga Kumbhaka), Mudras and Bandhas.

Although Tantra is one of the two greatest systems-paths of access to and activation of man's hyperconsciousness (the other is Raja Yoga), every interested person must, first of all, be trained in Raja Yoga, in order to be able to ascend correctly with Tantra yoga. Every Instructor should have as a priority to train his students in both these great esoteric practical systems of our world. On the other hand, we should not forget that there are psychosyntheses that suit one or the other of these two systems-methods more or that vibrate similarly and float together better.

The difference between Tantra Yoga and the other Upanishads is that Tantra Yoga abandons the Hermitism of the Upanishads, of the shapeless Brahman (Nirguna Brahman) in favor of a more concrete Brahman, endowed with qualities - definitions called Saguna Brahman (personal God).

Another difference of Tantra is that, though it itself also accepts the Upanishad principle of Maya, it does not scorn the external world as the Upanishads do. The Upanishads, even though they do not deny it completely, attribute only a relative existence to the external world (see the *books Raja Yoga, The Two- Volume Metaphysical Encyclopaedia, Omakoio Journal,* by Nikolaos A. Margioris).

Tapas: It is the third obligation of Niyama (Niyama is the second step - grade of Raja Yoga) and means discipline and endurance (with tolerance).

Tapasvin: It means 'warm man'. It is the person who has begun to discipline himself and to obtain different Siddhis.

Tat Tvam Asi: You are that or I am what you are.

Tattvas: They are the vibratory forms of matter, the elements of our experience of the world.

Tejas: Fire.

Totapuri: The naked monk, the Advaitist monk who gave Ramakrishna the ultimate initiation, Nirguna samadhi.

Turiya: It is redemption, transcendence.

Trikonasana: The Triangle Pose. It strengthens the heart, the shoulders and the rib muscles, as well as the belly and the knee muscles.
Technique: From a standing position with our legs apart and our hands stretched forward, we bend the torso towards the left, until the right hand touches the left toes, while the left hand is still extended. The knees remain straight. We repeat this exercise by bending the torso toward the right, and we also combine it with breathing exercises (see the book *Kriya Yoga* by Nikolaos A. Margioris).

Trimurti: It is the Hindu Triad: Brahma the Creator (M), Vishnu the Preserver (A) and Shiva the Transformer (U). See AUM in glossary.

U

Udana Vayu: It is a vayu situated at the thyroid gland. It constitutes word and speech.

Uddiyana Bandha: The 'Abdominal Lock' or the 'Flight Contraction'. It is an advanced technique of Yoga Upanishads aiming to elevate Kundalini. It took its name from the ancient Tantric Uddiyana kingdom, in Orissa (East India). The person who exercises it, contracts the stomach muscles, creating a void in the abdomen and the bladder.

Udos: It is the landing or the threshold or the connector or the bridge. Udos is an etheric organ of incredible value that when it doesn't function, man remains a foreigner to the etheric as well as to the physical events - phenomena. It is located on the forehead between the two eyebrows and its mission is to unite the two cerebrums of man (the two frontal lobes): the etheric with the physical cerebrum. Udos is a moving bridge or, otherwise, a rotating axis. This axis or bridge has four extremes, that is, it forms a tetractys. The left axis (horizontal) uses the left lobe and scans the details of our physical world, traversing it from one end to the other (it gives us hypervision). The right axis (horizontal) is higher, it uses the frontal right lobe and scans the etheric world (it conveys us the birth of phenomena). The upper axis brings messages from the spirit to the soul while the lower axis gives the secret revelations of our soul to the brain.

These two axes, the upper and the lower, form Insight. And the horizontal axes, the right and the left, give us Far-sight.

Ujjayi: 'The Victorious'. The word 'U' means high ground, to elevate and jjayi means a strong greeting. It is an exercise during which a characteristic sound is emitted. This exercise is accompanied by proper breathing and inhaling and holding breath. It has therapeutic effects for malaria, asthma, sinuses and so on. Also, it is a strong stimulus for Kundalini.

Upanishad: It is estimated that the Upanishads were written between 1000 BC and 300 AD. The word 'Upanishad' means 'by the Master's feet' or 'to sit devoutly by the Master'. As Upanishads complete and constitute the end of each of the four Vedas, they are called Vedanta, that is, the end (anta) of Vedas.
Nowadays, 108 Upanishads are intact, of which the hermit Shankara considers that at least 16 are indisputably true.
Upanishads deal with the esoteric conception of Truth, of Creation and of Beings, as well as the means by which a seeker or student can approach Enlightenment and Liberation, while living. They are also called Tantra Yoga or Sahaja Yoga, which is the interpretation-teaching and a clearly practical presentation of Upanishads by the Master or by the Instructor and concerns the preparation and the means that the student must bear in mind and must practise in order to awaken the Spiritual Power within him, Kundalini.
Among them are: instruction in Ekagrata, in Manolaya, in Mudras and in Bandhas and certainly, in the esoteric Kumbhaka, in holding air in (technical pranayama). All these must be performed with the continual and strict su-

pervision of the Mind, during their execution, always according to a Master's specific directions and suggestions.
Some of the most important Upanishads are: Yogatattva, Dhyana-bindu, Yogakundalini, Ksurika, Hamsa, Amritanada, Amritabindu, Mahavakya, Isa, Kena, Katha, Prasna, Mundaka, Mandukya, Taittiriya, Aitareya, Chandogya, Brihadaranyaka, Kaivalya, Svetasvatara.

Upasta: Reproduction.

Ushtrasana: The Camel Pose. It combats obesity, arthritis in the feet and hands and throat diseases.
Technique: From the prone position (face down), we bend the knees and bring our legs back till they touch the back. At the same time, our hands hold the soles and they press them backwards, as the head is raised from the ground. It is combined with breathing exercises (see the book *Kriya Yoga* by Nikolaos A. Margioris).

Utkatasana: The Chair Pose. It cures lumbago, strengthens the legs, the diaphragm and the belly muscles.
Technique: From the standing position, we bend the knees into a sitting position while we hold our waist with our hands and we keep our torso straight. Then, we stretch, rise or stretch our arms forward. Then, we return to the standing position. Then, during the second sitting, we slightly bend the torso forward, forming an obtuse angle, our hands on our waist. The exercise is combined with the appropriate breathing exercises (see the book *Kriya Yoga* by Nikolaos A. Margioris).

Uttama: A superior type of pranayama (rhythmical breathing) whereby inhalation lasts for 32", retention of breath for 128" and exhalation for 64". The two previous pranayama forms are Adhama and Madyama. (The presence and the guidance of an expert /instructor in esotericism (see glossary) is considered essential for the safe practise of pranayama and Yoga, in general.

Uttara Mimamsa: See *Vedanta* in glossary.

Utthita Pavanamuktasana: An exercise related to Pavanamuktasana, but with some complementary therapeutic qualities. It cures the tremors of old age (Parkinson), the hypertension that helps depression, abdominal bloating and chronic diseases.
Technique: From a standing position, we lift and bend our right leg, until our knee touches the edge of our raised head, while our hands hug the shins right below the knee. We repeat this with the other leg and we combine it with breathing exercises. (See the book *Kriya Yoga* by Nikolaos A. Margioris).

V

Vacashari: A great Indian Philosopher and Master of Yoga who, in the 9th century AD, filled the 'void' that the Father of Yoga, Patanjali, left.

Vaibasikas or Sarvastivadins: It refers to one of the 6 non-orthodox (non- Vedic) Indian philosophical systems (darsanas). It is Buddhi realism that was developed in the 3rd century BC. The principal text of this school is the Jnana Prasanna (systematization of knowledge).

Vairagya: Renunciation - Detachment.

Vaisheshika: The name Vaisheshika comes from the word Vishesa meaning 'peculiarity' in Greek. It is the second of the six orthodox philosophical systems (darsanas) of India that forms a pair with the Nyaya system. It is attributed to Kanada, who lived in the 3rd century BC, and is mainly occupied with cosmological problems. A later philosopher, Radhakrisnan, believes that Vaisheshika is more ancient even than Nyaya.

Vaisheshika together with Nyaya constitute the first pair of the Orthodox Indian Philosophy. It is written in Sutra Kanada and is composed of ten books. The first book examines the categories of substance, the second one the substances themselves apart from the soul, the third one the objects of the sensations, the fourth one the individual, the fifth one nature, the sixth one morality, the seventh one the categories of the ego while the last three deal with logical problems.

The six categories or parts of Vaisheshika are: 1) Substance (Dravya), 2) Quality (Guna), 3) Action - Obligation (Karma), 4) Race (Samanya), 5) Kind (Vivesa), 6) Relationship between Substance and qualities (Samavaya). Respectively, a 7th category is added (or a 6th if Substance is not considered a category): Abhava, non-existence, while Bhava is the total of the categories, the total of existence.

Vajrasana: The Diamond Pose. The perfect position. It cures stomach and intestinal disorders. It heals arthritis of the feet and rheumatism.

Technique: From the kneeling position, seated on our heels, we keep our torso straight and we place our palms on our knees. From this position, we lean our torso forward and backwards, our hands at the waist, in combination with breathing exercises (see the books *Hatha Yoga* and *Kriya Yoga* by Nikolaos A. Margioris).

Vajroli Mudra: 'The Thunderbolt Mudra.' According to Vajroli Mudra, an initiated couple has sexual intercourse, but without allowing either partner to reach the physical orgasm. On the contrary, the man as well as the woman holds the life seed, as the greatest possible training in self-discipline - self-control and mainly for higher-more spiritual aims concerning one of the non-orthodox ways of using the stored-up treasures of energy within us (Kundalini).

Vakrasana: An exercise that helps correct slumped shoulders and a flabby stomach.
Technique: Seated on the ground, we extend the legs forward and we keep the spine straight. Then, we raise the hands placing them forward parallel to the legs. From this position, we turn the torso slowly to the right and then to the left. Always in combination with certain breathing exercises (see the book *Kriya Yoga* by Nikolaos A. Margioris).

Vatsalya Bhava: It is one of the numerous relationships that a Bhakti can develop with his God. It is the relationship of fondness and tenderness of a parent to his child.

Vayu: Etheric winds. They are etheric vibrations (winds - prana states) of little pranic processes occupying different parts of our body and supervising certain functions of our organism. For the homovibration of vayus we practise pranayama. The first Vayu set of five is: Prana, Apana, Samana, Udana, Vyana. The second Vayu set of five is the following: Naga, Kurma, Krikara, Devadatta and Dhananjaya (see respective words in Glossary).

Veda or Vedas: They are the oldest and the most important texts that constitute the foundations of Hinduism. The term Veda has two meanings. The first and most narrow meaning refers to four religious works: Rig Veda, Atharva Veda, Sama Veda and Yajur Veda. These four Vedas are also called Samhitas, that is, a collection of hymns (mantras). In the second and broader meaning, the term Veda contains the total of the holy texts that are characterized as Sruti, that is, as revealed truths. In this sense, the Brahmanas, Aranyakas and Upanishads belong to the Vedas. The term Veda means knowledge, science. Etymologically, it is related to the Latin *video*: see.

Vedanta or Brahma Sutras or Uttara Mimamsa: It means the end of the Vedas. It is one (the sixth) of the 6 orthodox philosophical systems of Hinduism and forms a pair with the 5th philosophical system of Hinduism. It is also called Uttara Mimamsa because it deals with the Upanishads, that is, the last part of the Vedas. Finally, it deals with the Bhagavad Gita. The codification of the Brahma Sutras is attributed to Vyasa who lived between 500 BC - 300 AD. In contrast, the 5th philosophical system dealing with the first part of the Vedas is called Purva Mimamsa or Karma Mimamsa.

The Brahma Sutra has four chapters, each of which has four parts: the first one focuses on the Brahmanas, with their relationship to the ego and the exterior world and tries to reconcile the opposites which appear in the Upanishads. The second part refutes the arguments against the Upanishad beliefs concerning hermitism. The third part refers to the methods of attaining the supreme Knowledge of the Brahman and the fourth part is devoted to the outcome resulting from the attainment of the Knowledge of freedom.

Radhakrishnan says that the Brahma Sutra is to the Upanishads what the works of the Church Apostles are to the Gospel.

The basic Schools - Disciplines constituting the basis of

Vedanta Philosophy are three: The Dualist school (Dvaita) comes first, the second is the school of the Relative non-Dualism (Visistadvaita) and the third is the school of the Absolute non-Dualism or Oneness (Advaita).

Viasti: The partial, the little. Its opposite is Samasti.

Vibhuti: Supernatural powers. They are also called Siddhis.

Vidya: Correct Knowledge. The perception of Esoteric Truth as conveyed by the people who managed to experience it through transcendental conceptions and to transmit it in natural words and symbols so as to make it as intelligible as possible to every person.

Vijnanamaya Kosha: The sheath of the Intellect (Buddhi). It is the controller, the supervisor of our existence.

Vishnu: The Preserver (A). It is the second person of the Hindu Triad (AUM).

Vishuddha Chakra: It is the center of the throat and corresponds to the Thyroid Gland (Mantra Yoga). The color or prana introduced from Sutratma is light rose while the color coming from Antahkarana is phosphoric violet. It belongs to the 5th ray (Creativeness), to the Intellectual; it has 16 petals and is connected with hearing and ether. It has 144 third chakras – third stations - satellites in its authority.

Visistadvaita: Relative non-Dualism. School of the Vedantic philosophy (Vedanta) established by Ramanuja. In relative non-dualism, Creation came from God and God is found in it and is expressed through every formed and amorphous presence. Consequently, God is not outworldly but inworldly; with the difference that Brahman has two forms, Jiva and Matter. That is, it is worshiped as a God without any form, but with qualities.

Vitarka: Question.

Viveka: Distinction.

Vivekananda- formerly Narendranath Datta or diminutively Naren or even Kamalaksa which means 'with the eyes of a lotus': The authentic representative of all Yoga and of Indian (Dravidian, see glossary Dravidians) Esoteric Philosophy in the West. He is the greatest student of Ramakrishna, of the last Saint of India and the first one who made Yoga and the Philosophical systems that accompany it broadly known, popularizing it with the indisputable authority of his personality and with his supreme spiritual accomplishments: his participation in the World Congress of Religions in Chicago on February 1, 1893; hundreds of open speeches-lectures; courses to groups of students; the authorship of books. He was born in 1862 and died in 1902. He lived for only 40 years but his presence left an indelible mark of his passage through this world, with his immense spiritual-superhuman work and legacy that he left for every interested person-seeker-student (see his books *Raja*, *Karma*, *Bhakti*, with explanatory comments on the aphorisms of Patanjali, Divrys editions 1983 and Konidaris editions 1991, as well as *Jnana*, Konidaris editions 1981. Also, *Ramakrishna, the Demigod*, *Vivekananda, the Sage* by Romain Rolland, Divrys editions, Athens 1978, *Mystical Teachings*, 3rd Volume by Nikolaos A. Margioris and so on).

Vrittis: They are the intellectual waves - thoughts - stimuli - modifications that take place in our Mind continually. They are the result of either impressions - stimuli (samskara) conveyed by the activity of our five senses, or by the emergence of repressed personal thoughts in the thirteen channels of instincts we all have within us.

Vyana Vayu: It is one of the Vayus which functions and is activated as omnipotent, strengthening and helping all the other winds (vayu) for the function of the whole organism.

Vyasa: The organizer of the Vedas, the one considered to be the writer of Mahabharata and of the Brahma Sutras (Vedanta Sutras) and Sukadeva's father. Also, he was most probably Patanjali's Master who authorized him to write the Yoga Sutra (Raja Yoga).

Y

Yajur Veda: It is the fourth Veda containing the suitable psalms to be whispered during sacred ceremonies. In other words, it is the guide which states the actions a priest must perform and the words they must utter during the sacred ceremonies. The religion resulting from Yajur Veda is purely ritualistic. It is not characterized by any esotericity. Every prayer is combined with a ritual and aims to secure material benefits.

Yama: God of Death. Yama is also the first step of Raja Yoga and means Temperance and in extension 'death'. Yama has the significance of the death of many habits and tendencies we had in the past. That is, abstinence from every negativity and the dissolution of every ignorance that possessed us.

Yama contains five commandments or abstinences or restrictions: a) Avoiding presents (Aparigraha), b) Purity in everything (Brahmacarya), c) No envy and no theft (Asteya), d) Honesty (Satya) and e) Non-violence (Ahimsa).

Yantra: Yantra is the simplest Mandala used by Hinduism. Literally, Yantra is the object that holds/contains (tool, netting). It is a diagram we paint or we engrave on metal, wood, leather, stone, paper or that we just form on the ground or engrave on a wall.

Yoga: The word Yoga means 'joining-union'. This union defines the apogee of possibility within everyone, who, with the help of and training in Yoga, can bring his Mind and his Consciousness into direct contact and communion with his Hyper Mind, with his Hyper-Consciousness and to discuss-converse, be united with his own soul, his spirit and God (Perfection), who constitutes an inseparable part of his being.

In its esoteric etymology, the word Yoga may be freely translated as follows: 'The soul lives in eternity.' It is composed of three united words: the word *Yi* meaning *'life'*, the word *Oy* meaning 'this life goes through and exists in the Divine' and the word KA meaning 'soul'. Therefore, the three-syllable word Yoga means 'the soul lives its life, whether it wants to or not, within the Divine Being'.

The following are the accepted kinds of Yoga: Hatha Yoga, Kriya Yoga, Mantra Yoga, Laya Yoga, Tantra Yoga (Kundalini Yoga), Karma Yoga, Bhakti Yoga, Sambt or Logo Yoga, Jnani Yoga, Raja Yoga (see words in glossary). Yoga is not a religion; on the contrary, it is the fourth orthodox Indian (Dravidian) philosophical system (darsana) that forms a pair with the third system of Samkhya. On the other hand, it is not something ascetic or something that keeps us away from life and from action. On the contrary, it gives us the possibility to activate and to maximize the latent potential existing within us and to participate more responsibly, fully and actively, with more to contribute, in society. Also, it is by no means foreign to us - as many will have us believe - but as we shall see below, it is the Knowledge-Science of our ancestors, the Dravidians.

Therefore, Yoga is a very ancient practical Scientific method that concerns the health and the harmonious relationship between the body and the Mind, so that man may be able to realize and penetrate and control the deepest strata of Himself. That is, it is a completed method of self-therapy and of self-knowledge at the height of which the capable beings can touch the superior operations of their Mind (hyper-conscious) and form their own immediate experience of Truth (Mystic Actualization).

Briefly, training in Yoga is based on the internal moral development of man, with poses that are suitable for the balance and the correct operation of every part-limb of our body, using rigorously studied methods of rhythmical breathing techniques that have therapeutic and energizing value for our organism; techniques that teach us how to relax, how to detoxify our organism of every physical or intellectual burden. We learn how to concentrate, so that we may be able to direct our thoughts to any problem, matter, issue or anything else that occupies us at will, with ease and effectively. Meditation is the maintenance and focus of our thoughts on a specific object for long periods of time and the identification-union with the specific object that creates the transcendence of our known nature and, for the first time, the acknowledgement on our part of the Invisible Creation and of the Communion with the Divine Spark within us.

The roots, the origin and the antiquity of Yoga emanate from our ancestors, the fore-Greeks of the Aegean Sea, who were called Dravidians (see glossary). It is an antediluvian Science, invented thousands of years ago by the Dravidians (our direct ancestors, the inhabitants of Hinterland, the Mediterranean district covering the coasts of Asia Minor, of Greece and of North Egypt). Their surviving descendants formed the Greek Civilization while others went to seek a new country and ended up in the Indian Valley, where they created two huge cities, Mohenjo Daro and El Harrapa. There, they spread their spiritual enlightenment, as well as Yoga Science. This people together with other races such as the Arians who descended later, gradually merged with the native Dravidians and created the Indian Civilization.

Nowadays, it is believed that Yoga came from the East, but in fact, it is a product of our ancestors, the Dravidians. Unfortunately, we are oblivious to its quality as a practical art as well as the fact that it is a product of our own invention, despite all the recent archaeological discoveries and proof that confirm this fact, as well as the official reports of foreign and Greek archaeologists and scientists. See the books: *Dravidians, the Ancestors of the Greeks; The Reign of Minos, the Great King of Crete; The Two-Volume Metaphysical Encyclopaedia; Omakoio Journal;* Essay: *The Dravidians, the First Greeks of the Aegean Sea; Mystical Teachings, 3rd Volume* and so on, by Nikolaos A. Margioris.

Yogacara - Vijnanavada: One of the 6 non-orthodox (non-Vedic) Indian philosophical systems (darsanas). The school of Yogacara - Vijnanavada (4th - 5th century BC) means absolute idealism. Men can attain Buddha's absolute truth only through Yoga. The founders of this school are the two brothers: a) Asanga, writer of the book Yogacara Bhumi Sastra (steps of Yoga teaching) and Mahayana Sambarigraha (Mahayana manual), b) Vasubandhu, considered to be the writer of 27 works, the most principal of which are Abhidharma-kosa (Feast of Supreme Truth) and Vijnaprimatrata - Trimsika (A thirty-stanza essay on the world as a simple representation).

In Yogacara – Vijnanavada, a person's thought is the only reality and if it disappears, nothing remains. Yogacara results in identifying thought with God.

Yogakundalini Upanishad: The Snake Power (Kundalini). The Yogakundalini Upanishad includes exercises for the awakening of Kundalini such as the following: Ujjayi, Sitali, Bhastrika, Mula Bandha, Jalandhara Bandha and so on.

Yoga Mudra: Yoga that seals the yogi's face. It is combined with pranayama and asana. This exercise cures headaches, helps digestion and strengthens the waist muscles. It is not recommended for those who have a weak heart.

Technique: From the Lotus pose (padmasana) or, for greater ease, from the simple pose (Sukhasana), with our hands interlocked behind our back, we lean forward, trying to touch our left knee, then the right knee and then center forward (the floor) with our forehead. It is combined with the appropriate breathing exercises (see the book *Kriya Yoga* by Nikolaos A. Margioris).

Yogananda: An Indian Master of Kriya Yoga who brought it to the West. He was indirectly a student of Lahiri Mahasaya (Lahiri was the student of Master Babaji of the Eternal Wisdom). Also, Yogananda was a Swami and Vivekananda's student. He wrote the book *A Yogi's Autobiography* in which he describes the path of his personal search and actualization, his main guide being Kriya Yoga, a lost science that until recently, had completely vanished. It was Greek

Master Nikolaos A. Margioris who brought it back to life, teaching it to his students and writing the book *Kriya Yoga - A Practical Method of Psychosomatic Therapy*. In this book, he presents the first full and extensive public analysis of true Kriya Yoga which includes a comprehensive guide on how to apply it. The book *A Yogi's Autobiography* was translated into Greek by Ioannis Vorres, former mayor of Amaroussion. Master Nikolaos A. Margioris assisted him with the translation - interpretation of the Sanskrit and metaphysical terms into Greek.

Yoga Sutra: The aphorisms of Maha Yoga, the codified Raja Yoga by Patanjali. They are the salvaged contents of a non-existing book.

Yogatattva Upanishad: The true nature of Yoga. The Yogatattva Upanishad presents us with the 8 steps of Raja Yoga, the preparations that are indispensable in relation to the appropriate venue we use, the diet we follow, the arithmetical limits of pranayama for the gradual awakening of Kundalini, the 'Phenomena' and the 'Powers' we shall encounter in our organism and in our Mind, as we approach these limits. Also, the different Mantras corresponding to analogous chakras, as well as the Seals (Mudras) and Body Locks or contractions (Bandhas), such as Jalandhara Bandha, Kechari Mudra, Uddiyana Bandha, Mula Bandha, and so on.

Yogi: A Yoga student.

Yogini: A female Yoga student.

Yoni: The female genitals (uterus).

Yoni Mudra: The Uterus Lock Yoni (uterus - source) means the whole genital area and mudra is the seal. It is a yogic technique where all the sensory openings 'are closed' with the fingers, so that they stop the outward bound emission of Prana, that weakens man, through the unbridled and aimless scattering of the internal Life Force, driving him to physical and mental enfeeblement (diseases). An effort is made to seal the basic sensory channels and to cut the exit of energy flowing outwards and to gradually return it inwards.

Yuga-s: Cosmic Circles or Seasons. There are four similar seasons or circles: a) the Satya or Krita Yuga or the Golden Era (lasting 4,800 Divine years or 1,728, 000 earthly years), b) the Treta Yuga or the Silver Era (lasting 3,600 Divine years or 1,296,000 earthly years, c) the Dvapara Yuga or the Copper Era (lasting 2,400 Divine years or 864,000 earthly years) and d) the Kali Yuga or the Iron Era or the Black or Dark Era (lasting 1,200 Divine years or 432,000 earthly years). So, we have 4,800 + 3,600 + 2,400 + 1,200 = 12,000 Divine years and respectively 1,728,000 + 1,296,000 + 864,000 + 432,000 = 4,320,000 earthly years. The four seasons together give us a Maha Yuga or Manvantara (a long century), corresponding to twelve thousand Divine years. One Divine year is three hundred and sixty human years (360 earthly years). Consequently, the 12,000 Divine years are equivalent to 4,320,000 human years. One thousand Maha Yugas (12,000,000 Divine years) correspond to 4,320,000 human years and are one day of Brahman (Creator). Two thousand Maha Yugas (24,000,000 Divine years) correspond to 8,640,000,000 years and give us a Kalpa, meaning one day and one night of Brahman or one hundred Divine years. Consequently, Brahma's life or a Brahman's season or one hundred Divine years correspond to 311,040,000,000,000 earthly years.

Now, we are at the dawn of Kali Yuga that started on February 18th, in 3102 BC when Avatar Krishna died. However, in reality, Kali Yuga will not begin before 2899 AD

Yukta: Horses.

PART FOUR

DROPS OF WISDOM

PREFACE

The Drops of Wisdom constitute some passages and gleanings of various books by Master Nikolaos A. Margioris.

They contain the Eternal Truths, many pieces of important information, findings and new revelations, guidance, advice and encouragement that result from his deep Mystic Knowledge and Experience and are examples of his particular Unifying Vibration as well as of the kind and the quality of the works he has left as a legacy for anyone who really wants to discover the most appropriate way of penetrating his internal Being, the Esoteric Reality.

DROPS OF WISDOM
From various books by Master Nikolaos A. Margioris

"Without any personal freedom concerning the existence of God, Religious Faith is a ritualism, without any value or substance."
Three-dimensional and Four-dimensional World,
page 177.

"Every intellectual success is a new mistake of the Mind, which replaces the proven falsehoods of the past, with supposedly ascertained truths of our times."
Three-dimensional and Four-dimensionalWorld,
page 199.

"Mysticism is the headlight of Religion and the salvation of the Church. Where there is no Mysticism, there is ritualism and idolatry. Mysticism is the one and only path toward encountering the Holy Ghost.

Jesus Christ was the first Master of this path, of man's encounter with the Holy Ghost. I shall send you the Spirit of Truth, the Helper, who will help you on the return journey. Where Christ is, the Spirit is. Where the Spirit is, there is a Mystic. Where there is a Mystic, there is the presence of God-Christ."
Mysticism, page 317.

"Mystics are very well aware that their fellow-men are not ready to enter the high spiritual vibrations of God, The Essence of the Father, the spiritual transmission of thoughts, ideas and the will of God. For this reason, they recommend that the unprepared take the path toward the church, where they will find the future mystic life they will lead."
Mysticism, page 277.

"Allow Mysticism to become freely widespread and help it, because it is the only way for all of humanity to return to piety, to morality, to spiritual (Intellectual) health and to the peaceful co-existence of all the peoples of the human race."
Mysticism, page 73.

"Heresies are created and appear in Dogmas, in rituals, in the various interpretations, in the rhetoric and exoteric manifestations of Piety. In true Mysticism, all of these do not exist nor can they occur or take place because there is only One path and it needs FAITH in God and the WORSHIP of God and TRUE PERFECTION TO THE... FAITHFUL... Here, the words of the ritualism become weak and the holocaust of the EGO prevails through SACRIFICE."
Mysticism, page 259.

"Between Christian and Hindu Mysticism, there is a difference in the way the spirit-soul is released from its prison, which is the physical body of man. As strange as it may appear to you, it is so. Hindu Mysticism moves through the same body and encounters its spirit-soul somewhere in its abyssal depths and his disciple enters in shrunken form and...is united with the invisible and immortal reality, the BRAHMAN-SPIRIT OF GOD...

In contrast, in Christian Mysticism, the spirit-soul leaves

the body and travels high and is directed wherever the Lord's Divine House opens its barred doors to receive the prodigal and repentant son who has returned.

Of course, both paths will lead to the Lord's Gnophos. For both paths have the Eternal Father as their sole purpose... He, who is awaiting the arrival of His children."

Mysticism, page 290.

"What prevents man from finding Truth? It is the lack of a HEALTHY AND ENLIGHTENED MIND. Then, why does everybody bring forth the argument of the soul? Because they do not know the exact truth."

Mysticism, page 320.

"No system, no Religion and no Philosophy has the right nor the authority nor the strength nor the ability to impose on the human soul which path to follow in order to meet and unite with its Father in the heavens. Only the soul itself can guide its own being, its own vibration, its own direction and revel in the embrace of the Father.

It is quite funny and even absurd for others to want, under different pretexts, to direct the soul to places it does not wish to go and which it does not seek. Besides, above all, there is the steadfast beckoning of the Lord, who, with His Divine Grace, enabled the Soul to turn to the Spirit and the Eternal Source in order to find the reward it deserves.

The human laws, which in appearance only represent the will of God, are wrong to wish to steer the souls with their dogmatic dictates towards imaginary paths that are foreign to absolute reality, which is the permanent connection between God-man, the spirit-soul and the Holy Ghost.

When man is summoned, when he is called to HIS DESTINATION, when the mortal human being receives his message, then he rejects the temporary and without questioning anything, he walks toward this calling, guided by the Holy Ghost in accordance with the plans of our True Father and God and Benefactor."

Mysticism, page 49.

"Faith, due to external and intellectual necessity, will ultimately become KNOWLEDGE, which is naturally destined to lead to the communion between man and God. Concerning faith, Religion and the Church fulfill their holy duty. However, when it concerns KNOWLEDGE, it is Mysticism that undertakes to help the soul and to lead it to the Holy Ghost, where the communion of man and God is the outcome."

Mysticism, page 51.

"The power of Sacrifice surpasses the power of Love and the power of Justice."

The Birth and Death of the Worlds, page 21.

"A common misconception is that the soul is bad. The soul is by nature perfect and can be defined only as experienced or inexperienced, in our physical world."

The Last Day of Socrates, page 55.

"This is where we see modern man's inability to ascend the supersubstantial chambers of transcendence. The human race has degenerated. It allowed the line between the conscious-subconscious to close. Extroversion won the battle. Day by day, man is becoming more foreign because of the great speed with which he is distancing himself from the stars in space... He will lose all his qualities as a superior

animal. His so-called cold logic is nothing more than his identification with the exterior objects, with matter."
Kriya Yoga, page 344.

"The appropriate souls come and continually visit us and offer us their true teachings. In every generation and in every epoch, the guides, masters, prophets, leaders, saints and true saviors of the soul are incarnated. They again give us the lost method and show us how to pass the impassable path of actualization. What is actualization? It is the function of our Mind through another separate channel (vibration) besides our logic (the conscious) and the subconscious."
Kriya Yoga, page 346.

"What exactly does the strange word INITIATION mean? In Greek it derives from the word "μύηση" (myeses) which means to close. To close the senses to the world of sensible things where I am and where I belong. But I open another kind of sensitivity for the hypersensible higher world. Undoubtedly, our ancestors knew and studied this Hyperconsciousness of the conscious elevation to higher matter-frequencies-vibrations. Everything confirms that Socrates' Platonic THOUGHT was the use of the hyperconscious experience."
Raja Yoga, page 21.

"I mentioned above that each of these systems serves a particular period and a Root Race. So, I consider it necessary to reveal to you that in our times, Great Yoga, Maha Yoga or Raja Yoga has the upper hand and prevails over all her other Yoga sisters. When I say 'our times' I mean a period that began five hundred years ago and that will need about another one thousand five hundred years to reach its destination.

In Esotericism, we know that the present period is the Great Period of Great Yoga, that is, of Raja Yoga. These words are not only mine. Alice Bailey in *The Light of the Soul* presents us with the holy revelations of her Master, Djwal Khul. Vivekananda, the well-known student of India's last saint, Ramakrishna, and the great Yogi philosopher expresses, or rather emphasizes, the same thing in his unforgettable speeches."

Raja Yoga, page 38.

"Guided by the Light of Actualization, I ask my reader but also my student to reject whatever he does not personally experience, following a special training program in the wise Raja Yoga system of ascension to hyperconsciousness. One more piece of advice: The seeker should not proceed with his ascension to Hyperconsciousness by himself, without the guidance of a master."

Raja Yoga, page 16.

"In order for a student to dare to say that he has mastered the whole of Yoga (RAJA YOGA), he must definitely know how to tear away the blinders that permanently separate the Mind from the Supermind. If a student simply dabbles in the theory and philosophy, as unfortunately happens in our times, one does not succeed in rupturing the crystal ring surrounding hyperconsciousness or the Supermind."

Raja Yoga, page 29.

"All the suffering and all the hardships of every man and of every time, have as their basis and their cause this felonious concealment of our inner Self from the untrained and the vain outer ego."

Raja Yoga, page 38.

"Every idea of the Supreme Mind, after emerging from its Subjectivity and entering the Mind's Objectivity, is directed and stored in the Eternal Treasury - Archives and it becomes a matrix, a principle, an idea from which at one point in time in the Universe, it will be reproduced, it will become a creation, a Being, a new Universe, a Soul."
Light in the Dark, page 387.

"All the miracles on Earth have been created by the hyper-sensitive beings who possess a different kind of knowledge - information and create the musical compositions of Divine Harmonies (Beethoven), the color representations from the inexhaustible wealth of hues of the internal worlds (Michelangelo and El Greco), the sculpted depictions of Divine figures and other representations of harmony and achievements of beauty (Phidias), and finally, the eternal word, the expression and dissemination of revelatory wisdom (Plato)."
The Other View of Erich Von Daniken's Dogma, page 18.

"With only one simple and humble phrase, holy Mysticism announces this Esoteric PRINCIPLE of the whole of esoteric philosophy. What we call YOU does not and never did exist, nor does this false EGO exist.

YOU and EGO were always the ONE. WE and YOU, along with all the formed and unformed, never stopped being the ONE AND ONLY. From the very beginning, we were and still are the visible and the invisible, subjectively and objectively, beyond our past thoughts, ALL ONE and all together, we constituted and now here constitute the UNIFIED ONE.

Our so-called INDIVIDUALISM constitutes, according to the Mystics of all the centuries, the world famous DESCENT."
The Other View of Erich Von Daniken's Dogma, page 69.

"One of these is the Egyptian SPHINX which with its sculpted symbolism, gives us the required theorem concerning the immortality of the soul and the formation of the worlds. This construction was ancient, even before the first Egyptians appeared. It is a monument of the second to last civilization of the Atlanteans, a construction of the first period that was erected about 25.000 years ago, before the appearance and the submersion of Atlanteans on the continent of Atlantis, even before the second cataclysm-submersion in which the legendary hyperisland Posidonia, the last breath and existence of the Atlanteans disappeared."
The Other View of Erich Von Daniken's Dogma,
page 99.

"Perhaps while living as TERRESTRIAL BEINGS, we simultaneously live in the outer universes as EXTRA-TERRESTRIAL BEINGS all the while existing as HYPER-TERRESTRIAL BEINGS.

Do we perhaps exist as THREE-SUBSTANTIAL BEINGS? In my opinion, that's probably what we are.

From ancient revelations, we have learned much about it.

Thrice-Greatest Hermes, Osiris, Isis, Horus, the Hindu Triad Brahma = Creator, Vishnu = Preserver, Shiva = Catalyst, as well as the Christian Trinity, that is the Father, the Son and the Holy Spirit.

Perhaps, the body is on Earth. The soul itself is for the endless systems of the formed world and our Sacred and Holy Spirit is for our Esoteric Dimensions that are hidden from the world.

Therefore, we are TERRESTRIAL, EXTRA-TERRESTRIAL, HYPER-TERRESTRIAL BEINGS."
The Other View of Erich Von Daniken's Dogma,
page 260.

"It seems that the Order of the Seraphim, these angelic enlightened orders headed by Michael the Brigadier, know this science. They alone, I say, know this science, how to use this Power for their individual-materialization in the lower depths of the Esoteric Universes and here, on our three-dimensional existence."
The Other View of Erich Von Daniken's Dogma, page 346.

"This complementary text about the great work of Saint Patapios was both necessary and at the same time imposed upon me, his biographer, since for sixteen continual years I was near him trying to coordinate myself with him, grasping the great thoughts he left for humanity in its quest for perfection.

All this was based on my perceptiveness and were drawn from the etheric archives that were once registered, when the venerable figure of Saint Patapios existed in our physical world. I got the details of the Saint's works from these eternal etheric archives, and I express them here in the extroverted dialect, as I was inspired to."
Patapios, the Humble Philosopher and Saint from Egypt, pages 14-15.

"Saint Patapios was a religious Mystic. You should not consider this fact strange. There are mystics or otherwise ascended and enlightened men whose aim is to help some Religion. Every Religion has as the objective purpose to provide the soul with SPIRITUAL FOOD, to help man and particularly the man-mind to turn towards the spirit-mind and to instruct him on the problem of the phenomenon of death."
Patapios, the Humble Philosopher and Saint from Egypt, page 139.

"This knowledge of man's victory over the natural elements was called MAGIC and its workers were called MAGICIANS. Magic or the science of the wise-magicians constituted man's hyperscience on Earth during its times. For thousands of years, the entire East, from Greece and its islands to India and Egypt, was lucky enough to be served by the true Magic.

Some antediluvian and postdiluvian civilizations such as the Dravidians – the Hinterlanders, the Atlanteans, the Lemurians, the Antarktians and other unrevealed civilizations used and benefitted from Magic, the hyperconsciousness of their times."

White Magic, page 9.

"White Magic is the awakening and the use of all man's moral powers and the fight against the bad instincts and all the black thoughts and actions of himself and of his fellowmen. White Magic is the sowing and the use of the goods and holy ideas so that after a while, the crop of brilliant results may be harvested, results that were made and came from the initial sowing of White Magic."

White Magic, page 13.

"Because every esoteric law is the radiation of God, THE VIBRATION OF HIS SPIRIT, HIS THROBBING HEART, HIS DIVINE MIND emitting the absolute Perfection accompanying HIS LOVE."

Occultismology-Volume A, page 24.

"The first Karma, the first obligation has already been realized. How is this falling Karmic obligation paid for? It is paid for with death and with the rendering to matter-nature of all the elements received by the spirit-soul, for the construction of its physical body. That is how the Omni-universal Karmic Law operates."

Karma - The Law of Retributive Justice,
page 38.

"Only the blessed beings suffused with Substance, Manas, as we call it in Esotericism, are subject to Karma. This happens because only through Karma can every spirit-soul achieve the liberation and the release from the world of form.

For this reason, three seeds accompany the spirit-soul to the worlds of form:

A) The seed of Reincarnation.
b) The seed of Free Will.
c) The seed of Karmic Retributive Justice...

Karma - The Law of Retributive Justice,
page 43.

"Karma is not only limited to humanity. It is found in the whole of Omnicreation and constitutes the cohesive and controlling power overlooking all ranks of vibrations and their objective purposes."

Karma - The Law of Retributive Justice,
pages 53-54.

"As far as my experiences allow me to know, both occur: The Law of Retributive Justice and the reaction of matter compete and naturally rival each other. The Law has the soul of man as its eternal tool. Matter has the Mind of man as its faithful tool. The Mind and the Soul. Matter and Spirit. Everything takes place between the two poles and Karma is formed in this way."

Karma - The Law of Retributive Justice,
page 95.

"When Karma comes as a friend, it is your enemy and when it approaches you as an enemy, it is your friend. This paradox for human logic is the full and true Karmic image. It refers to the counterbalancing power that man has within him. When this power is increased, his spirituality - goodness is reduced. When this counterbalancing power is reduced, then his spirituality is increased."

Karma - The Law of Retributive Justice, page. 134.

"So, what is Karma? It is man's identity itself. It is his composed Being. It is the total of everything that formed his present character. This character was formed by the total of his actions, thoughts, words, infinite conclusions, the experiences he gathered and that constitute man's character at every moment."

Karma - The Law of Retributive Justice, page 163.

"The aim of Karma is to teach the spirit-soul about the results of opposites, which will consequently lead to man knowing about the results of the pulses (vibrations) in matter. Then, the carving of matter will follow, as will the planing, the smoothing out by the spirit-soul in order to produce its reaction, the existing Eternal Knowledge hidden within it that when applied-followed in the physical life, will render the mortal being immortal and the unwise wise."

Karma - The Law of Retributive Justice, page 138.

"So, how is it possible to avoid it? For this reason, man must be active, without having the result of his labor as his main aim. Whatever man does, he does it for the sake of

His Heavenly Father and not for the sake of his individual interests and of his own purposeless and vain satisfaction..."
Karma - The Law of Retributive Justice,
page 218.

"The training will be undertaken by seven root races. By seven subraces. By seven nations. By seven states. By seven collective groups. By a composite of subraces and by seven reconnections after the disappearance of the main root race. It is $7 \times 7 = 49$ steps which every spirit-soul must take, from the fallen angels. Every race is obliged to form 49 different but mutually complementary huge educational Centers by which the spirit-souls of the main root race will have to pass through in order to receive the necessary instruction and to become liberated.

It is highly likely that a person will pass through a root race as a master. Let us now examine the racial schools: 1st race 49, 2nd race 49, 3rd race 49, 4th race 49, 5th race 49, 6th race 49 and 7th and last race 49. We have $7 \times 49 = 343$ earthly schools which the seven root races will form in the lower form world."
Karma - The Law of Retributive Justice,
page 224.

"We estimate that every race needs 50,000 to 60,000 years to spread the truth, for our fellow-men to reject matter and return to their previous state, as pure, Divine angels, as perfect DEVAS, released from even the smallest trace of inhibitive matter. We have seven root races, each one for 50,000 earthly years $7 \times 50,000 = 350,000$ years to half a million years, as there is always a delay in the application of the programs of the Divine Plan, due to the issue of matter. Finally, one million (1,000,000) years are needed so that the main root races may be able to work productively.

I should inform you that 1,000,000 (one million) years have passed since the animal man felt his first enlightenment, his self-knowledge, his mental reaction and realized that he is different from the other animals, since his Mind moved. The fallen angel's spirit-soul entered man and their mental and intellectual functions operated IMMEDIATELY.

However, as soon as we entered the fifth (5th) root race - two main root races still remain - which means, according to the most moderate calculations, that the time limits will be greatly multiplied so that the masters may be able to teach the spirit-souls and so that the fallen angels may be liberated again. These angels look like the bees that fell in their own thick honey, got stuck there, filled up their stomachs and cannot escape from their own product, which they themselves produced to nourish others. In the same way, our spirit-souls became lethally attached to matter and it is now too difficult for them to become detached."

Karma - The Law of Retributive Justice,
pages 224-225.

"The Divine Plan is delayed and the ascending evolution of the spirit-souls is also delayed. This means the fulfillment of Karma by the spirit-souls which continually form new Karma. This behaviour is exhibited for two reasons: They refuse to feel pain, to pay, to attribute, to reunite the separated and to harmonize what they have decomposed from their Free Will.

The second reason following the avoidance of pain is their illusion that in the world of forms, they will become more activated and will apply their free will with more ease. This, however, is not true. On the contrary, the freedom of our will here is limited by the three-dimensional conditions, since no activity can escape place, time and causality. It has more to do with the withdrawal of the spirit-souls from THEIR SELF-KNOWLEDGE and their administration by the manmind that is a perfect tool of Mother nature-matter."

Karma - The Law of Retributive Justice,
pages 225-226.

"Every man bears his Karma within him. This directs him and guides him every step of his life. Man may - provided he knows how, of course - accept, react accordingly to what happens every step of the way. There is neither joy in the agreeable things nor sorrow in the disagreeable things. In everything, there is moderation. There should be caution everywhere, a gauging, how much Karma comes out of the unpleasant and how much Karma comes out of the pleasant matters."

Karma - The Law of Retributive Justice,
page 303.

"Now, thoughts about Karma guide me to the subject of suicide, an act that has plagued humanity from the very beginning of its existence. The greatest sin, the greatest Karmic reaction is the act of suicide, the technical and unnatural withdrawal of every living form from life.
He who commits suicide, in a cowardly and defeatist manner, allows the mission of retributive justice to fall behind."

Karma - The Law of Retributive Justice,
page 333.

"Those who commit suicide make the same mistake as the Fallen do. They neglect the return of their debts and stop their own evolution and liberation."
Karma - The Law of Retributive Justice,
page 333.

"Another thought torturing the esoteric seeker is: Is man allowed to explore the matters of God? His will and His works? Is it Karma for the spirit-soul, to try to probe into the Lord's plans? I shall try to answer from the point of view of our subject of analysis, Karma.

I steadfastly believe that man can and must explore the matters of God, because when he examines what concerns God, he conceives His perfection. And taking this perfection as an example, he enters the path of eternal joy and of divine revelation, learning the required truth. It is our sweetest moment when we discover the Will of Our Lord, for within it lies the whole Truth, whose purpose it is to attain the beloved perfection. Yes, we can study the wishes of Our Lord and Father. It is not karma when our spirit-soul tries to probe into His ultraviolet spiritual vibrations in order to perceive the least of His holy Plans."

For this reason, you must study the Scriptures. Yes, my dear reader. Do not neglect your daily opportunity to study the Scriptures of the Lord."
Karma - The Law of Retributive Justice,
page 337.

"But the current subject, Karma, is so great that all the books in the world cannot cover it. And that's because every man has his own unique case of his individual Karma

and every family, race and peoples have, in every historical period, their own personal Karma."
>
> *Karma - The Law of Retributive Justice*,
> page 343.

"When the Mind reflects the vision of the souls, it feels the memories of previous lives sailing within. Astonished, it then lives its infinite experiences, as a significant or as an insignificant person, as a head of a family or as a bachelor, as a rich man or as a poor man, as a quiet man or as an insatiable warrior, as a happy or as an unhappy being, and so on.

This reflection of man's previous lives is accompanied by numerous experiences that the visionary automatically realizes, uninterrupted by anything happening around him (earthquakes, thunder, explosions, demonstrations, war conflicts and all kinds of disturbances). This is the ecstatic state where the Mind is now attached to its soul, forgetting about the senses and the phenomena or the events taking place around him. He lives the eternal existences that formed his current personality, good or bad, holy or evil."
>
> *Reincarnation*, pages 22-23.

"As the newborn comes out of its mother's womb, the spirit-soul enters the baby from its little head covered now with its etheric protective suit.

Incarnation or reincarnation faithfully follows this path. There are definitely some exceptions. In some cases, the spirit-soul enters physical bearers of different ages and settles in the body, either after an invitation by the owner or even violently and forcefully. Also, the spirit-souls self-materialize and appear as well-known figures or as unknown persons.

These souls have missions to accomplish and as soon as this happens, they dematerialize and leave again returning to the worlds from which they came."
Reincarnation, page 28.

"When we call man 'a being with seven souls' we are not completely mistaken, since man has eight bodies. The Soul is surrounded by many bodies - thoraxes and each of these bodies has its own Mind and its own senses which start off as many but end up being five in our physical body. All these Minds work under the guidance and the supervision of the soul which is the representative of the substance - spirit."
Reincarnation, page 31.

"The incarnation of every spirit-soul takes place according to a predetermined plan by the critical committee of Karma. The spirit-soul, from the 12th dimension and below, is accompanied by a plan and by an explanatory note, on how the body, the exterior vessel will be formed. The etheric effigy-body, the netted prototype, the body of fire is constructed on the basis of this etheric plan, from which the physical body we have and know will be produced and woven."
Reincarnation, page 32.

"While incarnation takes place once, more specifically the first time, Reincarnation takes place as a repeated incarnation or as a reincarnation or as a rebirth or as a Metempsychosis, as some people call it, not knowing the meaning of this Pythagorean word."
Reincarnation, page 43.

"What is the aim of reincarnation? The absolute closing off of matter from the spirit-soul, so that man may be able to study - live - realize, experience, completely identify with it. After this in-depth acquaintance, the triumph of the awakening will be heard as will the resurrection of the spirit-soul, its abhorrence to matter and its great decision to forever release itself from the heavy bonds of matter, rising from the tomb of horror."

Reincarnation, pages 52-53.

"What clearly appears to be reincarnated and reborn is the immortal substance within us, our personality, our correct self, our spirit-soul, our eternal and immortal being, our right and true self, our spirit-soul.

This being of ours is reincarnated and reborn, it returns and re-enters the body of the infant, as it comes out of the mother's womb."

Reincarnation, page 83.

"I repeat: for the soul to express normal and correct behaviour, it is our duty and obligation to preserve the freedom of every spirit-soul. This means that every member of a family has the same preconditions for potential freedom that if used correctly, will allow the individual to obtain what it needs."

Reincarnation, page 98.

"If the spirit-soul were judged for one and only incarnation, surely the judgment would be unfair, because with only one incarnation, it is not possible to obtain all the opposing mysteries of our world, to try the demands of desire and to return to its initial purity. The spirit-soul would have been wrongly hanged. The Fallen angel would be pushed into Hades and being completely ignorant of its mysteries, would fall into its infinite traps; it would be blackballed, blemished, besmirched. That is why multiple reincarnations and infinite opportunities are given, so that the soul may restore to previous states all the abnormalities it had created in the past, all it had destroyed while it was drunk on matter and staggering about."

Reincarnation, page 102.

"Almost all the leaders of humanity come from the COLLECTIVE SOULS, not only because they are aware of their absolute compliance with the Divine Laws but also because they have been trained to have incredible patience and tolerance that only they have experienced and gone through."

Reincarnation, pages 115-116.

"Here, Metaphysics prevails with its inimitable esophilosophy. The enlightenment of our fellow-man concerning the Esoteric Truth is indispensable and necessary. If this is achieved, the ostensible man begins to have a different attitude and, little by little, he turns his search towards the afore-mentioned esoteric being within him (his esoteric self) and the eternal glory. From this moment on, the son of man instantly becomes the Son of God and the stimuli produced by his senses simply verify the synthetic inability of nature - matter, to offer something better, superior and more perfect, as the new psychical state of the enlightened being expects."

Reincarnation, page 127.

"As soon as these souls that are redeemed from our world, reach the last step of the lower intellectual area and are ready to enter the fifth step of the Intellectual world or the first step of the superior Intellect (the lower Intellectual world has four steps and the superior Intellectual world has three steps), the eternal question of our Most beloved Father is heard by all the successful - liberated spirit-souls.

The Father's voice says: 'Would you like to return, my

son, and teach my younger children? If you wish to return, you must undertake the task of teaching and enlightening your brothers and your sisters on how to prepare for deliverance as you too were delivered and are now immortal.'

The new spirit-soul thinks for a little. The Father's request is very warm. The freedom of his will is going to decide. Most people ask to continue the ascent into the Father's arms. Some others ask to return to our world, untouched now by Karma, as reincarnated Lords, as delegates, as Masters of Eternal Wisdom."

Reincarnation, page 143.

"The Posthumous Life is now written in my soul and not in my physical mind. My hand takes the pencil with the consent and at the suggestion of my soul, to write about its belief and the truth about life and death.

There is no death. Only the representations of form change and reappear rejuvenated due to the strengthening substance that is found in every form of expression, reasonable or unreasonable, in living or dead matter, as exoteric science calls it."

Posthumous Life, pages 9 -10.

"Have you ever really thought about it? What else is life than a point of friction (conflicts / clashes) of this radiation of Substance (which comes from Creator), on and in a region we call matter-form, which in its core consists of microbodies and electromagnetic planes that are supplied with life and force from this Divine Radiation."

Posthumous Life, page 10.

"Nobody else can nor knows how to turn or to handle the valve allowing the life substance to enter our etheric body. So, as soon as the baby emerges from the womb, it is re-

ceived or falls into the etheric network awaiting it. Immediately and automatically, the baby's soul opens this tap that will be closed at the final moment of the predetermined death of man's physical body."
Posthumous Life, page 36.

"Repentance for one's previous course of action creates the beginning and not the end, as many people believe, of the formation of a new, stellar shell."
Posthumous Life, page 53.

"He who passes through the first four areas and enters the fifth one which belongs to the superior intellect, becomes completely immortal and is not subject to a new obligatory incarnation."
Posthumous Life, page 56.

"However, in order for the common man to elevate his consciousness above his physical etheric body to the stellar one, he must first construct it. He begins with the well-known desires for food and the desire to remain in the physical etheric state; then, he forms the initial primitive stellar-like steps or areas and he elevates his consciousness to the point he has created. He awakens his soul to that extent."
Posthumous Life, page 73.

"Contact with our esoteric spirit occurs, even if our soul is still in the etheric stellar and in the thymoastric systems of these lower and denser worlds.

That is why the 'know thyself' has a deeper meaning and he who conceives it, becomes the ruler of wisdom. Mysticism and Meditation, philosophers and visionaries pursue this in life. An encounter with the holy and thrice holy SPIRIT existing within our being."

Posthumous Life, page 86.

"However a secret moment will come, a moment that will not be evident. One moment when the Universes, the Worlds and the creations will be absorbed. During that divine and holy moment of the contraction and reunion of the worlds and beings in the Father's arms, His exciting voice will be heard asking us to reveal our works and our days, in the outer and in the inner worlds.

Then, with a compelling leap, the spirit that holds the cosmic and eternal archives within it will transfer and empty them into the Father's being, the whole experience he gathered with the soul as an intermediary, as well as the different bodies from the innumerable incarnations in the universes and in all the dimensions."

Posthumous Life, page 101.

"Knowledge is symbolized by a snake. The snake bite hurts and this pain makes the soul feel how the gaining of experience functions. From a snake bite to a man's body...

That is how Buddha characterized pain and desire. Every desire is a pain. Where there is desire there is pain. Freedom comes when there are pains not derived from desire."

Posthumous Life, page 114.

"When the soul is ready to descend, it is accompanied by an etheric program on how to spend life in our physical world. In this program, the moment of birth and the moment of death are defined in incredible detail. Nothing is left out and nothing is forgotten."

Posthumous Life, page 126.

"Despite all this, the soul does not refuse the exterior world. On the contrary. Mysticism strengthens, regenerates and activates the human soul. It is as if the divine auras provide the soul with new potions for development and energetic awakenings, because they push men of vision and of Mystic experiences to higher deeds and to those of more general interest, in fact."

Posthumous Life, page 184.

"What do these mystic fellow-men of ours feel and see, that makes them accept and blindly believe what the other people consider to be unimportant childish fables? They see and live in other real worlds - dimensions - areas of another matter-state, where the souls together with other bodies, similar to what we know as our physical body, live, work and exist. Those who secretly know these cases become acquainted and flock together with these souls and then they continue their natural life, as if absolutely nothing had happened in the meantime."

Posthumous Life, page 190.

"Psychopathy of every type has so greatly spread in our times that it has surpassed the fears of cancer and of AIDs. It is a mental disease ruling the entire body. Our Mind, being made of the same matter as the whole body, suffers from the oscillations of the opposing elements of matter and... succumbs.

The stress of modern life breaks out on the Mind that, unable to solve our present problems and trying to escape from OUR PRESSURES refuses to conform to our absurd demands, and exhibits a completely different behaviour to the one defined by nature.

Man first falls victim to different phobias and then, he takes the easy way out by avoiding every necessary solution to his numerous problems, by focusing and working on other matters. In order to cover his inability to solve the projected problems, he plays the part of the ailing, of the psychopathic being. And this habit of acting becomes so strong that in the end it becomes second nature and his true nature is forever replaced by the role he is playing.

This conversion of one's natural behavior to its other one, to the false and unnatural one, forms psychopathy that brings its victim to the other side of physical life, to the diseased area where sick fantasies present good as evil, friends as enemies, lies as truth and vice versa."

Psychotherapeutics without medication, page 7.

"There are two brains in the head: The frontal brain and the dorsal brain. In our navel, there is the solar plexus whose presence is evident by the ventriloquists and other fellow-men who express themselves and talk with this Mind. The fourth brain is on the base of the vertebral column and possesses the control of the Universal energy that mortal beings inherit in order to pass through the physical life and to transmit it to their descendants so that they retain the matter that forms our physical body.

The correct cooperation of these four brains creates what we know as a classification of health that man presents and that we call the Divine Order, the HEALTHY MIND.

Psychotherapeutics without medication, pages 20-21.

"I return to the subject I touched upon in my preface. There are two kinds of ailing persons: Those who need esoteric therapy and those who are struggling to find an exoteric therapist. Experience is needed on the part of the therapist to detect them. He must by no means accept those who desire exoteric therapy, because they react to an incredible degree, they become too uptight, they become introverted and reject any effort on the part of the therapist to approach them.

On the other hand, there are others who, by nature, are completely ready to find their esotherapist, to become one with him and to allow themselves to open the gates of their subconscious and to help him repair the damage to consciousness."
Psychotherapeutics without medication, page 28.

"Exoteric science believes that everything in the human body comes from the cells. Although the muscular system as well as all the other systems resulted from the cells, the architect was the etheric model, which as a canvas, contained the weaving of the entire physical body, which of course was woven using thread of various colors made up of the cells of the muscular as well as of the other systems that constitute and form the human organism."
Psychotherapeutics without medication, page 32.

"First, the muscular and then the nervous system were created. The nervous system is the transmitter and the transporter of external vibrations; whereas, the muscular system is the receiver and the transporter of internal vibrations. The nervous system receives orders to release fishing systems whose vibrations will attract inwards the interest of the five senses.

The muscular system conveys vibrating orders and life

force from the Mind (subconscious) to all the cells of the organism. The muscular system feeds the whole body with energy and life. In a split second, it transmits news to the center of the brain and conveys all the Mind's orders to the cells through the subconscious."

Psychotherapeutics without medication.

"The blond animals used to drink only the milk of goats. These goats of the Asclepeion at Epidaurus used to eat only grass which grew on magnetic soil. This magnetic soil was brought from Pilion and Trikala, where the first two Asclepeions were located. The third one of Epidaurus was the most perfected and the biggest one in Greece. There they bred the Paris snakes, those blond animals, the therapeutic-magnetic snakes that were sent to all the Asclepeions of the world that were known at the time."

Psychotherapeutics without medication, page 63.

"The healthy Mind is always presented as the white Sorcerer. He is the good person, who, without delay, will make sacrifices for any of his fellow-men. The sick Mind is the bad Sorcerer who will not hesitate to benefit from his fellow-men, in order, as he alleges, not to be regarded as NAIVE. Because the cunning rationalists characterize the ethical, the just, the frank and harmless fellow-man as naive."

Psychotherapeutics without medication, page 80.

"I would say that this organ, man's tongue is the projection of the completed Mind. It contains within it the dynamism of the subconscious, the conscious and the hyperconscious. During this phase of the human race's evolutionary course, the tongue is captured by the conscious and isolated from the subconscious and the hyperconscious.

The tongue has close contact with the muscles and the subnerves, the fibers and the cells, the epiphysis and the hypophysis, with the circulatory system and with the ganglion, as well as with other systems unknown to the exoteric therapeutic systems, such as: the system of immortal water, Nectar and Ambrosia, which pull it from the depths of the brain and bring it down, where the two holes of the skull and the root of our tongue..."
Psychotherapeutics without medication, page 94.

"CHAOS means the UNSOWN PART OF THE OMNI-UNIVERSAL FLAME. Where chaos prevails, there is no vibrating ray and therefore EVERY TRACE OF LIFE AND EXISTENCE is absent."
Occultism, Volume A, page 197.

"THE SELF-SUFFICIENCY OF GOD AND THE HEAD OF THE RACE AND THE FATHER contains absolutely everything and then some: Good and evil, negative and positive, kind and wicked, love and hate. Because, if it did not contain all this, HIS SELF-SUFFICIENCY would be missing and it would not be what it had and has to be, that is SELF-SUFFICIENT."
Occultism, Volume A, page 323.

"The great dream of every member of the collective soul is the moment of completion with spiritual and psychical substance and its detachment from the group, possessing the new quality of the formidable individualization."
Occultism, Volume A, page 329.

"Even though the individualized spirit-souls of the collective souls are distributed in pairs within the group family, they rarely meet in their individualized presence-expression to share the experiences of the world of human form.

Due to this, they are radically different from the pairs born by the same Father at the base-seat-area of the Spiritual Beginning. There, in a splendid spiritual capsule, we witness the co-existence of two spirit-seeds born in an absolutely individualized form..."

Occultism, Volume B, page 80.

"However, the experience that such an individualized spirit-soul has, is immense and considerable. For this reason, the preeminent earthly beings, humans, came from one such spirit-soul. That is why we tell exquisite spirits that they probably come from below, from the mineral depths, from the depths of matter, where the Spirit is revealed as an eternal Force which bonds, overheats and accelerates the movement of particles in the core of the world."

Occultism, Volume B, page 79.

"However, Occultism and occultists do not interpret and do not teach whatever they find or whatever Mother Nature hides from our Mind. But they continually seek and preserve the invented, the revealed things. In contrast, Occultologists and Occultology teach in oral and in written form and by any other means, what has been learned, deciphered, discovered, found out, explained.

Personally, I am an Occultologist and at the same time an Occultist whose purpose it is to spread all knowledge as quickly as possible whether it is new or old or disputed or unaccepted by the so-called experts..."

Occultism, Volume A, page 99.

"In 1976, in Athens, Kolonaki, at 56 Omirou Street, the Omakoio of Athens was established to teach the true Pythagorean theory under the new title of ESOTERICISM. Then, with the help of another person, I established OMAKOIO. It was there that I wrote many books; it was there that I published the Omakoio journal. It was there that I was inspired and published *The Esoteric Key*. I also taught there for four full years: Mysticism and Occultism, Esoteric Philosophy and Esoteric Therapeutics, Esoteric Initiation, the Philosophy of Yoga with relaxation on its true basis. Finally, it was there that I wrote most of my essays and most of my Metaphysical notes which will remain forever unpublished. Afterwards, I moved to 17 Spyridona Trikoupi street, Exarchia, where I still live. Here I wrote my two last published books, *Posthumous Life* and *Raja Yoga*. Here also I wrote some new Essays and did the greatest part of my teaching.

Finally, it was here that I formed the Peripatetic School. I also established here the Raja Yoga and the Kriya Yoga School. Also, I taught Neoplatonism and Neo-pythagoreanism. Then my wife suddenly died. I went to Astoria, New York in self-exile. There, I wrote the complementary chapters of the *The Two-Volume Metaphysical Encyclopaedia* which reached one thousand (1,000) handwritten pages. My whole life was the Omakoio dream. Before I established it, I had written my first 5 books: *Light*, *Theurgy*, *Patapios*, *Daniken* and *Yoga*. I wrote the book *Theurgy* in Egypt. But my students will write the supplementary material. However, before I close with what I wrote, I mention here to you that I wrote my most beautiful book, which I called KRIYA YOGA- A Practical Method.

The Two-Volume Metaphysical Encyclopaedia -Volume B, page 611

"At this moment of my dedication, I feel that I am living beyond the limits of place-time, beyond the chains of nature-matter. I am living now in the bliss of perpetual spirituality. It is exactly this spiritual redemption that I offer my readers with this three-volume book."

Book: Mystical Teachings, Volume 3, page 8.

"No measure counts as perfectly as the measure of the soul."

From verbal teachings of Nikolaos Margioris

"As long as man doesn't light within him the spark of love, he remains without the secret knowledge of God."

From verbal teachings of Nikolaos Margioris

"For someone to become a Yogi, he need only to control his mind."

From verbal teachings of Nikolaos Margioris

PART FIVE

DEDICATION TO MODERN GREEK MASTER NIKOLAOS A. MARGIORIS

PREFACE

Arriving at the end of this book, I quote four texts - Dedications to the Master, which refer to his personality, his work and his actions. The first text constitutes the only public interview that Master gave to the metaphysical journal *Third Eye* (in December 1992), a few months before his departure.

The second text was written by the writer of this book, on behalf of the Master's closest students, after his physical death (6-5-93), as a tribute to his memory and it was published in *Third Eye* in September, 1993.

The third text was drawn up by Smaro Kosmaoglou, who is currently responsible for the Athens OMAKOIO, on behalf of all the students of the last decade as a memorial prayer after the one-year anniversary of the departure of the Master and it was published in *Third Eye* in May 1994.

The fourth passage-feature concerns Nikolaos Margioris who was made known as one of the 100 Great Greeks of ALL times in the open public vote held by the Greek television network SKAI TV in 2008. It was followed by the publication of a three-volume set with extensive features on the 100 Great Greeks, including the life and work of N. Margioris, and accompanied by DVDs with the original TV program. These features were first published in a series of sections in the Greek daily newspaper *Kathimerini*. The feature concerning the Modern Greek Philosopher and Mystic Nikolaos Margioris is republished in this book.

This chapter of Dedications to the Master closes exactly in the same way as the book begins, that is, with a letter. It is a letter from a female student and it is addressed to her Master wishing to pay, on behalf of everybody, a last tribute of appreciation, of respect, of love and of gratitude that we all feel for Him.

Through this spontaneous, internally-incited work – recently written (9-11-1995), a little while before this book was published - a great big THANK YOU is expressed to Him, for all that we gained from Him and for all that he instilled and inspired in us.

NIKOLAOS MARGIORIS
THE PATRIARCH OF GREEK OCCULTISM

Pythagoras and Omakoio. Two titles that immediately bring ancient Greece to mind. The man in charge, Nikolaos A. Margioris, the last representative of the 'old' esotericists feels a deep love for ancient Greek philosophy, combining it with eastern and Christian elements.

He is the nearly-80-year-old Master who has been teaching Esotericism for many years at OMAKOIO (an ambitious title indeed!) and who writes unceasingly.

His linguistic style, vivid and direct, compelled us to use his words exactly, without our intervention.

"I was born in 1913, on the island of Samos, in the village of Vourliotes. When I was very young, I left for Egypt. But I had very frequent contact with my island. I studied in and graduated from many schools, in Greece as well as in Egypt, until the moment, I went to India where I studied

Archaeology. There I was also initiated into the Hindu Philosophy and especially in Yoga and other matters, but to a higher and slightly superior level than the other people. When I returned to my country, the war between Greece and Italy had been declared. I fought in the Sahara Desert, I was wounded in El Alamein and then my brigade went to Rimini. Afterwards, I came to Greece as a refugee and I received the veteran's disability pension.

My Metaphysical experiences were very frequent because I grew up in a family composed of members who had metaphysical knowledge. My father had a very large library and, from a young child, I could explore any areas I had doubts about or inclinations in using French, English and other languages, and in this way I became informed about that world, the invisible world. From a very young age (12-13 years old), I had great experience in and broad Knowledge of another state of things. I saw many superior peoples and persons who as beings taught and instructed me. You must know that I am in a state of Absolute Control over my Mind and Thoughts. To an unbelievable extent. I am – strangely enough - both a scientist and a Metaphysicist. To this day, I follow the developments in Physics. I am also a Christocentric and Christocratic Mystic."

When I asked him if he accepts the Divinity of Christ he said:

"For the people, it is called educational, but in reality it is Theistic."

However, he accepts Reincarnation because it follows the Orighenian Dogmas. He said to us:

"The third professor who taught in the School of Alexandria was Admantios Orighenis who followed the line of Klimis of Alexandria, when metapsychosis was called 'regeneration'. Orighenis believed in it and for this reason, in the 6th century, during a special synod, he was excommunicated.

The Orighenian dogmas which are Reincarnation, Karmic Law and the Freedom of the Will were abolished. However, in many books we reveal that Jesus used them at many points.

I also accept other views of Eastern Philosophies, but the great masters were the Greeks. Plato persistently makes reference to Socrates and his 'thinking' in his *Symposium* and elsewhere. A way of thinking that was repeated by Plato and was taught in Pythagoras' OMAKOIO, in Croton of Great Greece and in Heraclitus, but which was also used by the Christian religion. Nicodemus, Simon, John of the Ladder, the pillars often fall into thought. Reflection is the vocation of monastic life. Of course, the Church does not consider them quite necessary and it does not accept them very much. As long as they live, it persecutes them, but when they die, it sanctifies them because without these Mystics the tree of Religion cannot develop. It needs the great faith of those who achieve the communion of the Invisible World with the visible one. And this can only be achieved through Mysticism, and Religion recognizes this (though the Church does not). We teach Plato's way of thinking in the form of Raja Yoga. Our Philosophy follows the familiar formula that there are three states of Mind: Consciousness, subconsciousness and hyper-consciousness. But how will the vibrations of hyper-consciousness come down as experiences to your conscious substance if they are not changed? You must therefore teach these vibrations of high length and intensity how to come down to your conscious world, to change and to become experiences, Knowledge."

NOTE.: The above interview by Master Nikolaos A. Margioris marks his first and last public appearance, five months before his physical death. At the same time, it is the first official recognition of his personality and of his work by the Greek metaphysical journal *Third Eye* which calls him 'The Patriarch of Greek Occultism and the last representative of the 'old' Esotericists.' The interview was held for the journal *Third Eye*, was published in issue 20, in December 1992 and is republished in the present book.

THE PATRIARCH OF GREEK OCCULTISM AND MYSTICISM HAS LEFT

After his recent physical departure from life (on May 6, 1993) and with the publication of the last completed work he left (*Mystical Teachings*, 3rd Volume), we present a brief biographical note for a first acquaintance of the reader with the Master's life, personality and work.

Nikolaos A. Margioris constitutes one of the greatest and most prominent figures in the area of Esotericism (Occultism and Mysticism). He is not only a recognized, but a fully-experienced Metaphysical Omni-Scientist-Master who was characterized as 'the Patriarch of Greek Occultism' in a relevant interview of the journal *Third Eye*, in its December 1992 issue. This was his first and his last public appearance.

Therefore, this is in memory of Nikolaos Margioris, who was a great Christocentric and Christocratic Mystic and modern Initiate, and we, a group of his closest students who followed him the last few years and were lucky enough to be taught the deep elements and aspects of the Universal Truth, to enrich our Occultist and Mystic Knowledge and to receive a part of the abundant LIGHT that he spread around him, feeling gratitude and sincere, not fanatic Love for him, would like to inform every seeker of the Truth, about the Master's life, personality and work.

Nikolaos Margioris was born on the island of Samos in the village of Vourliotes on the 15th of December, 1913. When he was 13 years old, he attained Samadhi-Enlightenment for the first time.

He was educated in India and in Tibet for almost 13 years. He lived with his relatives for many years in Alexandria of Egypt where he pursued his studies and made his career. He married Laitsa Papandreou with whom he had two children, Andreas and Kalia. He fought in World War II as a reserve officer in the Sahara Desert where he was wounded in El Alamein and in Rimini. For his services to the country, he was honored with many medals and with a veteran's disability pension. He was also honored twice with the Cross of Saint Mark for his offer to the church by Patriarch Nikolaos the 6th of Alexandria and Patriarch Timotheos of Jerusalem.

Apart from Egypt, he also taught in Greece, from the first day of his arrival in 1958 and at the same time he wrote books and essays, he circulated journals and he created a circle of students. He considered Metaphysics to be the only Truth and believed that man can attain Truth as Socrates did, through his famous MEDITATION (DHARANA-CONCENTRATION).

All his teachings, his books, his essays, his studies in Esotericism come and emanate from his deep Mystic experiences (Nirguna Samadhi-Theosis). Since he was very young, he was a participant in these transcendental states which he managed to transform in an incomparable way and to convey to his students and to the world as Knowledge, advice, guidance, for use, practise, training, therapy and personal experience.

His philosophical approaches on Creation, on Truth

(God), on the visible, perceptible and invisible, imperceptible Laws that rule the World and life, in general, are expressed with unique fluency, detail, analysis and depth. He also presented for the first time, a complete and sound Occultist and Mystic view of the Creation of All, using a torrential and overwhelming form of oral and written expression, which rivals, without exaggeration – for anybody who knows -, that of Paul the Apostle and Ramakrishna whom no obstacle, sickness, or anything else restrained (he came close to death at least three times).

Providing everything in abundance, offering continuous guidance, instruction and unceasing sacrifice and serving as an example of a model that is summarized in two words 'PERFECT MAN' and 'PERFECT GOD', without any advertisement, propaganda or proselytism was his belief. And he did this indeed with absolute respect for the freedom of every promising seeker.

He was a faithful soldier of our Lord Jesus Christ, a 'TRUE RAVI-CHRIST' and also His imitator, having always followed His Work and His Teachings, reviving it once more in our society of today. He created an Esoteric Metaphysical Academy in the tradition of Plato and a School (Athens Omakoio). Perhaps he is the new Pythagoras with an immense production of spiritual work.

A few words about his Multi-dimensional Work

After 23 years of Metaphysical publications (1970-1993), he wrote 33 books of clearly Esoteric subject-matter, with an incredible and unprecedented Metaphysical analysis which led to increasing popularity for those who know the subject. He also wrote multiple essays on various Esoteric matters.

He circulated the metaphysical journal *OMAKOIO*. He created a field of studies through correspondence courses under the name 'Esoteric Key'. In this field, the students received instruction characterized by a deep, theoretical and practical Esoteric analysis, in the following courses: MEDITATION, HYPNOTISM, ORTHOPSYCHISM, ESOTERIC PHILOSOPHY, ESOTERIC THERAPEUTICS, ASTROLOGY-ASTROSOPHY, ESOTERIC INITIATION, SCIENTIFIC SPIRITUALISM, DESYMBOLISM.

Every three months, he held seminars in SHIATSU lasting for many days in which he himself not only taught SHIATSU but a lot of other Esoteric therapeutic systems among which were also his own discoveries whose therapeutic potential is immense and whose success rate surpasses 80%.

Some of his discoveries, which he obtained through his own experience and deep Esoteric Knowledge, are mentioned in his books and were taught to his students. They are:

1. From the left palm of the hand, he identified the main terminals of certain internal organs of the human body.

2. FINGERTAPPING. It is a rapid method of stimulating the whole organism, the cells and the endocrine glands to secrete new hormones and heal the ailing person.

3. TONGUE THERAPY. With special kneading, pulling and massage movements on the tongue that have an immediate influence on the muscular and nervous system and on the whole organism for recovery and therapy.

4. HE REVIVED and used the ancient Greek Asclepian kneading-massage method that Asclepius, the father of Medicine invented and applied in ancient times, as well as the sleeping Method (Hypnotism).

5. HECTOPLASMATIC EXHALATIONS OR HECTOPLASMATIC EFFUSIONS

6. ENERGY TRANSFUSION
7. ICONOPLASTIC THERAPEUTICS.

Apart from teaching therapeutic systems, he himself applied therapies. Also, his students who had been instructed in these techniques applied these therapies. Meanwhile, a school of KRIYA YOGA was established where the first KRIYA female-teacher in Greece, Smaro Kosmaoglou, who had been instructed by him, started teaching. What's more, a school for Weight Loss using the system of Atmo-Liquefaction (his own invention) was established.

He himself taught the pure and complete RAJA YOGA, as well as all the Yoga systems: HATHA, KRIYA, MANTRAM, KARMA, BAKTHI, JNANA, TANTRA, KAMPALA, ESOTERICISM (OCCULTISM AND MYSTICISM).

All his lectures and didactic activities took place in his seat, in his Spiritual Laboratory, which, from its establishment in 1976, he called the OMAKOIO of ATHENS in memory of the OMAKOEIO which Pythagoras first established in Croton of South Italy.

In 1972, he established the Association "THE PIOUS PILGRIMS OF THE UNBUILT LIGHT, SAINT PATAPIOS", where he tirelessly held free lectures on various Esoteric subjects.

He was a steadfast, indefatigable Worker and guide of Good and of Perfection, an infinite and inexhaustible source of Divine Knowledge.

The above are recorded as the smallest tribute that we, his students, could pay, promising to continue and spread the legacy he left us.

NOTE: The above presentation of Master Nikolaos A. Margioris' personality, life and work was written by his student,

Ilias L. Katsiampas (on behalf of all the students he taught during the last decade).

In the beginning, the Master's biography was sent, on the writer's initiative, to foreign guides of metaphysical organizations and to different other metaphysical movements abroad. Then, after the Master's death it was revised and completed correctly by his student and the writer of this book and it was published for the first time in the metaphysical journal *Third Eye* in issue 28 of September 1993, four months after his departure.

Afterwards, it was included in the 3rd Volume of the Master's work *Mystical Teachings* that was published in 1994, as well as in the republished editions of the books *The Other View of Erich Von Daniken's Dogma* and *Dravidians, the Ancestors of the Greeks* as well as in the present book.

ONE YEAR WITHOUT MASTER NIKOLAOS A. MARGIORIS

On the 6th of May, exactly one year will have passed without Master Nikolaos A. Margioris. Last year, on this date, this great Master of Occultism as well as of Mysticism, left this world and departed, leaving behind him an immense body of spiritual work. This work of about 33 years of teaching in the Greek area is multi-faceted and multidimensional. But it is mainly separated into his oral instructive work and his written work (see issue 28, in *Third Eye*).

The instructive work includes lectures and courses from the whole Cycle of Metaphysical Philosophy and mainly matters concerning the origin of the souls, the Purpose of their Passage through the World of Form, the necessity for Redemption, but also the way in which the soul is awakened and Despiritualized.

He taught Esoteric Therapeutics and adjusted them to the SHIATSU method (finger pressing), he brought back the ancient Greek Asclepian Massage and discovered the Method of Finger-tapping.

He trained his students in Raja Yoga – the Royal Art or otherwise in Mind elevation from Consciousness to Hyperconsciousness, using the Mind itself with Thought-Will-Imagination or with the Awakening of Kundalini (see book *Raja Yoga*).

He reinstated Kriya Yoga and established it as a complete system of instruction and therapy for man's Mind and Body (see book *Kriya Yoga*). But he mainly spoke and wrote about the Truth. A Truth that can be heard from the mouth of a True Initiate and Mystic; Revelations about the Internal Worlds and the beings that exist within them; Revelations about the Birth of the Worlds and of the beings, but also about the End of Time (see his book *The Birth and Death of the Worlds*).

He spoke and wrote about the whole ring of Occultism but also of Mysticism. He particularly focused on Christocentric and Christocratic Mysticism (see *Mysticism-Christocentric and Christocratic Mysticism*) as he was an adorer of Jesus Christ but also His last soldier, as he modestly called himself. But what remains indelible in the souls of all those who sat by his side – and they were not few - mainly the close circle of his students during the last 10 years - is the living example of his way of life; Of his Love for man; Of his endless efforts for man's education. He was an inexhaustible source of esoteric Knowledge but also a living example. He proved that a man, who lived as a simple human being - he himself was a refugee from Egypt and worked hard in his life to support his large family - can be liberated by perfecting himself on a daily basis in expression, in action but mainly in thought. This is achieved by developing true Esoteric Love, a Love that is converted into Creative work for one's fellow-men, for the Whole, for the entire world, for Generality.

He broke the bonds of man from fear and from pain, crushing the egoism that holds him bound to Form-matter. He was a dynamic instructor of the souls who willingly accepted him as their Master. He granted them Internal Bliss releasing them from their small and humble human chains. But at the same time, he broadened the endless spiritual horizons for them, showing them the path the soul must follow in order to reach Redemption (see his last book *Mystical Teachings, Volume C*). He stood as a true Spiritual Beacon for any soul seeking guidance in finding the Internal Greatness of its true self, of its identification.

One year may have already passed since his departure to the Esoteric Worlds, but the bright course he traced for man emerges already in the horizon. He has not ceased directing, guiding and protecting us.

We, the group of his students, as the smallest token of gratitude and holy duty, have decided - as He indicated to us one week before his death - to continue his work and to disseminate his teachings in oral and written form. Also, to proclaim the way of life we were taught by him in the Athens Omakoio, as well as in his private institute in Anavyssos, where he built the Temple of his beloved Saint Patapios.

It is the Pythagorean bond, the bond of our souls that connects us. We are spiritually united, Master and students, in eternity. Love of God, Love for Man and the evolution of man to the Divine will always unite us.

It is a fact that a Master is irreplaceable for the soul of

each one of his students. But, after one year, his Omakoio still has its doors open for every soul that is thirsty for Truth, for every soul that is seeking help in healing psychical or physical pain.

Perhaps this is the only true memorial service that we, his students can offer him: to continue to teach, to advise, to cure and to spread his spiritual legacy.

Every seeker can be taught and trained in Esotericism or in Esoteric Philosophy, and can also obtain his 33 books and his numerous other essays and written lectures as well as his journals, in order to form a personal opinion about Master Nikolaos A. Margiori's work and personality.

NOTE.: The presentation of Master Nikolaos A. Margiori's personality, life and work was written by Smaro I. Kosmaoglou (on behalf of all his students of the last decade).

It was published in the third issue of the metaphysical journal *Third Eye*, in May of 1994, exactly one year after his natural death.

100 Great Greeks
THE GREATEST OF ALL TIME
Volume B´
NIKOLAOS A. MARGIORIS

Brief Curriculum Vitae of Nikolaos A. Margioris

Authorship-Editing: Ilias L. Katsiampas
Student of Nikolaos Margioris for a decade

***Introductory note by the biographer**: The following biographical summary of **Nikolaos A. Margioris**, a small part of which was broadcast on television on **16 and 23 February 2009**, has been published in the **second volume** of the three-volume publication by **SKAI CHANNEL** which is composed of the **100 Great Greeks of All Time** as elected by the public in the scope of an open vote that was organized by **SKAI CHANNEL** in **April 2008**. It was followed by the circulation of **2 DVDs** of the television presentation of the **90 Great Greeks** plus **6 DVDs** for the **first 10**, which were released and distributed throughout Greece as an insert in the newspaper '**KATHIMERINI**'. The television presentation of **Nikolaos Margioris** is included in the second DVD and his written work of a 1500-word analysis is included in the second volume. He held the **60th place** among the **100 Great Greeks of All Time**.

NIKOLAOS A. MARGIORIS (1913-1993)

Nikolaos A. Margioris belongs to the **100 Great Greeks** as he greatly contributed to the **formation, presentation and popularization** of current **Greek Metaphysical Philosophy** based on the comparative analysis of the most popular international philosophical views in this area with the corresponding Greek views.

At the same time, he presented his own studies and interpretations of **critical Ontological** and **Eschatological issues**. He regularly conveyed his thoughts in theoretical and practical ways by which the modern Greek and the modern man could **redefine** his **spiritual path and evolution** in the contemporary Greek or global environment of corruption and social disintegration. His contribution is engraved in **his 189 writings** and in his multi-faceted and invaluable preserved verbal **testimonies** and **teachings**.

Nikolaos A. Margioris was born on December 15th 1913 on the island of Samos and from a young age he settled in the **Greek Community of Alexandria** (GCA) that was flourishing in those days. The most creative part of his life was spent in the Alexandria of Cavafy where he was exposed to the multicultural civilization of the city. Furthermore, he spent many years in **India** and **Tibet** where he basically studied **Buddhism, Yoga** and was trained in **Meditation**. In 1958, he returned to Greece where he developed and promoted his work.

In **Egypt, N. Margioris** became acquainted with the mystical philosophy of **Helena P. Blavatsky** (Helena Petrovna Blavatsky) that is proposed in her books *Isis Unveiled* and *The Secret Doctrine*. Given that eastern metaphysical views constitute the basis of western mystical philosophy and in his effort to comprehend the depth of eastern philosophy, he was guided to India and Tibet where he was trained for many years in **ancient Brahmanism**, the **Vedas** and **Upanishads** of **Hinduism**, in **Raja, Jnani, Karma, Bhakti, Kriya** and other forms of Yoga as well as guided on the path of the elders of **Buddhism**.

It was there that he met his contemporary Jiddu **Krishnamurti** (he spent most of his life in the United Kingdom). They often discussed the connection between **Theosophy** and neo-orthodox mysticism. The catalytic influence of Krishnamurti in the early years of the master guided him to collaborate with **Kostas Melissaropoulos**, the late philosopher and theosophist. Later, he developed a different view concerning the work of Krishnamurti.

In pre-war British Egypt, he participated in study groups of eastern philosophy and its development into European Mysticism. Apart from **English** and French that was spoken by every Greek in Egypt, he also learned **Sanskrit, Arabic, Hebrew and Hieroglyphics**. His first master and educator in Alexandria was the great Alexandrian Mystic **Krino Salvador de Kastro** (his father was from Corfu and his mother was Hungarian, a relative of the great composer Liszt). Also, the name of his Indian master was **Baba**.

He fought in World War II as a reserve officer, where he was seriously injured in El Alamein and in Rimini. For his services to the country he was honored with many medals (it is worth mentioning the GRAND CROSS) as well as with the veteran's disability pension.

Being a **Greek Orthodox, he** also tried to explore the connection between the orthodox movements of monasticism and mysticism in the deserts of Egypt in the 3rd and 4th centuries after Christ and eastern metaphysical philosophy.

Christopher II, the blessed Patriarch of Alexandria, guided him in these philosophical quests and set him to work for years at the orthodox libraries of the Alexandrian Patriarchate and Saint Catherine's Monastery in the Sinai Desert. He had hour-long conversations with his student, he honored him with his friendship and he awarded him with the cross of Saint Marc, for his contribution to the **Church** and the **Alexandrian and the whole African Patriarchate**. The same happened with **Nikolaos the 6th**, the subsequent blessed Patriarch.

Furthermore, he became acquainted with and embraced neo-pythagoreanism and neoplatonism and he evolved into a staunch supporter of **Iamblichus** and **Porphyrios**, the Greek-Alexandrian neoplatonic philosophers but most of all of **Ammonius Saccas** and his student **Plotinus**, as they had already from the 3rd century AD combined neo-Pythagoreanism with eastern philosophical quests.

His love for these philosophers and their work, and especially for **Pythagoras**, inspired him to establish **Schools** by the name of **OMAKOIO** (from omou which means together and akouein, which means we listen to a Teaching) in **Alexandria (1946)**, in **Athens (1976)**, in **Lamia (1990)**, in **Trikala (1992)** and in other Greek cities.

From **1972**, he had already established the **Association of Saint Patapios** in **Athens**, where he unfailingly held free public open speeches. He **Expired in 1993** in **Athens**, being fortunate enough to be surrounded by his numerous students who continue to disseminate, preserve and analyze his oral and written work.

N. Margiori's **lived** the **metaphysical philosophy** from a young age and his enthusiasm spread to his **students**. In the introductory note of the interview that he gave to the magazine *Third Eye* (December 20, 1992-issue 20) he was characterized as '**The Patriarch of Greek Metaphysical Philosophy**' and it was the first and last public appearance in his life. One more extensive presentation dedicated to **Greek Mystics** was published in *Avaton* magazine (October 2002-issue of September) while similar presentations have been published on websites and writings related to his work.

The "**Master**" as he was called by his students all over the country, was an **enlightened leader** for thousands of Greeks in the miraculous world of eastern philosophy and ancient Greek and Christian theory because of his efforts to detach them from the neo-Greek materialism, the extreme cynicism and the perpetual quest for the chimera.

Nikolaos Margioris was a uniquely-gifted modern esoteric experiential personality, of multiple talents and of unprecedented dynamism and productivity, who noiselessly passed the threshold of our country, delivered the quintessence of integrated spiritual experiences that summarizes the interaction of a metaphysical worldview in the oriental cultures and the ancient Greek, Hellenistic and Christian Orthodox view of life and death.

N. Margioris' teachings consist of the harmonious coexistence of the **ancient Greek, Egyptian and Indian philosophical theories** with the **esoteric Christian tradition** through the filter of his personal actualization. At the same time, he provides comprehensive personal answers with unprecedented explanations on **Cosmological-Ontological** and **Eschatological Issues** as a result of his personal '**mystical life.**'

His written work could be divided into **historical**, **ancient Greek** and **mystical**, **scientific** books, books of **alternative therapeutics**, of **Yoga systems** and their practices as well as **mysticism**, **occultism**, **esoteric theology** and **philosophy**, desymbolism of Greek Mythology, meditation, ancient

Greek Asclepian massage and **hypnotism, scientific spiritualism, philosophy of Astrology and so on.**

Among them, the **following** are worth mentioning: *The Two-Volume Metaphysical Encyclopaedia, Pythagorean Arithmosophy, The Eleusinian Mysteries, Dravidians, the Ancestors of the Greeks, The Last Day of Socrates, The Reign of Minos, the Great King of Crete, The Secret of Hatha Yoga, Kriya Yoga, Karma, Raja Yoga, The Pharaohs Akhenaten and Tutankhamun, The Chiroplastic Therapeutics of SHIATSU, Psychotherapeutics without medication, The Birth and Death of the Worlds, Posthumous Life, Mystical Teachings, Saint Patapios, Mysticism-Christocentric and Christocratic Mysticism, The Other View of Erich Von Daniken's Dogma* **and so on** (www.omakoio.gr)

Moreover, **16 years** after his physical end, many **reputable authors** and **researchers** have repeatedly consulted and derived material from his writings with **specific references** in their literature. Already many of his writings and books have been translated into the English language.

He left behind a **prodigious** and **diachronic wealth of reserves** (theoretical and practical) for **study** and **exploitation**. If it were possible to print his work in respective documents, they would probably be comparable in volume to the works of **Adamantios Orighenis**.

In fact, for the preservation, safekeeping and promotion of all this invaluable material, his representatives and his students are considering the **establishment** of an **ACADEMY** for the study and dissemination of his work. The first Academy was established by his students under the leadership of Ilias Katsiampas in July 2012 in Trikala by the name **"Yoga Academy of Nikolaos Margioris-Omakoio".**

His philosophical and practical work is continued in the Omakoio Schools that he founded as well as in the newer Schools that were established after his death in Greece, while his writings are promoted by his natural heirs. Finally, his teachings are continued by his students as is the publication of newer books based on his personal verbal testimonies and teachings.

* We must express our special thanks to the son of Nikolaos A. Margioris, Andreas N. Margioris for his contribution to the creation of this biography. Finally, we thank the student of the OMAKOIO of Trikala, Vivian Doufa, for her translation of this biography from Greek to English.

Biographer's Notes[*]

Nikolaos A. Margioris was deeply knowledgeable about eastern religions, including Hinduism and Buddhism, as well as modern Esoteric Philosophy and Metaphysics and their determinative interaction with the classical Greek and Hellenistic education and the contemporary Orthodox movements such as monastic mysticism and others.

The philosophical system that he created is above all

---

[*] **Ilias L. Katsiampas** is a professor of physical education (TEFAA), a journalist and the author of 5 books and many studies, the editor of a magazine as well as the publisher of a daily political newspaper in Trikala, *THE SEARCH*. For a decade, he was a student and partner of Nikolaos Margioris as well as the founder and director of the neo-Pythagorean philosophical schools **the Omakoio of Trikala and Thessaloniki** and president of the Association "**Yoga Academy of Nikolaos Margioris-Omakoio**". He is married to Sophia Skoumi and he has two children, Lampros and Maria. He lives and works in Trikala, Greece.
E-mails: omakoio@omakoio.gr & omakoeio@gmail.com
(www.omakoio.gr & https://omakoio.blogspot.com)

Helleno-Centric and is based on a fully experiential esoteric metaphysical education combined with all these philosophical systems in a flowing unity. He popularized the wealth of this knowledge through his modern, explanatory, simple and truly elegant way of speaking.

He deeply believed that every human being could become connected with the roots of his existence and his inner self, using a meditation system based on the classical Socratic stochasmos (meditation), on the absolute concentration of Hindus, on Christocentric Mysticism and on more current psychoanalytical findings all combined to suit the idiosyncrasy and the individuality of every individual.

He personally presents this work in **189 philosophical** and **practical writings** (34 books, 34 special essays, 49 issues of the Omakoio magazine and 7 treatises of metaphysical courses that contain 10-11 different lectures).

It is worth mentioning that his salvaged oral presentations constitute an extremely important and notable treasure grove of philosophical and practical material that is still unexploited.

A Letter to Master

November 11, 1995

My beloved Master,
Looking at your photo today, I felt an intense urge to write something about You. Something simple, plain, that I thought could be included in the chapter of dedications in the present book. I had neither the time nor the intention of composing and editing something special. I just wrote down some thoughts that sprang to mind instinctively, feeling strong emotions and gratitude at the same time.

Our dearest Spiritual Master,
This book is the first work that a close, devoted and beloved student of yours edits. He is the student who literally bombarded you with his endless questions during our meetings. But you enjoyed it very much, since it gave you the opportunity to offer the 'spiritual food' all of us needed so generously. I refer to this book as the first one because I feel that it is only the beginning and that sooner or later

– it doesn't matter when - other works of esoteric subject matter will follow, written by your other students (close or far, known or unknown, of today or of tomorrow), inspired by the pulse and by the giving-transmission of your perfect Spiritual Completion, from the touch and coordination of your Vibrating Ray. Besides, you yourself refer to it in your writings, during one of those moments when you brought forth certain... revelations! And it could not be otherwise. You instilled so many things in us. You broadened our spiritual horizons. You emancipated our thought from the closed, restricted and stagnant borders of reasoning. Our Mind was enriched. We became activated. New orientations, new perspectives and new aims appeared. You cultivated our morality and you awakened our Christian element.

You imparted this liberation, certainty and feeling of safety that comes from the deep knowledge and understanding of things to us. You activated the lethargic forces within us. You gave us the necessary stimulation so that our miserable soul may be awakened. You sowed your high quality seeds and at a certain moment the time will inevitably come for them to bear fruit.

Our beloved Master,

The present book is the first one that has You as its starting point. For this reason, it could only be dedicated wholly to your person, to your esoteric work, to this Superior Being that you represented and represent in Eternity and that few people essentially understood in the end. Nevertheless, even for those who did not comprehend your Esoteric grandeur, you were an excellent, unique Father, brother, friend, guide, fellow-traveler, assistant, MASTER. Could it be the Light that you sent out... the super-abundant Energy that you had and effused... that calmed, soothed, cured, changed everybody around you? Yes! You sent forth Strength, power, vitality, action, serenity and harmony, decisiveness, certainty, justice, honesty, goodness, even austerity when you had to but above all, you radiated LOVE. So much Love... My God, where did you draw it from? And it was so Real that even when you reproached somebody he felt deeply in his heart that you loved him and that you suffered more than he did. Really, how catalytic the effect you had upon the personalities and the souls of the people who met you was! Often, only one glance, one word, one movement of yours was enough! You allowed them to probe and to truly get to know themselves, to expand the operation of their Mind, to replace their evil, cunning and ill thoughts with pure, correct and balanced ones, to become more moral elements, to reject their egoism, to turn towards and help their other ego (their fellow-man), you taught them how to truly love, to justify and to forgive.

Our Beloved,

We, your closest students feel the greatest gratitude since we were lucky enough, - some more and others less, depending on what corresponded to each - to be trained by you, to witness your Esoteric Greatness, to receive and bear important knowledge and revelations of the transcendental Truth of Omnicreation and to acquire the equipment that is useful for our life and for our spiritual evolution. The change that has taken place in our Being, Internal and External, is something more than perceptible. The simplest result is that we lead a much more conscious life today.

Master, you were an inexhaustible source of Wisdom, Knowledge, Revelation but also of Inspiration for us. You conveyed to us the message of Hope, the power of Faith. You provided us with such a radiation of Love that we also learned how to love deeply, sincerely, without any self-interest and hypocrisy. You taught us well.

Everybody without exception received something from You.

Some people took many things, very many things. Some realized it, others not yet. But one thing is quite obvious: All your students ascended one or more steps of the spiritual ladder. You taught the path of Love and of Truth that you yourself experienced. You clearly indicated the path we were to follow to reach Truth-God. As you once said... before you left... you have explained EVERYTHING to us as analytically as possible, so that nothing else remains for you than to take our hand and to guide us There. We thank you just for having said this. Yes! You nearly did this too! Only the last step remains... the one that depends on our own powerful Will and Faith to ascend it.

WE THANK YOU
humbly and sincerely
for EVERYTHING,
V. K.

OMAKOIO SCHOOLS IN OPERATION IN ATHENS, LAMIA AND TRIKALA

For the readers' information, I list below the three Schools that have been established and operate in the Greek area. They are: Omakoio of Athens, Omakoio of Lamia and Omakoio of Trikala.

We mention them because all three schools belong to students-instructors of Master Nikolaos A. Margioris. They were established while he was alive and they follow his spiritual legacy and instructions.

Of course, every Omakoio school does not cease to constitute a separate and autonomous entity-spiritual school with its own identity-history and work and with its own personality and instructor.

ATHENS OMAKOIO
SMARO I. KOSMAOGLOU
METAPHYSICAL STUDIES
YOGA AND SHIATSU
17 SPYR. TRIKOUPI STREET
10683 ATHENS
TEL.: 210-3808365

LAMIA OMAKOIO
DIMITRIS AND KOULA TSAPARA
METAPHYSICAL STUDIES
YOGA AND SHIATSU
31 MILTIADOU STREET
35100 LAMIA
TEL.: 2231-32888

TRIKALA OMAKOIO
ILIAS L. KATSIAMPAS
METAPHYSICAL STUDIES
YOGA AND SHIATSU
21 KEFALLINIAS STR.
42100 TRIKALA, GREECE
0030-24310-75505 MOBILE: 0030-6974-580768
Web Site: http://www.omakoio.gr
https://omakoio.blogspot.com
E-mails: omakoio@omakoio.gr or omakoeio@gmail.com

IN OMAKOIO OF TRIKALA THE FOLLOWING
DEPARTMENTS ARE IN OPERATION:

A) PUBLICATION - SALES OF BOOKS

WHOLESALE - RETAIL

All the books written and published by the Metaphysicist, Master Nikolaos A. Margioris (189 books in total) are distributed through the Omakoio of Trikala, Greece. Please ask for the relevant price-list. Also, ask for Ilias L. Katsiampas' (Nikolaos A. Margioris' student) book *From the Master's Mouth to the Student's Ear, with a thorough glossary of Sanskrit (philosophic dictionary, 400 words) for the students of Yoga.* The following books by the same author are in press a) *A Comprehensive Analytical Dictionary of Metaphysical Terms*, b) *The Systems of Esoteric Therapeutics*.

B) KRIYA YOGA SCHOOL

PSYCHOSOMATIC - THERAPEUTICS

It started operation for the first time in Trikala, in January of 1992. Master of Metaphysics, Yoga and SHIATSU N. Margioris revived and established the authentic Kriya Yoga. He brought back the genuine Kriya from obscurity and made it known again. He taught it in Greece for the first time in 1981 in the Omakoio of Athens and he wrote his first book without a Master, *Kriya Yoga - A Practical Method of Psychosomatic-Therapy*. In this School many physical exercises are taught in combination with rhythmical breathing exercises (Pranayama), so that the Nervous and the Muscular system may become stronger, resulting in health and serenity, as well as the release of the trainee from the stress and internal psychological disturbances. Kriya is the only path which properly prepares the trainee for his initiation to Concentration (Raja Yoga).

C) RAJA YOGA SCHOOL

MIND ELEVATION FROM CONSCIOUSNESS TO HYPERCONSCIOUSNESS

It was established and has been in operation in Trikala since December 5, 1991. Instruction is accompanied by Master Nikolaos Margioris' book *RAJA YOGA*. In Raja Yoga, the advanced students are trained only in intellectual exercises aiming to perfect and balance the Mind. The trainee strengthens his will and acquires a larger and clearer understanding of every matter that may occupy him, particularly in Metaphysics. Special exercises in concentration and hyperconcentration only found in Raja Yoga are executed with the purpose of ultimately and gradually reactivating the third and highest Mind function, hyperconsciousness.

Also all the Yoga systems such as Karma, Bhakti, Mantra, Jnani, Kundalini (Tantra) and so on, are taught.

D) SEMINARS OF SHIATSU - SUGGESTION - HYPNOTISM

Every year, many seminars on Therapeutics without medication based on the Japanese technique of SHIATSU (Namikoshi) are held, while at the same time the ancient Greek method of Massaging (Asklipieia-Amfiaraeia), of Finger-tapping (Nikolaos A. Margioris' method), of Sleep Therapy (suggestion, hypnotism) and others are taught.

E) SEMINARS AND SPEECHES OF ESOTERIC PHILOSOPHY

In these seminars, topics concerning the entire field of Esoteric Philosophy, Occultism and Mysticism, such as the other Dimensions; the Law of Free Will, of Karma and of Reincarnation; the life and work of great Sage Masters: Body-Mind-Intellect-Soul-Spirit; the Divine Plan and the Evolution of Creation and so on, are presented.

F) ATMOLIQUEFACTION SCHOOL
SLIMMING ONLY FOR WOMEN

This department of the Omakoio of Trikala operates once or twice a year and its program lasts for about three months.

Special physical exercises in combination with the proper breathing exercises (Pranayama- N. Margioris' system) are taught. These are very effective in activating the organism, resulting in perspiration and the burning of fat. At the same time, it strengthens muscles without any mechanical means or medicine.

G) ESOTERIC KEY
STUDIES BY CORRESPONDENCE COURSE IN THE FOLLOWING BRANCHES OF ESOTERICISM

1) ASTROLOGY - ASTROSOPHY
2) ESOTERIC PHILOSOPHY
3) SCIENTIFIC SPIRITUALISM
4) HYPNOTISM - ORTHOPSYCHISM
5) ESOTERIC THERAPEUTICS
6) ESOTERIC INITIATION
7) MEDITATION
8) DESYMBOLISM

Those who would like further information and analytical prospectuses about every branch, may request them from the OMAKOIO OF TRIKALA, 21 Kefallinias Str., 42100 Trikala, Greece, or call Mr. Ilias Katsiampas at the telephone number 0030-24310-75505 or 0030-6974-580768 (mobile).

In the Omakoio of Trikala, all the books, essays, journals and correspondence courses by Master Nikolaos A. Margioris, founder of the Omakoio of Athens, are available.

THE WRITER'S BIBLIOGRAPHY

Apart from a small part of Master N. A. Margiori's oral teachings as well as their personal correspondence that he used for the writing of this book, the writer also took the following bibliography into consideration:

I) PUBLISHED BOOKS BY NIKOLAOS A. MARGIORIS
(copyrights belong to his heirs)

1. **Patapios, the Humble Philosopher and Saint from Egypt**, 1st edition in 1970 (156 pages), 2nd edition in 1987 (220 pages), with supplementary and explanatory material, 3rd edition in 2005 (220 pages).
2. **Light in the Dark**, 1st edition in 1975 (300 pages), 2nd edition in 1987 (429 pages) with supplementary and explanatory material, 3rd edition in 2005 (429 pages).
3. **Theurgy Teaches the Eternal Path of the Soul**, 1st edition in 1975 (318 pages), 2nd edition in 1987 (408 pages), with supplementary and explanatory material.
4. **The Other View of Erich Von Daniken's Dogma**, 1st edition in 1976 (318 pages), 2nd edition in 1994 (372 pages), with supplementary and explanatory material. ISBN: 960-7484-00-2.
5. **The Secret of Hatha Yoga**, 1st edition in 1976 (111 pages), 2nd edition in 1977 (155 pages). ISBN: 960-7484-04-5.
6. **Pythagorean Arithmosophy**, 1st edition in 1977 (168 pages), 2nd edition in 1987 (271 pages), 3rd edition in 1993 (276 pages) with supplementary and explanatory material, 4th edition in 2000 (276 pages), 5th edition in 2004 (282 pages). ISBN: 960-7152-06-09.

7. **The Eleusinian Mysteries**, 1ˢᵗ edition in 1978 (99 pages), 2ⁿᵈ edition in 1987 (159 pages), 3ʳᵈ edition in 1993 (178 pages) with supplementary and explanatory material, 4ᵗʰ edition in 1999 (183 pages). ISBN: 960-7152-11-5.

8. **The Last Day of Socrates**, 1ˢᵗ edition in 1978 (111 pages), 2ⁿᵈ edition in 1988 (152 pages), with supplementary and explanatory material.

9. **The Pharaohs Akhenaten and Tutankhamun**, 1ˢᵗ edition in 1978 (151 pages), 2ⁿᵈ edition in 1991 (311 pages), with supplementary and explanatory material. ISBN: 960-7152-00-X.

10. **Birth and Death of the Worlds**, 1ˢᵗ edition in 1979 (195 pages), 2ⁿᵈ edition in 1990 (p 323 pages), with supplementary and explanatory material, 3nd edition in 2009 (323 pages). ISBN: 960-85024-5-4.

11. **Dravidians, the Ancestors of the Greeks (Synopsis) in English**, 1st edition in 1979 (45 pages).

12. **The Reign of Minos, the Great King of Crete**, 1ˢᵗ edition in 1979 (88 pages), 2ⁿᵈ edition in 1997 (105 pages). ISBN: 960-7484-06-1.

13. **Dravidians, the Ancestors of Greeks**, 1st edition in 1979 (88 pages), 2ⁿᵈ edition in 1989 (143 pages), with supplementary and explanatory material, 3ʳᵈ edition in 1996 (167 pages), 4ᵗʰ edition in 2004 (166 pages).

14. **Eastern and Western White and Black Magic**, 1ˢᵗ edition in 1979 (134 pages),

15. **White Magic**, 2ⁿᵈ edition in 1992 (227 pages) with supplementary and explanatory material. ISBN: 960-7152-03-4.

16. **Barefoot They Dance on Fire (Anastenaria)**, 1ˢᵗ edition in 1980 (95 pages).

17. **Posthumous Life**, 1ˢᵗ edition in 1982 (256 pages), 2ⁿᵈ edition in 1993 (262 pages), 3ʳᵈ edition in 2010 (262 pages). ISBN: 960-7152-09-3.

18. **Raja Yoga**, 1st edition in 1983 (208 pages).
19. **The Two-Volume Metaphysical Encyclopaedia**, 1st edition in 1985/86 (Volume A, 443 pages, Volume B, 752 pages).
20. **Kriya Yoga – A Practical Method of Psychosomatic Therapy**, 1st edition in 1988 (357 pages), 2nd edition in 2000 (359 pages).
21. **The Desymbolism of Greek Mythology**, 1st edition in 1988 (521 pages), 2nd edition in 2002 (562 pages).
22. **The Three-Dimensional and Four-Dimensional World**, 1st edition in 1989 (214 pages), 2nd edition in 2007 (222 pages). ISBN: 960-85024-3-8.
23. **Mystical Teachings, Volume A**, 1st edition in 1991 (346 pages). ISBN: 960-85024-1-1 SET 960-85024-7-0.
24. **Karma. The Law of Retributive Justice**, 1st edition in 1989 (373 pages), 2nd edition in 1996 (373 pages), 3rd edition in 2009 (373 pages). ISBN: 960-85024-0-3.
25. **Reincarnation**, 1st edition in 1990 (286 pages), 2nd edition in 2009 (286 pages). ISBN: 960-85024-4-6.
26. **The Chiroplastic Therapeutics of SHIATSU, VOLUME A**, 1st edition in 1990 (533 pages). ISBN: 960-85024-6-2.
27. **Psychotherapeutics without Medication**, 1st edition in 1991 (325 pages). ISBN: 960-85024-8-9.
28. **Mysticism. Christocentric and Christocratic Mysticism**, 1st edition in 1991 (331 pages). ISBN: 960-85024-9-7.
29. **Occultism (Occultology), Volume A**, 1st edition in 1991 (391 pages). ISBN: 960-7152-01-8, 960-7152-02-6.
30. **Occultism (Occultology), Volume B**, 1st edition in 1992 (428 pages). ISBN: 960-7152-01-8, T.2. 960-7152-04-2.
31. **The Chiroplastic Therapeutics of SHIATSU, Volume B**, 1st edition in 1993 (395 pages). ISBN: SET 960-7152-07-7, 960-7152-08-5.

32. **Mystical Teachings, Volume B**, 1st edition in 1993 (388 pages). ISBN: SET 960-85024-7-0, 960-7152-05-0.
33. **Mystical Teachings, Volume C**, 1st edition in 1994 (379 pages). ISBN: SET 960-85024-7-0, 960-7152-10-7.
34. **The Chiroplastic Therapeutics of SHIATSU, Volume C**, 1st edition in 1993 (255 pages).
35. **Occultism (Occultology), Volume C**, 1st edition in 1997, 103 pages. ISBN: 960-7484-05-3.

II) ESSAYS BY NIKOLAOS. A. MARGIORIS

1. SCHOOL OF ASKLEPIANS - HYPNOTHERAPISTS
2. CARL VON REICHENBACH
3. SCHOOL OF AESKLEPIANS - SPIRITUAL THERAPISTS THEOPHRASTUS PARACELSUS
4. MAGNETOTHERAPY
5. ASKLEPIAIA AND AMFIARAEIA
6. THE THERAPY FROM BEFORE TIME
7. THE CELL AND LIFE MYSTERY
8. ECTOPLASM
9. ESSENES
10. APPARITIONS OF IDOLS OF LIVING PEOPLE
11. ANASTENARIA
12. CREATION OF THE WORLDS
13. MYSTICISM
14. DRAVIDIANS, THE FIRST GREEKS OF THE AEGEAN SEA
15. THE CONTROL OF VIBRATIONS
16. WHAT IS ESOTERICISM?
17. THE HOLY SCROLLS OF THE ESSENE RULES
18. EROS AND LOVE

19. PROPER NUTRITION, PROPER DIET, WEIGHT LOSS
20. THERAPEUTICS WITHOUT MEDICATION
21. THERAPEUTICS THROUGH HYPNOTISM
22. THERAPY OF PSYCHOPATHY
23. SHIATSU. THERAPEUTIC METHOD TWO VOLUMES (1st seminar)
24. SHIATSU. THERAPEUTIC METHOD TWO VOLUMES (2nd seminar)
25. SHIATSU. THERAPEUTUC METHOD TWO VOLUMES (3rd seminar)
26. SHIATSU. THERAPEUTIC METHOD TWO VOLUMES (4th seminar)
27. SHIATSU. THERAPEUTIC METHOD TWO VOLUMES (5th seminar)
28. SHIATSU. THERAPEUTIC METHOD ONE VOLUME (6th seminar)
29. SHIATSU. THERAPEUTIC METHOD ONE VOLUME (7th seminar)
30. SHIATSU. THERAPEUTIC METHOD ONE VOLUME (8th seminar)
31. SHIATSU. THERAPEUTIC METHOD ONE VOLUME (9th seminar)
32. SHIATSU. THERAPEUTIC METHOD ONE VOLUME (10th seminar)
33. SHIATSU. THERAPEUTIC METHOD ONE VOLUME (11th seminar)

III) OMAKOIO JOURNAL
BY NIKOLAOS A. MARGIORIS (49 issues)
The best **metaphysical** and **occultist magazine** of our country. Its every article *is a* revelation. Its every page is an en-

lightenment. It contains **well-documented** *and* **rare metaphysical analyses** (on plenty of esoteric matters. It comes in hexads. It was in circulation for **8 years (1977-1985)** in bimonthly publications. The first issue is number 2 and the last is number 49 (total of pages: 1658). There are 8 hexads at **25.00€** per hexad.

IV) ESOTERIC KEY BY NIKOLAOS A. MARGIORIS

Esotericism and **Metaphysics** are presented in complete form in their practical application and they give the student the **KEY OF KNOWLEDGE**.

Seven Branches *of* **Esotericism**, with **thirty** or **thirty-three** treatises of lessons. Every Branch contains approximately ten or eleven triads or thirty to thirty-three chapters – lessons. See summaries and contents for every branch separately in our site: www.omakoio.gr

Every lesson – triad costs **15,00 Euro. Enrolment** is a one-time fee of **10,00 Euro**. Ask for informative printed enrolment forms for the Esoteric Key branches of study by correspondence course.

The Branches are the following:

1) MEDITATION
2) HYPNOTISM - ORTHOPSYCHISM
3) SCIENTIFIC SPIRITUALISM
4) ESOTERIC PHILOSOPHY
5) ESOTERIC INITIATION
6) ASTROLOGY - ASTROSOPHY
7) ESOTERIC THERAPEUTICS
8) DESYMBOLISM

Nikolaos Margiori's books that are translated into English or that are currently in the process of being translated, are the following:

1) Dravidians, the Ancestors of the Greeks (translated, in a book), **2) Posthumous Life** (translated), **4) Birth and Death of the Worlds and of Beings** (matter, antimatter, hypermatter, universe, antiuniverse, hyperuniverse) (under translation), **4) Kriya Yoga** (translated) and **5) Raja Yoga** (translated).

BOOKS BY ILIAS L. KATSIAMPAS (N. MARGIORIS' STUDENT) OMAKOIOS OF TRIKALA AND OF THESSALONIKI, GREECE (AND YOGA ACADEMY OF NIKOLAOS MARGIORIS – OMAKOIO)

My own books (**Ilias Katsiampas**, student of **Master N. Margioris**) that relate directly with Margioris' work, translated into English, are the following:

1) **From the Master's Mouth to the Student's Ear, with a thorough glossary of Sanskrit (philosophic dictionary, 400 words) for the students of Yoga,** 1st edition 1995 (270 pages), dimension 24X17, ISBN: 960-85735-0-5. In the Greek language, it is available in book form. The English translation is also available in an A4 thermal-bound edition 1995.

2) **The Apocalypse of John as Explained by Master Nikolaos A. Margioris,** (A bilingual Greek-English edition, supervised and with extensive analytical annotations by his student, Ilias L. Katsiampas), 1st edition 1999, ISBN: 960-85735-1-3. Second Award from the International Union (Company) Greek Man of letters (DEEL).

3) Bilingual Greek-English Magazine "New Omakoio",

size A4, 1ˢᵗ issue, of 100 pages. All the 189 writings of Master Nikolaos Margioris are included in Greek and in English, with a photo of the cover, summaries and contents for each one separately, esoteric articles and the Schools-Omakoios that function in Greece.

4) **Handbook – Guide for Staff and Instructors of Esotericism According to Master Nikolaos A. Margioris' work.** It exists **in Greek** in an A4 thermal-bound edition (202 pages), 1ˢᵗ edition 2003 and **in English** as a separate edition (206 pages), **only for the members of the Omakoios.**

5) 10-year anniversary of the establishment of the Omakoio of Athens by Master N. A. Margioris. A bilingual **Greek-English 1999 edition** in an A4 thermal-bound edition, the Greek text consisting of 34 pages and the English text of 33 pages.

6) **Inauguration of the Omakoio of Lamia by Master N. A. Margioris.** A bilingual **Greek-English 2000 edition** in an A4 thermal-bound edition, the Greek text consisting of 36 pages and the English text of 22 pages.

7) **Inauguration of the Omakoio of Trikala by Master N. A. Margioris.** A bilingual **Greek-English 1999 edition** in an A4 thermal-bound edition, the Greek text consisting of 57 pages and the English text of 38 pages.

8) **Esoteric and Spiritual Experiences of Master Nikolaos A. Margioris.** A bilingual **Greek-English edition**, in an A4 thermal-bound edition. 1ˢᵗ edition 2004.

9) **Collection Articles –Advice & Interviews** of Ilias L. Katsiampas, 1ˢᵗ edition in an A4 thermal-bound edition. October 2004. First Reward from the International Union (Company) Greek Man of letters (DEEL).

10) **Prayer Book and Poems of Master Nikolaos A. Margioris**. A bilingual **Greek-English edition**. In book form. 1st edition 2004. First Reward from the International Union (Company) Greek Man of letters (DEEL).
11) **From Deep Metaphysical Correspondence**. In Greek, 1st edition 2007, 400 pages.
12) **Meditation and Mysticism, Raja and Kundalini Yoga (Theory and practice)**, in press.
13) **Asklepian Art and the Systems of Esoteric Therapeutics**, in press.
14) **Plagues and provocations of our time. The Metaphysical View**. In press.
15) **A Full and most Analytical Dictionary – Guide of Metaphysical Meanings**, in press.
16) **The Question of Aliens**. In press.
17) **The Mystery of Death and the Posthumous Course of the Soul**. In press.

Information
Ilias Katsiampas
21 Kefallinias str., 42100 Trikala, Greece
Tel. and Fax 0030-24310 – 75505 or mobile: 0030-6974-580768
Website: http://www.omakoio.gr or https://omakoio.blogspot.com
E-mails: omakoio@omakoio.gr or omakoeio@gmail.com

PRESENTATIONS ON YOUTUBE AND ON FACEBOOK OF 189 WRITINGS OF MODERN GREEK MYSTIC, NIKOLAOS A. MARGIORIS (1913-1993) AND OF 15 BOOKS OF HIS STUDENT, ILIAS KATSIAMPAS

IN ENGLISH
VIDEO PRESENTATION IN ENGLISH OF 35 BOOKS OF MODERN GREEK MYSTIC, NIKOLAOS A. MARGIORIS (1913-1993)
DURATION: 61 MINUTES.
The video was posted at http://youtu.be/GUbJ3RbhpIQ
https://www.youtube.com/watch?v=GUbJ3RbhpIQ&feature=youtu.be

VIDEO (PRIVATE) OF THE INAUGURATION OF THE NEOPYTHAGOREAN SCHOOL - OMAKOIO OF TRIKALA BY GREEK SPIRITUAL MASTER NIKOLAOS A. MARGIORIS THAT TOOK PLACE ON SATURDAY, JANUARY 18th 1992, 8:00 p.m.
Part A of VIDEO (Duration: 2:02:44)
http://youtu.be/KU3JalIc5HI or
https://www.youtube.com/watch?v=KU3JalIc5HI&feature=youtu.be

VIDEO (PRIVATE) OF THE INAUGURATION OF THE NEOPYTHAGOREAN SCHOOL-OMAKOIO OF TRIKALA BY GREEK SPIRITUAL MASTER NIKOLAOS A. MARGIORIS THAT TOOK PLACE ON SATURDAY, JANUARY 19th 1992, 8:00 p.m.

Part B of VIDEO (Duration: 1:26:15)
http://youtu.be/YR3I-WqVawI or
https://www.youtube.com/watch?v=YR3I-WqVawI&feature=youtu.be

IN GREEK
VIDEO PRESENTATION of 35 BOOKS of MODERN GREEK MYSTIC NIKOLAOS A. MARGIORIS
Duration: 29 Minutes
The video was posted at: http://youtu.be/950X-21eiis
https://www.youtube.com/watch?v=950X-21eiis

VIDEO PRESENTATION of 35 STUDIES of MODERN GREEK MYSTIC NIKOLAOS A. MARGIORIS
Duration: 45 Minutes
The video was posted at: http://youtu.be/oPXVjvj_GcM
https://www.youtube.com/watch?v=oPXVjvj_GcM&feature=youtu.be

VIDEO PRESENTATION OF 8 TREATISES - SECTORS OF STUDY OF ESOTERICISM THROUGH CORRESPONDENCE
Duration: 35 Minutes
The video was posted at: http://youtu.be/oNBMqt-S3_0
https://www.youtube.com/watch?v=oNBMqt-S3_0&feature=youtu.be

VIDEO PRESENTATION OF 49 COPIES OF METAPHYSICAL MAGAZINE "OMAKOIO" OF MODERN GREEK MYSTIC NIKOLAOS MARGIORIS
Duration: 50 Minutes
The video was posted at: http://youtu.be/FYwWD6BURZE

https://www.youtube.com/watch?v=FYwWD6BURZE&feature=youtu.be

VIDEO PRESENTATION OF 6 BOOKS AND 10 STUDIES BY ILIAS KATSIAMPAS, STUDENT OF NIKOLAOS MARGIORIS AND OF ONE BOOK OF HIS STUDENTS SMARO KOSMAOGLOU AND DIMITRIS TSAPARAS
Duration: 31 Minutes
The video was posted at: http://youtu.be/V9lo89LCUpM
https://www.youtube.com/watch?v=V9lo89LCUpM&feature=youtu.be

FACEBOOK PAGES

NIKOLAOS A. MARGIORIS – A GREEK SPIRITUAL MASTER (A MODERN SPIRITUAL FORM)
https://www.facebook.com/pages/NIKOLAOS-A-MARGIORIS-A-MODERN-GREEK-SPIRITUAL-FORM/110183632346517?ref=bookmarks

GROUPS ON FACEBOOK

YOGA ACADEMY OF NIKOLAOS MARGIORIS – OMAKOEIO (CLOSED)
https://www.facebook.com/groups/848311315181471/

ESOTERICISM FOR ALL - GROUP AND FRIENDS OF NIKOLAOS A. MARGIORIS
https://www.facebook.com/groups/310048335902/

PROFILE FACEBOOK ILIAS KATSIAMPAS – ADMINISTRATOR OF PAGES-GROUPS
https://www.facebook.com/ilias.katsiampas

SECOND FACEBOOK PROFILE OF ILIAS KATSIAMPAS ADMINISTRATOR OF PAGES – GROUPS
https://www.facebook.com/ekatsiampas?fref=ts

CURRICULUM VITAE OF ILIAS KATSIAMPAS

Ilias L. Katsiampas was born on October 30th 1965 in Trikala of Thessaly (Greece), where he grew up and lives today. He is a graduate of Physical Education (TEFAA), he has worked as a journalist for the last twenty-two years and he is the writer and publisher of 15 philosophical works. He is married to Sofia A. Skoumi with whom he has two children, Lampros and Maria.

From a very young age, he expressed a strong esoteric interest in looking for the essence of things, the real meaning of life. He studied many philosophical systems as well as volumes of books on Esotericism of every kind, time and country until he met **Nikolaos A. Margioris**, the **Greek Master** of **Esotericism** (1913-1993), in whose spiritual work he recognized the presence of substantial Knowledge, the supreme real truth. He became his student and remained close to him from 1983 to his physical passing on May 6th 1993.

Among other things, he was taught the pure form of Raja Yoga and he was trained in numerous other esoteric fields of interest (Esoteric Philosophy, Esoteric Theology, Mysticism, Astrology-Astrosophy, Hypnotism-Orthopsychism, Scientific Spiritualism, Esoteric Therapeutics and so on) and gradually ascended the steps of his spiritual evolution.

The fiery and indomitable tendency and willingness of the writer to explore the Beyond in combination with his intensive training, apprenticeship and direct close relation with his Master N. Margioris for almost a decade, contributed decisively to his gradual formation of an integrated experiential clear perception-point of view on the whole field of Metaphysics as well as the practices of meditation and mysticism.

On **January 18,1992** with the full encouragement, guidance and in the presence of his Master, he inaugurated the **Omakoio of Trikala**, an educational-spiritual center, where all the **Yoga** systems (Mantram, Kriya, Raja, Karma, Jnani, Bhakti, Kundalini, Sahaja, Atmoliquefaction), **Esoteric Philosophy, Alternative** and **Esoteric Therapeutics** and generally **Esotericism** (Occultism and Mysticism) are taught to this day.

Since 1999, he has been active in the **Omakoio of Thessaloniki**.

On **July 2012**, he established, with his partners and his students, the Association **"YOGA ACADEMY OF NIKOLAOS MARGIORIS-OMAKOIO"** as a tribute to his Master **N. Margioris** for a more complete application of his philosophical and practical work.

He proclaims and highlights the paramount need for the widespread teaching of **Esotericism** (Introversion-Self Knowledge) in order to create healthy and balanced minds and a truly New Spiritual Man characterized by self-awareness, self-reliance, autonomy, an open mind, with a giving disposition, free of materialistic pettiness and repressed desires, an ability to better adapt and respond to the challenges of modern reality as well as to every future time of Humanity.

SUMMARY OF THE WORK

- A **book-document** which contains an unprecedented, fascinating, revealing and rare **metaphysical example of correspondence** between a **Spiritual Master** and his **student** and defines **the ideal method of teaching an esoteric course.**
- A landmark **book** with **honest** and **interesting essays written in layman's terms** which succeeds in bringing together - in condensed form - deep, burning **Esoteric Knowledge** on the whole spectrum of **genuine Metaphysics** (Occultism and Mysticism).
- A **unique book** with an analytical and thorough **Glossary of Sanskrit (philosophical dictionary of 400 words)** which constitutes a **reference point** and a **guide** for all seekers or students of Yoga and of **Esotericism.**
- A **book containing Drops of Wisdom** from the 189 works of the contemporary Greek Spiritual Master, **Nikolaos A. Margioris**, who is a steady source of aid, knowledge, inspiration, sound and firm guidance in various Esoteric matters.
- A piece of **work** in the circle of **Esotericism** whose ambition it is to offer the reader initial guidance and clarification on the Esoteric path as well as on the formation and completion of **his Esoteric Being.**
- A **book containing dedications** to the person and to the immense work of a great Greek Master of Esoteric Metaphysics and Spirituality, **Nikolaos A. Margioris.**

FROM THE MASTER'S MOUTH TO THE STUDENT'S EAR

A bold and remarkable book recently released in Trikala, Greece. A book that deals with the limits of Metaphysical philosophical thought.

The writer of the book succeeds in conveying, in original form, the personal relationship that he developed with his Master, including all the small and unimportant – though they are not - details of a heart-warming correspondence which is also the beginning of the acquaintance with his Master.

All these small details are relevant to the whole work because they highlight the sincerity, the passion, the spontaneity, the agony, the hesitation, the doubt - and why not - the youthful contempt and finally, the humiliation; details that forced Ilias L. Katsiampas, the author, to write a book which surpasses the limits required for the subject. The result is a clear analysis in layman's terms of the path of knowledge in Esoteric Metaphysics.

A book with complex questions is made readable, understandable, and accessible to every reader.

A pleasant read for anyone wishing to approach the field of **Esoteric Metaphysics** through the path of *THE MASTER'S MOUTH TO THE STUDENT'S EAR*

The book is supplemented with a Sanskrit Glossary (an analytical philosophical dictionary of 400 words).

www.ingramcontent.com/pod-product-compliance
Lightning Source LLC
LaVergne TN
LVHW041247080426
835510LV00009B/619